Old Testament Exegesis, Fourth Edition

A Handbook for Students and Pastors

Douglas Stuart

WESTMINSTER
JOHN KNOX PRESS
LOUISVILLE · KENTUCKY

Book design by Sharon Adams
Cover design by Mark Abrams

Library of Congress Cataloging-in-Publication Data

Stuart, Douglas K.
  Old Testament exegesis : a handbook for students and pastors / Douglas Stuart.—4th ed.
    p. cm.
  Includes bibliographical references and indexes.
  ISBN 978-0-664-23344-0 (alk. paper)
  1. Bible. O.T.—Hermeneutics.   2. Bible. O.T.—Homiletical use.   3. Bible. O.T.—
Bibliography.   I. Title.
  BS476.S83 2008
  221.601—dc22   2008039353

PRINTED IN THE UNITED STATES OF AMERICA

To
Gayle, Joanna, Eliza, Eden, Missy,
Hannah, Maria, Delia, and Jon

Contents

Abbreviations

ABD	*Anchor Bible Dictionary*, ed. David Noel Freedman, 6 vols. (New York: Doubleday, 1992)
ANET	*Ancient Near Eastern Texts Relating to the Old Testament*, ed. James B. Pritchard, 3rd ed. (Princeton: Princeton University Press, 1969)
ATLA	American Theological Library Association
BDB	Francis Brown, S. R. Driver, and C. A. Briggs, *A Hebrew and English Lexicon of the Old Testament* (Oxford: Clarendon, 1907)
BH³	*Biblia Hebraica*, 3rd ed. (Stuttgart: Württembergische Bibelanstalt, 1937)
BH⁵	*Biblia Hebraica Quinta* (5th ed. of *BH*) (Stuttgart: Deutsche Bibelstiftung, 2004–)
BHQ	another abbreviation for *BH⁵*
BHS	*Biblia Hebraica Stuttgartensia* (4th ed. of *BH*) (Stuttgart: Deutsche Bibelstiftung, 1977)
CAD	*The Assyrian Dictionary of the Oriental Institute of the University of Chicago*, ed. I. J. Gelb et al. (Chicago: Oriental Institute, 1956–)
DJD	Discoveries in the Judaean Desert
DSS	Dead Sea Scrolls (Qumran)
ed.	edited by/editor/edition
IDB	*Interpreter's Dictionary of the Bible*, ed. G. A. Buttrick, 4 vols. (Nashville: Abingdon, 1962)

ISBE	*International Standard Bible Encyclopedia*, ed. G. W. Bromiley, 4 vols. (Grand Rapids: Wm. B. Eerdmans, 1979–88)
IRBS	International Review of Biblical Studies
JSNT	Journal for the Study of the New Testament
JSOTSup	Journal for the Study of the Old Testament Supplements
MT	Masoretic Text
NIDOTTE	*New International Dictionary of Old Testament Theology and Exegesis*, ed. Willem A. VanGemeren, 5 vols. (Grand Rapids: Zondervan Publishing House, 1997)
NT	New Testament
OHB	Oxford Hebrew Bible
OT	Old Testament
OTA	*Old Testament Abstracts*
Q	Qumran (Dead Sea Scrolls)
Quinta	another abbreviation for *BHQ*
repr.	reprint
rev. ed.	revised edition
SBL	Society of Biblical Literature
TDNT	*Theological Dictionary of the New Testament*, ed. Gerhard Kittel and Gerhard Friedrich, trans. G. W. Bromiley, 10 vols. (Grand Rapids: Wm. B. Eerdmans, 1964–76)
TDOT	*Theological Dictionary of the Old Testament*, ed. G. J. Botterweck, Helmer Ringgren, and Heinz-Josef Fabry, trans. J. T. Willis, G. W. Bromiley, and D. E. Green, 15 vols. (Grand Rapids: Wm. B. Eerdmans, 1974–2006)
TLOT	*Theological Lexicon of the Old Testament*, ed. Ernst Jenni and Claus Westermann, trans. M. E. Biddle, 3 vols. (Peabody, MA: Hendrickson, 1997)
TWOT	*Theological Wordbook of the Old Testament*, ed. R. L. Harris, G. L. Archer Jr., and B. K. Waltke, 2 vols. (Chicago: Moody Press, 1980)

Preface

T hose few students and pastors who control several ancient and modern languages, read the scholarly literature regularly, and have already gained some confidence in their ability to do exegesis will certainly not need this primer. It is written for those who cannot read a Hebrew psalm at sight and who are not sure what "Vetus Testamentum" would mean or contain (the words mean "Old Testament" in Latin and are the title of a major OT scholarly journal). It is for those who have no idea what *homoioteleuton* might mean ("same kind of ending," a factor in certain textual problems). It is for the vast majority of all seminary students and pastors. It is predicated on the conviction that even the most intelligent people cannot understand procedures and concepts that are not somehow explained to them, and that there is no shame in seeking such explanations in spite of the fact that most seminary professors do not volunteer them. Old Testament exegesis has regular procedures and concepts, and these can be taught to almost anyone willing to learn. It is a tragedy that so few seminary students ever really feel sure of themselves in doing OT exegesis—and most pastors apparently abandon the practice altogether.

I have set out, therefore, to present a step-by-step guide to OT exegesis that will be nontechnical and simple without being simplistic, that will explain not only the procedures but also the goals of exegesis, and that will serve as a handbook for reference as the student or pastor does the actual work of exegesis.

My approach to exegesis has certain conscious biases for which I make no apologies. Perhaps the most debatable is my insistence that exegesis should include guidelines for application of the passage being studied. Exegesis is patently a theological enterprise, and a theology that is not applied to the lives of God's people is sterile. For this reason, too, I have purposely deemphasized some of the critical techniques (e.g., structuralism, redaction criticism) which, though fascinating to the scholar, yield meager rewards theologically and are, in the final analysis, of minor value homiletically, much as that value judgment may displease some scholars. Likewise and for similar reasons, I have not given attention to various subjective hermeneutical approaches such as ethnic-based, gender-based, or life-status-based interpretational filters. I have tried to set a fair balance between synchronic and diachronic techniques (i.e., techniques concerned with the text as it stands [synchronic] and with the history of the developments that led to the text as it stands [diachronic]), but only insofar as these also hold promise of practical, theological benefit. The end of exegesis is preaching and teaching in the church. Seminary students and pastors know this instinctively and demand relevance from exegesis and other biblical studies, as well they should.

This primer recognizes that very few American students and pastors can read German or other scholarly languages. Of what advantage, therefore, is it to pretend that they can? The bibliographical guidance in chapter 4 is thus restricted as much as possible to English works.

A unique feature of this book is found in chapter 3, which outlines an abbreviated, limited-time exegetical format for pastors. At least in a general way, seminary students usually learn how to produce formal exegesis term papers, based on dozens of hours of research and writing. But no one tells them how they can transfer that ability to the weekly preaching task, where perhaps only *a few* hours may be available for the exegesis part of the sermon preparation. Exegesis can be done responsibly even if not exhaustively in a few hours' time. The pastor should first try to understand the fuller form of the guide in chapter 1. Chapter 3 represents a condensation and economization of the same material, with special attention paid to homiletical interests.

Those aspiring OT exegetes who know no Hebrew should still be able to make good use of the guidance given here—but there can be no denying that at least some knowledge of Hebrew is a precious advantage for student and pastor alike. I have done everything possible to encourage those whose Hebrew is weak to use it anyway. The helps discussed in chapter 4 can go a long way toward overcoming the disadvantages, especially via computer concordances that can instantly provide a range of Hebrew-English resources once found only at great effort. Indeed, the pastor who faithfully works from the biblical languages in sermon preparation, no matter how rusty one's knowledge of them may be at the start, cannot help gaining *more and more* language mastery as time goes by. I hope this primer will encourage many to try.

For the fourth edition I have changed the order of some of the steps and the advice within them, adjusted explanations, added or deleted reference works to continue to reflect what is actually available in print, updated the listings of works that have been revised, and included much more information on electronic and online databases. Thus this edition is revised and expanded substantially. I am very grateful to my students John Beckman and Robert Jennings for their opinions on how best to describe the actual usage of some of the newer online databases that I mention in this latest edition. It is a joy to work with students who love learning and want others to share their delight. I am also grateful to Jon Berquist, a seasoned scholar and skillful editor, who has worked with me on behalf of a wonderful publisher, Westminster John Knox Press.

The widespread use of the first three editions, including their foreign language translations, has been very gratifying and is evidence of an ongoing hunger for preaching and teaching based accurately and confidently in the Scriptures.

Analytical Table of Contents
(For Cross-Reference Use)

The reference system used in this book functions as follows:

4.1.7. refers to chapter 4, section 1, subsection 7 of this book.
Thus 4 (Exegesis Aids and Resources), 1 (Textual Criticism), 7 (The
  Masorah).
Likewise, 1.3.5. refers to chapter 1, section 3, subsection 5 (etc.).

Introduction

An exegesis is a thorough, analytical study of a biblical passage done so as to arrive at a useful interpretation of the passage. Exegesis is a theological task, but not a mystical one. There are certain basic rules and standards for how to do it, although the results can vary in appearance because the biblical passages themselves vary so much.

To do OT exegesis properly, you have to be something of a generalist. You will quickly become involved with the functions and meanings of words (linguistics); the analysis of literature and speech (philology); theology; history; the transmission of the biblical writings (textual criticism); stylistics, grammar, and vocabulary analysis; and the vaguely defined yet inescapably important area of sociology. Natural intuitive skills are helpful but no substitute for the hard work of careful, firsthand research. Exegesis as a process can be quite dull. Its results, fortunately, can often be exciting. Exciting or not, the results should always at least be of genuine practical value to the believer; if not, something is wrong with the exegesis. Although this book is a primer and hardly an exhaustive analysis of exegetical presuppositions or techniques, it ought to serve you well if your reason for learning exegesis is eventually to apply its benefits in Christian preaching or teaching.

An exegete must work from many books and sources. Four kinds are especially valuable for the methodological and bibliographical guidance they contain relating to exegesis. You should own all four kinds, of which the following are representative samples:

OT Introductions

Tremper Longman III and Raymond B. Dillard, *An Introduction to the Old Testament*, 2nd ed. (Grand Rapids: Zondervan Publishing House, 2006).

J. Alberto Soggin, *Introduction to the Old Testament*, 3rd ed. (Louisville, KY: Westminster John Knox Press, 1989).

Both of these introductions contain lucid, concrete explanations of OT literary types and divisions, scholarly approaches, book-by-book content and criticism, canon and text. Moreover, there is much to be gained from either book's bibliographical guidance.

OT Tools Overviews

Frederick W. Danker, *Multipurpose Tools for Bible Study*, rev. ed. (Minneapolis: Fortress Press, 2003).

Danker provides backgrounds, definitions, and explanations for all sorts of books, methods, sources, and styles in biblical exegesis. His work is a standard resource for such information.

OT Handbooks

Richard N. Soulen and R. Kendall Soulen, *Handbook of Biblical Criticism*, 3rd ed., rev. and expanded (Louisville, KY: Westminster John Knox Press, 2001).
John W. Rogerson and Judith M. Lieu, eds., *Oxford Handbook of Biblical Studies* (Oxford: Oxford University Press, 2006).

Handbooks offer basic explanations and collections of definitions. Most of the exegetical terms and techniques you will run across are explained. They also fill you in on many of the trendy/subjectivist interpretational schools.

Bibliographies

Joseph A. Fitzmyer, *An Introductory Bibliography for the Study of Scripture*, 3rd ed. (Chicago: Loyola University Press; Rome: Editrice Pontificio Istituto Biblico, 1990). Also available in CD-ROM.

Fitzmyer's *Bibliography* is one of the best annotated listings (through its publication date) of lexicons, texts, grammars, concordances, and other technical aids used by exegetes. Excellent online bibliographies also exist, which have the advantage of being updatable constantly. An example is that of

Jean Louis Ska, "Old Testament Basic Bibliography," http://www.biblico.it/doc-vari/ska_bibl.html.

We discuss several of these in chapter 4.

With these four kinds of texts in hand, you will know what the issues in exegesis are, what kind of resources are available, and where to find them.

In addition to these four sorts of books, you ought to have in your library, either in book form or electronic form or both, a "critical" edition of the Hebrew OT. For the time being, the one you want will be the *BHS*, the *Biblia Hebraica Stuttgartensia* (the fourth edition of a carefully edited Hebrew Bible published in Stuttgart, Germany). It has replaced the older *BH³* (the third edition, also known by the name of its main editor as the "Kittel") just as it will, in time, be replaced by the fifth edition, *BHQ* (*BH⁵*) or *Biblia Hebraica Quinta*. The Quinta, like its predecessors, uses the Leningrad Codex of AD 1008 as its basis, with its text carefully checked against photographs of that codex taken in the 1990s.

Unlike its predecessors, however, it includes a commentary explaining the Masorah (the medieval Jewish text notational system) and discussing the significance of the textual variants it gives in its footnotes. Moreover, it contains the Masorah magna (a compendium of medieval Jewish text notes), which was available only via a supplementary volume in the case of the *BHS*. Controversially, its editors cite relatively few variants from other medieval Hebrew manuscripts since the editors are convinced that such variants are of little value.

The *BHQ* books of Ruth, Canticles, Qoheleth, Lamentations, and Esther appeared in a fascicle published in 2004; Ezra and Nehemiah appeared in 2006, and Deuteronomy in 2007. It was originally scheduled gradually to be completed in 2010, and may, we hope, actually appear by about 2012.

You will surely want to have at hand also a Hebrew-based concordance, a Hebrew lexicon, a Hebrew grammar, a comprehensive history of Israel, a Bible dictionary, and a "critical" commentary series (if possible). Any and all of these are available in both electronic and book form. Examples of the specific works are discussed in chapter 4. The concordance, history, dictionary, and commentary series are essential even if you do not know Hebrew. Without the proper tools, an exegesis cannot go far. The more of these sorts of works you have via computer software, including online access, the faster your exegesis work can go because of the time saved in searching. On the other hand, speed is not always an advantage: searching through a book forces you to see things in context in a way that searching via search engines *prevents* you from doing.

Remember as you use this guide that all the steps do not apply equally to all OT passages. For example, some passages will require major attention to historical issues and little attention to their form or vocabulary;

others will be just the opposite. There is no way to be sure of this automatically in advance. As you become familiar with a passage, it will tend to become obvious to you how to assign the relative weight of each step, and the subpoints thereof.

This primer is organized into four sections. Chapter 1 provides a nontechnical format for extensive, formal exegesis projects including, but not limited to, term papers. Chapter 2 gives illustrations for the steps of an extensive exegesis. Chapter 3 gives a simple, condensed version of the longer format and centers especially on sermon preparation. Chapter 4 discusses various exegetical aids and resources, especially bibliographical, including how to access them and how to use them.

Chapter One

Guide for Full Exegesis

The outline that we provide here is supplemented with many comments and questions intended to help you leave no stone unturned in doing a thorough exegesis. These comments and questions are primarily suggestive and not to be followed slavishly. Indeed, some questions overlap and some may seem redundant to you. Some may not be relevant to your purposes or the scope of your particular exegesis needs in any given passage. So be selective. Ignore what does not apply to your passage and task. Emphasize what does.

Pastors and others who will work mainly from the guide for sermon exegesis in chapter 3 should familiarize themselves with the content of this chapter first, since it constitutes the basis for the condensation in chapter 3.

1.1. Text

1.1.1. Confirm the limits of the passage

Try to be sure that the passage you have chosen for exegesis is a genuine, self-contained unit (sometimes called a pericope). Avoid cutting a poem in the middle of a stanza or a narrative in the middle of a paragraph—unless that is the assignment you are working under, or unless you explain clearly to your reader why you have chosen to exegete a section of a full passage. Your primary ally is common sense. Does your passage have a recognizable beginning and end? Does it have some sort of cohesive, meaningful content that you can observe? Check your decision against both the Hebrew text and modern translations. Do not trust the OT chapter and verse divisions, which originated in medieval times. They are not original and are often completely misleading.

Note: You may find it confusing to begin with the textual analysis of your passage if your knowledge of Hebrew is not yet adequate. In that case, first prepare a rough, even wooden translation of the passage from the Hebrew. Do not delay yourself needlessly at this point. Use a trustworthy modern translation as your guide, or an interlinear if you wish (see 4.2.2 [chapter 4, section 2, subsection 2]). Once you have a working idea of what the Hebrew words mean, you can resume the textual analysis with profit.

1.1.2. Compare the versions

From as many as you can read of the Greek, Syriac, Aramaic, Latin, and Qumran versions of the passage, isolate any words or phrases that do not seem to correspond to the Hebrew text you are working on. Since all of these ancient language versions have English translations (see 4.2.2), you can actually work from them profitably even if you do not know one or more of these languages.

Refer to the critical apparatus in the *BHS* (and perhaps the apparatuses in the older *BH³* if you have access to it and/or whatever part of the the newer *BHQ* [*Quinta*] has been published as of the time you are doing your exegesis), even though none of them is complete and any comment in an apparatus can be difficult to decipher because it is typically written in abbreviated Latin (!). Fortunately, the deciphering guides mentioned in 4.1.5 are very helpful. Examine the differences (called variants). Try to decide, as best you can, whether any of the variants is possibly more appropriate to the passage (i.e., possibly more original) than the corresponding words in the Hebrew text. To do this, you must translate the variant back into Hebrew (normally via English) and then judge whether it fits the context better. Often you can see exactly how a variant came to result from a corruption (an ancient copying mistake that became preserved in the subsequent copies) in the Hebrew text. Make these decisions as best you can, referring to critical commentaries and other aids (see 4.1) for their guidance. Sometimes, especially in a poetic section, a corruption will simply be insoluble: the wording may not make much sense in the Hebrew as it stands, but you cannot figure out a convincing alternative. In such cases, leave the received text alone. Your task is to reconstruct as far as possible the text as originally inspired by God, not to rewrite it.

1.1.3. Reconstruct and annotate the text

Make your best guess at the original Hebrew text. Normally you should print out the reconstructed original text in full. If your reconstruction omits any words or letters from the received text, mark the omissions by square brackets: [ ]. If you insert or replace any words or letters, place the new part inside angle brackets: < >. Mark each such spot with a raised letter (letters are better than numbers for these sorts of notes, since they cannot be confused with verse numbers) and in the footnotes keyed to those letters, explain clearly and simply your reasons for the changes. It is advisable also to footnote any words you did not change but which someone else might think ought to be changed. Provide an explanation of all your significant decisions for or against changes in the text, not just those that result in actual changes.

Normally, this reconstructed text should constitute the beginning of your exegesis paper/project, following immediately upon the table of contents (if any), preface (if any), and introduction. Fortunately, textual problems are rarely so frequent or major as to affect the sense of a passage. So a proposed textual revision (i.e., revision of the MT) that materially affects the sense of the passage will probably require a major discussion at this point in the paper/project.

1.1.4. Present poetry in versified form

In most cases you can expect the *BHS* (or *BH³* or *BHQ*) to identify poetry properly and to arrange the lines of poetry according to the editor's sense of parallelism and rhythm (meter). The process of arrangement and the arrangement itself are both referred to as stichometry.

The parallelism between the words and phrases is the main criterion for deciding the stichometry. A secondary criterion is the meter (see 4.6.4). If you decide on a different stichometry for your passage from the one indicated by the *BH* editor (their stichometries can be quite subjective and are not always right), be sure to give your reasoning in a footnote. The modern English translations usually arrange poetry stichometrically. Consult them as well, because their sense of how the parallelism works can be both instructive and time-saving, providing a good check on the *BH* editor's approach.

1.2 Translation

1.2.1. Prepare a tentative translation of your reconstructed text

Start fresh, from the beginning. Look up in a lexicon such as Holladay's (see 4.4.1) all words whose range of meaning you are not absolutely certain of. For the more significant words, try at least to skim the more lengthy lexicon articles in major lexicons such as Koehler-Baumgartner or Brown-Driver-Briggs (see 4.4.1). For any words that appear to be central or pivotal for the meaning of your passage, it is advisable either at this point or in connection with your analysis of the lexical content (exegesis step 1.4.3) to consult the detailed word studies (concept studies) in the aids referred to in 4.4.3. Remember that most words do not have a single meaning, but rather a range of meaning(s), and that there is a difference between a word and a concept (at step 1.4.3 we explain this further). A single Hebrew word rarely corresponds precisely to a single English word but may range in meaning through all or parts of several different English words. Translation therefore almost always involves *selection*.

1.2.2. Check the correspondence of text and translation

Read your Hebrew text over and over. Know it as a friend. If possible, memorize parts of it. Read your translation over and over (out loud). Do the Hebrew and your English seem the same in your mind? Have you used a rare or complicated English word to translate a common or simple Hebrew word? If so, does the resulting precision of meaning outweigh in value the disruptive effect on the reader or hearer? Have you considered the possibility of using several English words to convey the meaning of one Hebrew word? Or vice versa? Does your passage contain words or phrases that originally were genuinely ambiguous? If so, try to reproduce rather than mask the ambiguity in your English translation. A good translation is one that creates the same general impression for the hearer as the original would, without distorting the particular content conveyed.

1.2.3. Revise the translation as you continue

As you continue to exegete your passage, especially as you examine carefully the grammatical and lexical data, you will almost certainly learn enough to make improvements in your tentative translation. This is because the word(s) you choose for a given spot in the passage need(s) to fit the overall context well. The more you know about the whole passage, the better you will have a proper "feel" for selecting the right word, phrase, or expression in each part. The part should fit the whole. Also, as you make decisions about the literary and theological contexts of your passage, you will likewise be developing better judgment about the translation. Try to evaluate the use of a word, phrase, or expression both in its broad contexts (the book, the OT, the Bible as a whole) and its immediate contexts (your passage, the chapter, the surrounding chapters). The difference can be significant. For example, although you might have assumed that the Hebrew word בַּיִת means "house" in your passage, a wider look at its uses throughout the OT shows that in an expression like בֵּית דָּוִיד it can mean "family," "dynasty," or "lineage." Which suits your passage better? Which makes your passage clearer to the reader? By asking these sorts of questions, you help to guarantee that you will not overlook potentially useful translation options.

1.2.4. Provide a finished translation

After your research is complete and you have benefited from the secondary literature as well as all the other steps of the exegesis process and are ready to write the final draft, place the finished translation immediately following the text. Use annotations (footnotes—again, for these note call characters, letters are less likely to cause confusion with verse numbers than digits are) to explain choices of wording that might be surprising or simply not obvious to your reader. You are not obliged, however, to explain any word that was also chosen by several modern versions unless it seems to you that their choice, even if unanimous, is questionable in some way. Use the footnotes to tell the reader other possible translations of a word or phrase that you consider to have merit. Do this especially wherever you find it difficult to choose between two or more options.

1.3. Grammatical Data

1.3.1. Analyze the significant grammatical issues

A correct understanding of the grammar is essential to a proper interpretation of the passage. Are any grammatical points in doubt? Could any sentences, clauses, or phrases be read differently if the grammar were construed differently? Are you sure you have given proper weight to the nuances of meaning inherent in the specific verb conjugations and not merely the verbal roots? Slight variations in syntax can convey significant variations in meaning. Are the syntactical formations in your passage clearly understood? Does your translation need revision or annotation accordingly? Are there genuine ambiguities that make a definite interpretation of some part of the passage impossible? If so, what at least are the possible options? Is the grammar anomalous (not what would be expected) at any point? If so, can you offer any explanation for the anomaly? Pay attention also to ellipsis, asyndeton, prostaxis, parataxis, anacoluthon, and other special grammatical features that relate to interpretation. (For definitions, see Soulen's *Handbook*—mentioned in the introduction.)

1.3.2. Analyze the orthography and morphology for date or other affinities

All major texts of the Hebrew Bible contain an orthography (spelling style) characteristic of the Persian period (postexilic), since the texts selected for official status by the rabbis of the first century AD were apparently copies from the Persian period. At many important points, however, traces of older orthographies are discernible (in 4.3.2, see Freedman, Forbes, and Andersen, *Studies in Hebrew and Aramaic Orthography*). Does the passage have any of these older spellings or traces of special ancient morphological features? Morphology refers to meaning-affecting parts of words, such as suffixes and prefixes. (For examples, see David A. Robertson, *Linguistic Evidence in Dating Early Hebrew Poetry* [Missoula, MT: Scholars Press, 1972].) If so, they may help to indicate the date or even the geographical origin of your passage; their presence elsewhere may help you to classify your passage in comparison to others. At least an intermediate-level knowledge of Hebrew is required for this task.

1.4. Lexical Data

1.4.1. Explain all words and concepts that are not obvious

Bear in mind that there is a difference between a word and a concept. A given concept may be expressed by many different words or wordings. An excellent reminder of this is Jesus' parable of the Good Samaritan in Luke 10. He tells the parable to demonstrate what it means to love neighbor as self, yet the parable does not contain the word "love" or the word "neighbor" or the word "self"—even though it teaches powerfully the concept of loving neighbor as self. It therefore is important to realize that your purpose in analyzing the lexical data is to understand the individual concepts of your passage, whether these concepts are conveyed by single words, groups of words, or by the way all the words are put together into a coherent pericope.

Work in descending order of size from whole sentences or even groups of sentences (if applicable) through clauses (if applicable) through phrases (such as idioms) to words and parts of words. Using the various helps available (see 4.4), try to define for your reader any concepts, words, or wordings that might not be clear or whose force would not be noticed without attention being called to them. Some of these explanations may be quite brief, others fairly detailed. Proper nouns almost always deserve some attention. So do idioms, since by definition an idiom is a wording that cannot be translated literally, meaning word for word. When citing words from the passage, use either the Hebrew letters or an underlined transliteration of them.

1.4.2. Concentrate on the most important concepts, words, and wordings

Working in descending order of size, isolate whatever you consider especially significant or pivotal for the interpretation of the passage. Assemble a list of perhaps six to twelve such important concepts, words, or wordings. Try to rank them in order from most crucial to least crucial. Focus on these, telling your reader why they are important to the interpretation. The meaning of a passage is built up from the meaning of its concepts, and the more clearly they are explained, the more clearly the passage is likely to be understood.

1.4.3. Do "word studies" (really, concept studies) of the most crucial words or wordings

Using the procedure outlined in 4.4.3, try to analyze the most crucial—therefore not a large number—of the key words or wordings in the passage. Present a summary of your procedures and findings to the reader. (Much of the statistical or procedural information may be relegated to footnotes.) Do not neglect the specific theological meaning(s) of words or wordings in considering the various ranges of meaning. In addition, be sure that you do not merely analyze individual words but also words in combination—including combinations sometimes separated from one another by intervening words—because combinations of words convey concepts as well. Be as inductive as possible, checking your conclusions against, rather than deriving them from, the theological dictionaries.

1.4.4. Identify any special semantic features

The semantics (the relation between content and meaning) of the passage is often affected by such features as irony, anaphora, epiphora, paronomasia, metonymy, hendiadys, formulas, loanwords, purposeful archaizing, and etymological oddities. Look for these, and bring them to the attention of your reader. Where possible, show how they affect interpretation.

1.5. Form

1.5.1. Identify the general literary type (genre)

First, locate the passage within the broad, general categories of literary types contained in the OT. Decide whether your passage is a prose type, a saying, a "song," or a combination (such basic categories are defined in any of the general guides to form analysis listed in 4.5.1).

1.5.2. Identify the specific literary type (form)

Describe more precisely what sort of prose type, saying, or song the passage actually is. For example, if you decide that it is a historical narrative, you must then go on to judge whether it is a report, a popular history, a general autobiography, a dream-vision account, a prophetic autobiography, or some other specific kind of historical narrative. This is important: You must do your best to identify the specific type because that is what allows you to compare it to other such types elsewhere in the Bible (and sometimes in literature outside the Bible) and thus learn what elements in your passage are *typical* of its literary form and what elements are *unique* to your passage alone and thus of special value for interpreting your passage as opposed to others.

You must know both the general and the specific literary type of your passage before you are in a position to analyze its form or forms. Only the specific—not the general—types have "forms." That is, every specific literary type is identifiable because it has certain recognizable features (including both its contents or "ingredients" and the order in which those ingredients occur) that make it a form. For example, each "dream account" in the OT tends to have certain features that it shares with all the other dream accounts. The specific contents of the various dream accounts may be different, but the features are not; each dream account contains roughly the same sorts of things. They are said to have the same form, which we call the "dream account form."

There is a complication here that you must be aware of: scholars may use different terms to refer to OT forms because no standardized system of terminology exists. Therefore, what one scholar might refer to as a "dream account form," another might call a "dream report," another might call a "dream narrative," another might call a "sleep revelation narrative," and so on. Moreover, scholars sometimes use Hebrew words in their names for forms, so what one scholar calls a "covenant lawsuit form," another might call a "*rîb* form" (*rîb* being the Hebrew word for "lawsuit/legal case"), yet another might call a "רִיב form" (using the actual Hebrew alphabet to spell *rîb*), and so forth. It would be nice if the terminology were standardized, but that has not yet happened, and it is not likely to happen anytime soon.

1.5.3. Look for subcategories

A main purpose of form analysis is to compare your passage with others of like form and to exploit the knowledge that results from that comparison. It is therefore best to describe a form as specifically as possible without making it entirely unique. For example, if your passage contains a dream account that includes a conversation between an angel and a prophet, you will probably gain more fruitful exegetical data from a comparison of your dream account with others that also contain a prophet-angel dialogue, rather than with all dream accounts found anywhere in the OT. You might even decide that you will tentatively call your form a "prophet-angel dialogue dream account." As we have already noted, the terminology used by scholars in form analysis is not very standardized, certainly not so standardized as to rule out a cautiously exercised freedom of terminology on your part. However, do not try to subcategorize your form to the extent that it becomes one of a kind. At that point it is meaningless even to speak of a form, and the crucial benefits of comparison are lost. The elements that cannot be compared are the special elements that call for careful attention elsewhere in your exegesis and that distinguish your passage from all others. Their uniqueness does not, however, define the form. The form is defined rather by what is typical or shared with other passages.

1.5.4. Suggest a life setting

Try to link the passage (in the sense of its form or forms) with the real situation of its use. Sometimes the text itself does this for you. Otherwise you must work inferentially and with caution. It may be obvious that a prophet has borrowed the funeral dirge form from the life situation of funerals and reused the form in a prophetic way, such as singing a predictive funeral dirge for Israel, which is to be destroyed by Yahweh. But it is not so obvious where the life setting of a "community lament" psalm is to be located. Knowing the original life setting (often called the *Sitz im Leben*) usually helps you to understand the passage in a concrete way. But an overemphasis on the life setting can be counterproductive. The fact that a psalm, for example, has the form of a royal accession song should not lead to the conclusion that it has no function or meaning in the OT (or among Christians today) other than as a part of the ancient Jerusalem coronation ritual. Its original setting as a form is one thing; its potential for adaptation and reuse for a whole variety of secondary settings (literary, cultural, theological, etc.) is another. Try, then, to balance a sensitivity to the theoretical origin of the form with its actual use in the context of your passage.

1.5.5. Analyze the completeness of the form

Compare your passage to other passages that have the same form. In the particular instance of your passage, how completely is the given form represented? Are all its usual elements present? If so, is there also anything extraneous to the form that is present? If not, what elements are lacking? Are they lacking because the passage is logically elliptical (it leaves certain obvious elements unexpressed) or because it is purposely modified? Does the ellipsis or modification tell you anything about what the passage is focusing on or what its special emphases are? The differences between your passage and all others of the same essential form are what make your passage unique and give it its special function in the Bible. Try to understand as well as you can that uniqueness and that function.

Does your passage contain more than one form, as many passages do? If so, how are the forms to be separated out? Does the passage contain a mixture of forms or a form within a form (e.g., a riddle within a dream account, or a messenger speech within a woe oracle)? Or is your passage part of a larger form, the full extent of which goes beyond the limits of your passage? If so, what part does your passage and its form(s) play in the greater form?

1.5.6. Be alert to partial and broken forms

Most of the time, all the known elements of a given form will not be present in any specific instance of its use. The more common the form, the more likely it may be that the form is partial, thus containing only some of all the possible elements that might be found in the fullest, most complete exemplar of such a form. For example, when the prophets repeat the word of Yahweh in the *rîb* (covenant lawsuit) form, they sometimes present only one aspect, such as the speech of indictment or the judgment sentence. Presumably their audiences immediately recognized from the partial form that a divine lawsuit was being described, in the same way that we can recognize from just the words "We interrupt this broadcast to bring you . . ." the form used today when an important news story is breaking. A partial form functions to suggest the purpose, tone, style, and audience of the full form without the needless detail and bulk necessitated by the full form. A form may also be broken (segmented) by the inclusion of other material within the form so that its constituent parts are rather widely separated from one another. Sometimes the beginning and end of a form are used to sandwich material technically extraneous to the form proper. Such a sandwiching is known as an *inclusio*. The material sandwiched in such an inclusio is usually related to but not technically part of the form. Try to analyze the effect of any such structure on the interpretation of the passage.

Be careful about historical assessment and atomization. Considerable criticism has been leveled against these two past practices of many form critics. Historical assessment was the practice of calling into question some or all of the accuracy of the historical content in a given form, on the theory that certain kinds of forms preserved more genuine historical data than others. Atomization was the practice of assuming that the most basic forms were found in the smallest units—those of a verse or two in length—and that larger units were secondary. Both of these practices rested on assumptions that are now widely questioned. You should avoid them in your own exegesis.

1.6. Structure

1.6.1. Outline the passage

Try to construct an outline that genuinely represents the major units of information. In other words, the outline should be a natural, not artificial, outgrowth of the passage. Note how many components are included under each topic (quantitative) and also the intensity or overall significance of the components (qualitative). Let the passage speak for itself. When you see a new topic, subject, issue, concept, or the like, you should construct a new topic for your outline. There are no automatic criteria for outlining. Do not be fooled by suggestions that you can count repetitions or identify "transitional" words (such as לָכֵן, "therefore") and mechanically derive your passage's outline. Instead, your outline must be your best judgment as to how the major units of information in the passage group together logically. Some learning theorists suggest that the best outlines

will contain from three to five major units, since most people have diffi-
culty comprehending or remembering six or more abstract elements at
once, and fewer than three elements hardly constitute an adequately
descriptive outline. Nevertheless, your outline must be a reflection of your
best judgment about the logical structure of your passage, and the number of elements in the outline must therefore reflect the major units of
information, however many they may be.

After outlining the major divisions, work on the more minor divisions,
such as sentences, clauses, and phrases. These should be visibly subordi-
nated under the major divisions. The outline should be as detailed as you
can make it without seeming forced or artificial. From the outline you can
then go on to make observations about the overall structure.

1.6.2. Look for patterns

Any biblical passage whose limits have been properly identified will have
a self-consistent logic made up of meaningful thought patterns. Try to
identify the patterns, looking especially for such key features as developments, resumptions, unique forms of phrase, central or pivotal words, parallelisms, chiasms, inclusios, and other repetitious or progressive patterns.
The keys to patterns are most often *repetition* and *progression*. Look for any
evidence of repetition of a concept, word, phrase, expression, root, sound,
or other identifiable feature and analyze the order of the repetition. Do
the same with progressions, analyzing them as well. From this analysis
may come helpful insights. Poetry, by its very nature, will often contain
more (and more striking) structural patterns than will prose. But any passage, properly defined, has structural patterns that should be analyzed and
the results interpreted for your reader. Especially point out the unex-
pected or unique, since these are part of what makes your passage different from any other and thus contribute to its special character and
meaning.

1.6.3. Organize your discussion of structure according
to descending units of size

First, discuss the overall outline pattern, the three to five (or more) major
units. Then discuss what you feel is important among the subpatterns
within the major units, one at a time. Move in order from largest to smallest unit: from passage to paragraphs, to verses, to clauses, to words, to

sounds. Where possible, describe whether you feel that a pattern is primary, secondary, or simply minor, and how important it is to the interpretation of the passage.

1.6.4. Evaluate the intentionality of the minor patterns

Given enough time, most people can find all sorts of not very obvious minor patterns in a passage: a preponderance of certain vowel sounds here, the repetition of a verbal root there, the occurrence of a certain word exactly so many words after another word in two different verses, and so forth. The question is, did these minor patterns happen to appear at random (according to what some people call the "law of averages"), or were they constructed *intentionally* by the ancient inspired speaker or writer? We assume that the major patterns, because they are so obvious, were intentional. We also assume that many minor patterns were intentional, especially when we can see such patterns occurring repeatedly throughout a given OT book or portion thereof or in parallels from other books. But how can we be sure? There is only one criterion: Ask whether it is likely that the ancient speaker/writer composed the pattern for a purpose, and/or whether the ancient hearer/reader could reasonably be expected to have noticed the pattern while listening to or reading the passage. In your judgment, if it is likely that the answer is yes, then evaluate the pattern as an intentional one. If no, then identify the pattern as probably unintentional or the like and be cautious about making exegetical inferences from it.

1.6.5. If the passage is poetic, analyze it accordingly

Using semantic (meaning) parallelism as the guide, arrange the lines of poetry in parallel one to another. Then try to identify the meter of each line. If you can, revocalize the text to reflect the original pronunciation as much as possible, and describe the meter according to syllables per line (the most accurate method). Otherwise, describe the meter according to accents (less precise but still helpful). Note any special metrical features or patterns. Identify any groupings suggested by the metrical count. Although the concepts of stanza and strophe are not native to Hebrew poetry, you may divide a poem into sections or parts if you think such a division actually seems to be inherent in the poem, based on a shift of scene, topic, or style. Rhyme or acrostic patterns are rare but deserve careful attention if present. Watch also for formulas (words or phrases used in more than one place in the OT, in comparable metrical contexts and patterns, to express a given idea). Formulas are "stock phrases" of poetry, especially musical poetry.

Compare the use of a given formula in your passage with its use elsewhere (see also step 1.4, Lexical Data). Watch also for epiphora (repetition of final sounds or words) and other patterns that frequently appear in poetry. Identify any intentional instances of assonance (repetition or juxtaposition of similar sounds), paronomasia (wordplay, including puns), *figura etymologica* (variation on word roots, often including names), and other such poetic devices. However, do not look for rhyme. Because so many Hebrew words have similar endings (most feminine singulars ending in -*â* [-*āh*], most feminine plurals ending in -*ôth*, most masculine plurals ending in -*îm*), rhyme was too easy and would have been considered "cheap." Other poetic devices were far better tests of a poet's skill and to an audience indicated quality in poetic expression in a way that rhyme simply could not.

1.7. Historical Context

1.7.1. Research the historical background

Try to answer the following questions in your research: What is the setting of the passage? Exactly what events led up to this point? Did major trends or developments in Israel or the rest of the ancient world have any bearing on the passage or any part of its content? Are there any parallel or similar passages in the Bible that seem to be related to the same historical conditions? If so, do they provide any insight into your passage? Under what historical conditions does the passage seem to have been written? Might the passage have been written also under very different historical conditions? If not, why not? Does the passage represent or bring to an end some particular stage in the progress of any events or concepts?

From this point and onward, take note of how the information you have learned about your passage has an effect on its interpretation. Explain how this historical information helps one to understand or appreciate the passage in some way. Be sure to exploit any archaeological data that may exist concerning the passage. In some instances it may not be possible to determine anything specific about the historical background of your passage. For example, this is sometimes the case with poetic passages, such as psalms or proverbs intended to be meaningful at all times and places. If so, explain this to the reader. Describe the implications of the lack of a clear historical context, if any, for your passage.

1.7.2. Research the social setting

Try to answer the following questions: Where in Israel's life are the content or events of the passage located? What social and civil institutions bear upon the passage? How do they illumine the passage? Is the passage or some portion of it directly relevant only to an ancient Israelite (i.e., culturally "bound") or is it useful and meaningful today, and to what extent? Over what range of time or what breadth of Israelite (or other) culture would events of the passage (or its concepts) have been possible or likely? Are the events or concepts uniquely Israelite, or could they have occurred or been expressed elsewhere?

1.7.3. Research the historical foreground

What comes next? What does the passage lead to? What ultimately happens to the people, places, things, and concepts of the passage, and how is that significant? Does the passage contain information essential to understanding something else that occurs or is said later? Is the passage at the start of any new developments? Where does the passage fit in the general scope of OT history? Are there any implications that follow from its placement?

1.7.4. Research the geographical setting

Does the passage have a provenience (a geographical setting or "origin")? In which nation, region, tribal territory, or village do the events or concepts of the passage apply? Is it, for example, a northern or southern passage (i.e., either reflecting a northern or southern origin, or else focusing especially on northern or southern kingdom matters), or an intra-Israel or extra-Israel passage, or is that impossible to discern? Does it have a national or regional perspective? Is it localized in any way? Do issues such as climate, topography, ethnic distribution, regional culture, or economy play a role? Is there anything else about the nature of the geography that illuminates the passage's content in some way?

1.7.5. Date the passage

If the passage is a historical narrative, seek the date for the events as described. If it is a prophetic oracle (revealed message to a prophet), seek the date when it might have been delivered by the prophet. If it is poetry of some other sort, try to determine when it might have been composed.

Arriving at a precise date is not always possible. Be especially cautious in using secondary literature, since a scholar's critical methodology largely determines to what extent one will tend to consider portions of the Bible as "authentic" (genuinely representative of the time and events of which they speak) or not "authentic" (actually products of a later historical period) and will date them accordingly.

If you cannot suggest a specific date, at least suggest the date before which the passage could not have occurred or been composed (called the terminus a quo) and the date by which the passage surely must have already taken place or been composed (called the terminus ad quem). The context and content of the passage, including its vocabulary, are your main guides to date.

Dating prophetic passages precisely is often difficult or impossible. In most cases the only way to proceed is to try to link the message of the passage with historical circumstances known from OT historical portions and other ancient Near Eastern historical sources. This is typically what the commentaries do in such cases. Sometimes it is possible to identify a historical circumstance that forms the background for or subject of an oracle. Many times it is not, and the oracle can be dated no more precisely than within the limits of the book as a whole.

1.8. Literary Context

Some overlap is bound to exist between the historical context and the literary context. The Old Testament (OT) is a historically oriented revelation, and therefore its literary progressions and orderings will tend to correspond to the actual history of Yahweh's dealings with his people.

1.8.1. Examine the literary function

Is your passage part of a story or a literary grouping that has a discernible beginning, middle, and end? Does it fill in, add on, introduce, bring to completion, or counterbalance the book or section of a book of which it is a part? Is it self-contained? Could it be placed elsewhere, or is it essential to its present context? What does it add to the overall picture? What does the overall picture add to it?

1.8.2. Examine the placement

Just how does it fit within the section, book, division, Testament, Bible—in that order? What can you discover about its style, type, purpose, degree of literary integration (degree to which the passage is linked or "woven into" the rest of the book), literary function, and so forth? Is it one of many similar texts in the same book or perhaps in the OT as a whole? In what sense is its nature unique to the surrounding material and/or its position within that material somehow unique?

1.8.3. Analyze the detail

How comprehensive is the passage? If it is historical, how selective has it been? What things does it concentrate on, and what does it leave unsaid? Does it report the events from a special perspective? If so, what does that tell you about the special purpose of the passage? How does its perspective relate to the larger context? If it is poetic, how narrow or broad is its range? Do any details help you decide whether it was written in connection with a specific cultural or historical situation? Do any details give you insight into the author's intentions?

1.8.4. Analyze the authorship

Is the author of the passage identified or identifiable? If the author can be identified, how certain is the identification? If the passage is anonymous, is it possible to suggest generally the probable human source or milieu out of which God communicated his word? Can the time of its composition be discerned, whether or not the identity of the author can be known for sure? Is it possible that material originally written by someone else has been reused, adapted, or incorporated into a larger structure by a later inspired "writer" or "editor"? Does this tell you anything theologically? Does it help you follow the logic of the passage better? If the author is known either explicitly or implicitly, does this knowledge help you connect the passage, including its motifs, style, vocabulary, and so forth, with other portions of Scripture from the hand of the same author? Is this in any way instructive for the interpretation of the passage? Does the author here reveal any unique features (stylistically, for example), or is the passage typical of the author's writing elsewhere?

1.9. Biblical Context

At this point you must begin tentatively drawing together in your mind the essential discoveries from the previous sections for the purpose of focusing on the specific "message" of the passage as it relates more broadly to the message of both its immediate and its wider context. In other words, you can no longer pay attention only to individual features of the passage. How the passage as a complete entity actually fits into a broader body of truth now calls for attention.

At this stage you may find it helpful to summarize for yourself what you consider to be the passage's message—including its central point(s), essential characteristics, unmistakable implications, or the like. Such a summary is necessarily quite tentative, but it helps to focus your attention on the biblical and theological significance of the passage. The three procedures outlined next are designed to help you make headway as regards the passage's connections with the rest of Scripture, and the three that follow in step 1.10 should help you relate the passage to the more general discipline of dogmatic theology.

1.9.1. Analyze the use of the passage elsewhere in Scripture

Is the passage or any part of it quoted or alluded to anywhere else in the Bible? How? Why? If more than once, how and why, and what are the differences, if any? What does the reference made elsewhere to the passage tell you about how it was interpreted and is to be interpreted? If it is alluded to, how does the allusion shed light on how the passage was understood within the context where the allusion is found? If it is quoted, how does the circumstance under which it is quoted aid in its interpretation? The fact that a portion of a passage is quoted elsewhere in Scripture may say a great deal about its intended impact, its uniqueness, its foundational nature theologically, or the like. The way a later inspired biblical writer uses the words or concepts of an earlier biblical passage can take you a long distance toward appreciating the point of that earlier passage.

1.9.2. Analyze the passage's relation to the rest of Scripture

How does the passage function dogmatically (i.e., as teaching or conveying a message) in the section, book, division, Testament, Bible—in that order? Does it have any special relationships to any apocryphal or pseudepigraphic writings or any other extrabiblical writings whose content or perspective might illumine the passage ? How does it or its elements compare to other Scriptures that address the same sorts of issues? What is it similar or dissimilar to? It may be necessary to address these questions with various portions of the passage if you judge that various portions make individual assertions. But the primary goal is always to see the mes-

sage of the passage as a whole as it fits within and contributes to the overall biblical revelation.

1.9.3. Analyze the passage's import for understanding Scripture

What hinges on it elsewhere? What other elements in Scripture help
make it comprehensible? Why? How? Does the passage affect the meaning or value of other Scriptures in a way that crosses literary or historical
lines? Does the passage concern issues dealt with in the same or different
ways elsewhere in Scripture? Does the passage exist primarily to reinforce
what is already knowable from other portions of Scripture, or does it make
a genuinely special, perhaps even unique contribution? Ask yourself the
following question: Suppose the passage were not in the Bible at all. What
would be lost, or how would the message of the Bible be less complete if
the passage did not exist? Answering that question should yield useful
results for appreciating the biblical context.

1.10. Theology

1.10.1. Locate the passage theologically

Where does the passage fit within the whole corpus of revelation consti-
tuting Christian theology? Under which covenant does it fit? Are aspects
of it limited in part or in whole to the Old Covenant as, for example, certain cultic sacrificial practices or certain rules for tribal responsibilities
would be? If so, is it still relevant as a historical example of God's relationship to human beings, or as an indication of God's holiness, standards, justice, immanence, transcendence, compassion, and so forth? (The reason
theology is called *theology* [literally, the study of God] is that the better one
understands God, the better one understands what life is about, what truths
and practices are essential or important, and what values best protect
against disobedience to God. One can understand much about God from
the covenant God revealed to Israel even if various aspects of that covenant
are superseded by the New Covenant.) Is the passage related to far broader
theological concerns that encompass both covenants and are not strictly
bound by either? To which doctrine(s) does the passage relate? Does it have
potential relevance for the classical doctrinal conceptions of God, human-
ity, angels, sin, salvation, the church, eschatology, and so on? Does it relate
to these areas of doctrine because of its vocabulary or subject matter, or
perhaps because of something less explicit? (A passage that shows the

nature of God's love for us may not happen to mention love, God, or us directly.)

1.10.2. Identify the specific issues raised or solved by the passage

Go beyond the general areas of doctrine touched on in the passage and identify the specific issues. What are the problems, blessings, concerns, confidences, and so forth about which the passage has something to say? How does the passage speak to these? How clearly are they dealt with in the passage? Is the passage one that raises apparent difficulties for some doctrines while solving others? If so, try to deal with this situation systematically and also in a manner that is helpful to your readers.

1.10.3. Analyze the theological contribution of the passage

What does the passage contain that contributes to the solution of doctrinal questions or supports solutions offered elsewhere in Scripture? How major or minor is the passage's contribution? How certain can you be that the passage, properly understood, has the theological significance you propose to attach to it? Does your approach agree with that of other scholars or theologians who are known to have addressed themselves to the passage? How does the passage conform theologically to the entire system of truth contained in Christian theology? (It is a basic and indeed necessary assumption that a proper theology should be consistent overall and univocal: coherent and noncontradictory.) How does your passage comport with the greater theological whole? In what way might it be important precisely for that whole? Does it function to counterbalance or correct any questionable or extreme theological position? Is there anything about the passage that does not seem readily to relate to a particular expression of Christian theology? (Remember that the Scripture is primary and theological systems are secondary.)

What solution can you offer for any problems, even tentatively? If a solution is not readily forthcoming, why? Is it because the passage is obscure, because you lack knowledge, or because the presumptions and speculations required would perhaps be too great to be convincing? The Bible contains some things that from a human point of view may seem difficult to comprehend or even paradoxical. Does your passage deal with an area where there are so many unknowns that you must refrain from trying to identify some aspects of its theological contribution? If so, your reader deserves to be told this, but in a constructive rather than a destructive way. Do everything you can to milk the passage for its theological value, but do not force anything from or into the passage.

1.11. Application

Everyone agrees that exegesis seeks to determine the meaning of a passage of Scripture. Many exegetes believe, however, that their responsibilities stop with the past—that exegesis is the attempt to discover what the text *meant*, not what it *means* now.

Placing such arbitrary limits on exegesis is unsatisfactory for three reasons. First, it ignores the ultimate reason why the vast majority of people engage in exegesis or are interested in the results of exegesis: they desire to hear and obey God's word as it is found in the passage. Exegesis, in other words, is an empty intellectual entertainment when divorced from application. Second, it addresses only one aspect of meaning—the historical—as if God's words were intended only for individual generations and not also for us and, indeed, for those who will follow us in time. The Scriptures are our Scriptures, not just the Scriptures of the ancients. Finally, it leaves the actual personal or corporate existential interpretation and use of the passage to subjectivity. The exegete, who has come to know the passage best, refuses to help the reader or hearer of the passage at the very point where the reader's or hearer's interest is keenest. The exegete leaves the key function—response—completely to the subjective sensibilities of the reader or hearer, who knows the passage least. Naturally, the exegete cannot actually control what the reader or hearer does in response to the passage. But the exegete can—and must—try to define the areas within which a faithful response will be found and likewise to warn about putative areas of response that the passage might seem on the surface to call for but that turn out not to be justified by the results of good exegesis.

Making decisions about application is more an art than a science; it is qualitative, not quantitative. Nevertheless, the following procedural steps will help you isolate the applicable issues of the passage systematically and will maximize your chances of relating those issues properly to the persons or groups for whom your exegesis should have benefit. An application should be just as rigorous, just as thorough, and just as analytically sound as any other step in the exegesis process. It cannot be merely tacked on to the rest of the exegesis as a sort of spiritual afterthought. Moreover, it must carefully reflect the data of the passage if it is to be convincing. Your reader or hearer needs to see how you derived the application as the natural and final stage of the entire process of careful, analytical study (exegesis) of your passage.

Subjectivity is the primary enemy of good application. When people think that they can derive from a passage an application somehow relevant to them but not to others, or somehow unique to one passage but not even comparable to the applications of genuinely similar passages, the probability of logical consistency is reduced and the likelihood of accuracy is threatened.

Objectivity in application is best assured by following the sort of systematic process outlined next. See also "A List of Frequent Hermeneutical Errors" (in appendix 2) for brief explanations of some of the most common hermeneutical fallacies that undermine the likelihood of proper application.

1.11.1. List the life issues

A starting point for the proper application of a passage is comparing life issues. To apply a passage, you must try to decide what its central issues are and what issues in it are only secondary. In other words, what aspect(s) of life is the passage really concerned about? You must try to decide how such issues are or are not still active in the lives of persons or groups today. What do "I" or "we" encounter today that is similar or at least related to what the passage deals with? The life issues will emerge from the exegetical data on the one hand, and from your own knowledge of the world on the other.

First identify all potential life issues included in the passage. Then identify issues transferable from the passage to the current situation, using the following steps to help make the transfer accurate. The audience for whom you are doing your exegesis can have an effect on the way you isolate the issues but should not per se change the issues themselves.

1.11.2. Clarify the nature of the application (does it inform or direct?)

Applications may generally be of two kinds: those that basically inform the reader and those that basically direct the reader. A passage that functions to describe some aspect of God's love might be considered primarily to inform. A passage that functions to command the reader to love God wholeheartedly primarily directs. Obviously there is considerable overlap between informing and directing, and a passage can contain elements that are at the same time informative and directive. Nevertheless, the force of your application will be much clearer and more specific if you divide the applicability in this way, at least tentatively. At first, maximize—include all the possibilities, knowing that you will discard some or most later, after more analysis. Caution: Narrative passages do not generally teach something directly; rather, they illustrate what is taught directly elsewhere.

1.11.3. Clarify the possible areas of application (faith or action)

Applications may fall into two general areas: faith and action. In practice, faith and action should ultimately be inseparable—a genuine Christian could not display one without the other. But even though they must belong together in the Christian's life, faith and action may be considered distinct entities, and a given passage, part or whole, may concentrate on one more than the other. Try therefore to decide the potential areas of application for the material contained in the passage, tentatively dividing the areas into categories of faith and action. Be inclusive at first; reject and discard later.

1.11.4. Identify the audience of the application

There are primarily two audiences to whom the application(s) may be seen to be directed: the personal and the corporate. What in the passage gives information or direction regarding faith or action to individuals? What to groups or corporate structures? If such a differentiation cannot be made, why not?

If the passage informs or directs individuals, what kind of individuals are they? Christian or non-Christian? Laypersons or clergy? Parents or children? Powerful or weak? Haughty or humble? Desperate or confident? What in the passage makes this clear? How does the passage address the object of its informing or directing? If the passage informs or directs groups or corporate entities, which kind are they? Church? Nation? Clergy? A profession? A societal structure? A family? People who are closely allied? People who are at enmity with one another? Some other group or combination of groups? And so on.

1.11.5. Establish the categories of the application

Is the application directed toward matters primarily personal in nature or primarily interpersonal in nature? Matters that relate to sin, or perhaps to doubt, or perhaps to proper piety? Or to the relationship of God and people? Is the concern social, economic, moral, religious, spiritual, familial, financial, or other areas? And so on.

1.11.6. Determine the time focus of the application

Does the passage call primarily for a recognition of something that has occurred in the past as a way of orienting us to what God has done, what God is like, or who we are in relation to him, or the like? Or does it expect present faith or action? Does it perhaps look primarily to the future? Does the application involve a combination of times? Is there a concern for immediate action? Or is what the passage calls for more a matter of steady, consistent response over a long period of time? Does the timing of the application depend on the nature of the audience or some other factor? And so on.

1.11.7. Fix the limits of the application

This is an important step: it often is as valuable and necessary to explain how a passage does *not* apply as to explain how it does. Does the passage call for a response that could possibly be misunderstood and then taken too far? If so, how can you define what is too far? Does the passage call for an application that is secondary rather than primary? That is, does your passage function more as a background or support, or part of a further or larger passage that more specifically suggests an application than does your passage? Is your passage one of several that all function together to indicate a given application that none of them individually would quite indicate, or at least quite indicate in the same way? Are there any applications that at first might seem appropriate to the passage but which upon more careful examination are not? If so, briefly identify these for your reader and give your reasoning. Does the passage have a double-barreled application, as certain messianic passages do—one application having immediate reference for the people who first heard it in OT times, the other having more of a long-range reference, for people in our day? If so, are both applications of equal weight now? Were they of equal weight when the passage was first spoken or written?

In general, it is probably safest to limit potential applications as much as possible. Rare is the passage that calls for several applications, all of equal relevance or practicability. Try to decide what *single* application is most central to and follows most naturally from the passage. If you are convinced that the passage demands more than one application, at least try to rank these in order of either universality of application or urgency of application. Remember: You are not responsible for discussing all the possible ways in which the passage might strike the fancy of the reader or be put to use—wisely or not—by the reader. Rather, you are responsible for educating the reader about what the passage itself calls for or leads to in terms of application. If the passage is so brief or specialized that you are at a loss to suggest any application for it (even as part of a greater whole), you would be wiser to suggest no application than to suggest one that is ultimately unsound. By all means, an application must derive demonstrably from the data of the passage and not from preconceived notions to which the passage is then forced to conform.

1.12. Secondary Literature

1.12.1. Investigate and learn from what others have said about the passage

Even though you will have consulted commentaries, grammars, and many kinds of other books and articles in the process of completing the preceding eleven steps, you should now undertake a more systematic investigation of the secondary literature that may apply to your passage. In order for the exegesis to be your work and not merely a mechanical compendium of others' views, it is wise to do your own thinking and to arrive at your own conclusions as much as possible before this step. Otherwise you are not so much doing an exegesis of the passage as evaluating others' exegeses—and therefore potentially prejudicing yourself not to go beyond what they have achieved.

Now, however, is the proper time to ask what various scholars think about the passage. What points have they made that you have overlooked? What have they said better? What have they given more weight to? Or conversely, what do you feel you must reject in their views? Can you point out things they have said that are questionable or incorrect? If in your opinion any of these scholars is to be disagreed with, you can point this out by using footnotes for minor differences and the body of the paper for more significant ones. As a rule, it is considered far more convincing to disagree with a scholar's views if you have also given that person proper commendation for the views that you do agree with, and to state your own conclusions modestly rather than stridently. If you cannot describe with appreciation and respect someone else's earnest attempt to explain a position and defend it, even though you disagree with it, you will surely undercut the degree to which your own arguments seem convincing as you try to refute it.

1.12.2. Compare and adjust

Have the conclusions of other scholars helped you to change your analysis in any way? Do other scholars analyze the passage or any aspects of it in a manner that is more incisive or that leads to a more satisfying set of conclusions? Do they organize their exegesis in a better way? Do they give consideration to implications you had not even considered? Do they supplement your own findings? If so, do not hesitate to revise your own conclusions or procedures in steps 1.1 through 1.11 (textual analysis through application), giving proper credit in each case. But never feel that in your exegesis you must cover everything that the others do. Reject what does not seem germane, and limit what seems out of proportion. You decide, not they.

1.12.3. Apply your discoveries throughout your paper or project

It should not be necessary to include a separate section of findings from secondary literature in any draft of your paper/project. So do not view this step as resulting in a single block of material within the paper. Rather, this step will show itself generally in the quality of the paper, in the suitability of your interaction with the views of others, in the footnotes, and in the bibliography. Thus step 1.12, consulting secondary literature, is a step in your research process but not something you need to discuss in your final written product. At many points throughout the exegesis, your discoveries should produce additions or corrections or both. You must always be willing to go back and adjust what you have previously thought you understood. Try to be sure that a change or addition at one point does not contradict statements made elsewhere in the paper. Consider the implications of all changes. For example, if you adjust the textual analysis (step 1.1) on the basis of what you have now learned from something in the secondary literature, how will this affect the translation, lexical data, and other parts of the exegesis? Aim for consistency and evenness throughout. This will considerably influence the reader's ability to appreciate your conclusions. Carefully give due credit to secondary sources in the footnotes and bibliography. Every source that has contributed to your conclusions requires citation somewhere in your paper/project, lest you implicitly claim that ideas you received are ideas you generated.

Moving from Outline to Paper

After completing the research in step-by-step fashion, you will want to organize the results into a format that presents them effectively to the reader.

There are many acceptable formats. If a given one is specified for you by a professor or editor, you will obviously follow that. Otherwise you might wish to consider using one of the three most common options. The first is the topical format, which proceeds much in the same order as the twelve steps above, but with sections and headings rearranged, combined, expanded, or otherwise adjusted according to your own best sense of how the material of the passage can be drawn convincingly to the attention of the reader. The second is the commentary format, which moves more or less verse by verse through the passage, marshaling relevant data and conclusions as they apply to individual parts of the passage, yet not excluding appropriate additional sections, such as introductions, excursuses, and summaries. The third is the unitary format, in which the passage is discussed in a relatively free-flowing fashion, apart from a strictly systematic or methodical outline, with or without the use of formally identified sections, subsections, headings, and so forth.

Any of these formats—and others—can serve you well. Do not hesitate to be innovative, as long as the format you choose aids in getting the full impact of your findings across to your readers clearly.

Chapter Two

Exegesis and the Original Text

The purpose of this chapter is to help you get a better feel for the process of exegesis by providing illustrations of how certain parts of the process might work in various OT passages. A number of passages are used selectively here—in some instances more than one for a given exegesis step—in an effort to provide you with an exposure to the OT's rich diversity of material. Therefore you will not see a systematic exegetical coverage of any single passage; for examples of the latter, recent technical and exegetical commentaries such as the Word Biblical Commentary series or the Hermeneia series (see 4.12.4) will prove helpful, as will, occasionally, the exegesis articles in a journal such as *Interpretation* (4.12.2).

Those who cannot read Hebrew will still find the content of this chapter helpful and generally comprehensible. For those who know Hebrew, regular reference to *BHS* (or *BH*³ or *BHQ*) is essential for a sense of the full contexts from which this chapter's selections are taken.

For convenience, the divisions in this chapter correspond to those in chapter 1. Not every step should require an illustration, but wherever one might genuinely be helpful, at least one has been provided. Longer or multiple illustrations have been provided when it seemed that they might help to clarify the exegesis process.

2.1. Text

2.1.1. Confirming the limits of the passage

There are two places to which you can turn immediately for help in confirming proper limits for a passage: (1) the Hebrew text itself in *BHS* (or

BH³ or *BHQ*), and (2) virtually any modern translation. Examine their paragraphing. In the case of the Hebrew text, the biblical material is set off in paragraph form by means of right-margin indentation variation. When the margin location changes, either by going further into the middle of the page or by going further back out to the right edge, that is signaling the editor's opinion that logically a new section has begun. In the case of the modern English versions, simple indentation of the first word in a sentence indicates a new paragraph. By examining the arrangement of your passage, ideally in both Hebrew and English, you can quickly tell whether your own tentative identification of a passage conforms to scholars' judgments about the natural groupings of subject matter.

Decisions about paragraphing are sometimes subjective, and you will find that the various editors' groupings of content do not always agree. But if you decide to start your passage where no editor has begun a paragraph, or end your passage where no editor has ended a paragraph, then it is your responsibility to argue fully for your decision to select or configure the passage as you have done.

2.1.2. Comparing the versions

To analyze the contribution of the various ancient language versions of the OT for confirming or questioning the Hebrew text, you must in effect translate each one back into Hebrew at least to the extent that you can tell whether it reflects the MT or runs contrary to it. Since this process can be complicated, most people find it helpful, at least at first, to chart the versions one above another, line by line, so that your ability to compare readings is facilitated. Remember to compare the wording of the versions for the whole passage. If you try to consult the versions only when the MT seems problematic, you will miss all the variants resulting from MT corruptions that once were obvious but later were smoothed over and rewritten into readable Hebrew (but not necessarily the original Hebrew) by well-meaning scribes of old.

A word-by-word comparison in the case of 1 Samuel 20:32 (where the Qumran version happens to exist) would look something like the chart on the next page.

By writing out the Hebrew of the MT, then listing selected versions (including the LXX) directly underneath, according to the Semitic word order from right to left, you can easily see how the versions line up. In the chart, the parentheses are a convenient way to indicate that both the

Qumran text and the LXX omit any correspondence to the MT אֵלָיו, suggesting that this word might be an expansion (in this case, a simple explanatory addition) in the MT. However, the LXX also omits any correspondence to the MT and Qumran words ויאמר אביו. This perhaps reflects a haplography (a loss of something once present) in the Hebrew text that was used by the LXX translator. The Peshitta and Targum follow the MT, as they usually do. The Vulgate also follows the MT, as it typically does. (The Peshitta, Targum, and Vulgate are much less often truly "independent" witnesses to an original that differs from the MT than the LXX is. Even the Qumran scrolls, themselves Hebrew, will much more often reflect independence from the Hebrew MT than the Peshitta, Targum, or Vulgate will.)

In the chart we have included the English translation according to the Semitic word order. You may find it helpful to do this, at least as you begin learning the method. You may also wish to include the English translation under any spot where the versions contain a wording different from the MT, especially if you cannot translate the various versions at sight! Refer to Brotzman's *Old Testament Textual Criticism: A Practical Introduction* or Tov's *Textual Criticism of the Hebrew Bible* or McCarter's *Textual Criticism: Recovering the Text of the Hebrew Bible* (see 4.1.2) for examples and explanations of the principles involved in deciding which version best reflects the original.

1 Samuel 20:32

אביו	את שאול	יהונתן	ויען	MT
his father	Saul	Jonathan	And answered	
"	"	[first two words obliterated]		Qumran
( )	τῷ Σαουλ	Ιωναθαν	καὶ ἀπεκρίθη	LXX
"	" "	"	" "	Syriac
"	" "	"	" "	Targum
				Vulgate

עשה	מה	יומת	למה	אליו	ויאמר
has he done?	What	must he die?	Why	to him	and said
"	"	"	"	( )	"
πεποίηκεν;	τί	ἀποθνῄσκει;	῞Ινα τί	( )	( )
"	"	"	" "	"	"
"	"	"	" "	"	"
"	"	"	" "	"	"

2.1.3. Reconstructing and annotating the text

Two examples are given here to illustrate the process of reconstructing and annotating the text. Many times a passage will require no reconstruction at all. After you have compared the versions, you will decide that the passage as printed in the *BHS* or *BH³* or *BHQ* (all three contain the wording of the Leningrad Codex of AD 1008) adequately preserves the original. But when the ancient versions disagree significantly, you must try to determine how that disagreement might have arisen. Thus you must look for an original wording that would best account for the present divergent wordings. This means working backward from what is present in the various ancient versions to what theoretically must have been in the original text.

Hundreds of differences in translation among modern English versions of the OT are due simply to translators' reconstructions of the Hebrew text. No modern translation follows the *BHS/BH³/BHQ* Hebrew text slavishly. All translators will modify a text whenever they think that the evidence from the ancient versions points to an original Hebrew text different from that preserved in the Leningrad Codex. As a result, they are often translating into English from a reconstructed Hebrew text. Thus, if for no other reason than to understand why modern translators have done what they have done, you need to know something about how reconstructing a text works. The examples below should help.

Reconstructing two Hebrew names: Joshua 7:1
A careful comparison of the ancient versions confirms what the *BHS* textual footnotes 1a and 1b alert you to in abbreviated form. That is, the Hebrew (MT)

עָכָן בֶּן־כַּרְמִי בֶן־זַבְדִּי

is possibly the result of a miscopy at some point in the long history of the transmission of the text of Joshua. For the name עָכָן (Achan) you find that a number of important Septuagint (Greek) texts, as well as the Syriac Peshitta, have the equivalent of עָכָר (Achar), which is the form this name has in the Hebrew text as well at 1 Chronicles 2:7. Moreover, the name of this person's grandfather, זַבְדִּי (Zabdi) in the Hebrew, is rendered in a number of important Septuagint texts as the equivalent of זִמְרִי (Zimri), which is also the form the name has in 1 Chronicles 2:6.

Which is correct: Achan grandson of Zabdi or Achar grandson of Zimri? Three considerations help you decide. First, you take the approach that the Greek (LXX) evidence must be evaluated seriously. (See 4.1.3 for further comment on the value of the LXX relative to the MT.) It makes the choice at least a toss-up. In the instance of the first name, the addition of Syriac evidence adds even more weight. Second, you note that the comparative readings in Chronicles are very strong evidence for Achar and Zimri, respectively. Why? Because the Chronicler, writing long after the book of Joshua was complete, reflects an independent rendering of the names. We have no evidence to suggest that the Chronicler would alter a name, and plenty to suggest that his concern for accurate genealogies might preserve a name more precisely than even a copy of the book of Joshua would. Third, you see that the passage makes an issue of the mnemonic device, a pun, by which Israelites remembered the valley where Achan/Achar was stoned. They called it (Josh. 7:26) עֵמֶק עָכוֹר, "Trouble Valley," the word for "trouble" (עָכוֹר, Achor) having the same consonants as Achar, but not those of Achan.

You must then give this evidence and your reasoning (whether briefly or at length depends on the scope of your paper/project) for the originality of Achar and Zimri, in annotations to the text as you print it out. Using the bracket system recommended in chapter 1, you may make your reconstructed text look something like this:

$$\text{וַיִּקַּח עָכָ<ר> }^{a}\text{ בֶּן־כַּרְמִי בֶן־זִ<מְר> }^{b}\text{יִ}$$

The superscript letters [a] and [b] will alert the reader to look for explanations of these reconstructions in your annotations.

Reconstructing a common term: 1 Samuel 8:16

Near the middle of the verse, the Hebrew (MT) reads:

וְאֶת־בַּחוּרֵיכֶם הַטּוֹבִים
and your fine/choice young men

A careful examination of the ancient versions reveals to you, however, that the Greek (LXX) at the same point in the verse has

τὰ βουκόλια ὑμῶν τὰ ἀγαθά
your fine/choice cattle

Which was the original—"cattle" or "young men" or neither—and how do you decide? First, following the most basic principle of text criticism (as explained for you in any of the basic guides to text criticism listed in 4.1.2), you try to determine what original wording would, in the history of copying/miscopying the passage, have produced both "young men" in the Hebrew and "cattle" in the Greek. To do this you must translate the Greek back into Hebrew, because the original wording was not Greek but Hebrew. Here, by consulting Hatch and Redpath's *Concordance to the Septuagint* (see 4.4.2) or by using one of the computer concordances to trace Hebrew equivalents for Greek words (see 4.4.2) or by using Tov's text comparison concordance (see 4.4.2) you can find at once that βουκόλια is how the LXX frequently translated the Hebrew בָּקָר, "cattle."

Now, just two more steps. First, you compare בָּחוּר and בָּקָר. The words are the same except for the middle consonant, ח or ק. The *shureq* vowel (וּ), though written with *waw*, is only a vowel and represents a vocalization decision by copyists long after 1 Samuel was first written (cf., e.g., Cross and Freedman, *Early Hebrew Orthography* [4.3.2]). What original word would account for both בָּחוּר and בָּקָר? Your answer is בָּקָר, "cattle." The ח of בָּחוּר is probably the miscopy. Second, you confirm this decision by analyzing the immediate context. After "male slaves" and "female slaves" (a logical pair), "young men" and "donkeys" would hardly go together. But "cattle" and "donkeys," another logical pair, certainly would.

Finally, you summarize the evidence and your reasoning for your reader, at whatever length is appropriate to your paper. Your reconstructed text might look like this:

וְאֶת־בְּקַ[ר]^aרֵיכֶם הַטּוֹבִים

The [a] would refer the reader to your annotation, that is, your summary of the textual evidence and explanation, in the footnotes or endnotes.

2.1.4. *Putting your passage in versified form*

To save space, the *BHS* (as did *BH³* and as will *BHQ*) arranges poetry so that an entire couplet (bicolon) or triplet (tricolon) appears on one printed line. But in an exegesis paper, it is usually better to list each part of a couplet or triplet on a line of its own. In this way the correspondences from line to line are much more evident.

Here is Numbers 23:8–9 versified in such a manner:

How can I curse   מָה אֶקֹּב לֹא קַבֹּה אֵל[8]
  whom God has not cursed?

| And how can I denounce | וּמָה אֶזְעֹם לֹא זָעַם יהוה |
| whom Yahweh has not denounced? | |

| For from the tops of the mountains | ⁹כִּי־מֵרֹאשׁ צֻרִים אֶרְאֶנּוּ |
| I see him, | |

| And from the hills I view him. | וּמִגְּבָעוֹת אֲשׁוּרֶנּוּ |

| Look, the people dwells alone | הֶן־עָם לְבָדָד יִשְׁכֹּן |

| And among the nations | וּבַגּוֹיִם לֹא יִתְחַשָּׁב |
| does not consider itself. | |

From such an arrangement it is much easier to see that the couplet in verse 8 is a simple word-for-word synonymous parallelism, while the couplets in verse 9 represent more complicated synonymous parallelisms.

By the way, unless you actually intend to analyze the Masoretes' medieval chanting system or count their (chanting) accents as a rough way of analyzing the meter of a poem (see the Masorah introductions by Kelley et al. or Ginsburg in 4.1.2 for help in doing this if it is what you wish to do), there is no point in including the accent marks in your own written text.

2.2. Translation

The purpose of the following illustrations is to encourage you to produce your own translation of a passage rather than simply relying on translations found in major modern versions. These brief examples all involve relatively simple Hebrew wordings, which nevertheless have not always been translated clearly or even properly.

What right have you to disagree with translations produced by "experts"? You have every right! Consider the facts: All the modern translations (and all the ancient ones for that matter) have been produced either by committees working against time deadlines or by individuals who cannot possibly know the whole Bible so well in the original that they produce flawless renderings at every point. Moreover, in the modern business of Bible publishing, the more "different" a translation is, the more risk there is that it will not sell. Thus there is a pressure on translators, committees, publishers, and others responsible to keep renderings conservative in meaning, even though, happily, usually up-to-date in idiomatic language. Finally, most people hate to go out on a limb with a translation in print. Many translation problems are matters of ambiguity: there is more than one way to construe the original. But space limitations do not permit translators to offer an explanation every time they might wish to render something from the original in a truly new way. So they almost always err on the side of caution. As a result, all modern translations tend, albeit with perfectly good intentions, to be overly "safe" and traditional. In the working of a translation committee, the lone genius is usually out-voted by the cautious majority.

Therefore, every so often you might actually produce a better translation than others have done because you can invest much more time exegeting your passage than the individuals or committees were able to afford because of the speed at which they were required to work. Besides, you are choosing a translation suitable for your particular reader(s) rather than for the whole English-speaking world. Remember: A word does not so much have an individual meaning as a *range of meanings*. Choosing from that range of meanings is often subjective and should be something you do for the benefit of your audience, rather than something you leave entirely to others who have no knowledge of your audience and must translate strictly for the masses. Fortunately, in an exegesis paper/project you can explain briefly to your reader, in the annotations to your translation, the options you had to choose from and your reason(s) for choosing the particular English word that you did. Those who worked on the various ancient or modern versions did not have such an opportunity.

2.2.1. A translation that clarifies a prophet's behavior: Jonah 1:2

וּקְרָא עָלֶיהָ כִּי־עָלְתָה רָעָתָם לְפָנָי

The usual translation of the last part of the verse is something like this: "Proclaim against it because its evil has come up before me." This translation, however, has always been problematic. It represents only one way of rendering some Hebrew words that have extensive ranges of meaning, and it does not fit easily the point of the overall story. After all, this is a command that Jonah tries to disobey by refusing to go to Nineveh. Yet as typically translated, it sounds like a command Jonah would love to obey. Why would he not be glad to preach against a city that God has declared to be *evil*—a city occupied by the enemies of his people?

In 1.2.1 you are advised to "start fresh, from the beginning." Following that advice, and determined not to accept the usual translation as the only reasonable option just because it is the usual one, you consider the meaning of the Hebrew words afresh by looking at their definitions in a good up-to-date lexicon such as Holladay or Koehler-Baumgartner (4.8.1). Here is what you find: עַל can mean "against" but also "concerning." כִּי can mean "because" but also "that." רָעָה can mean "evil" but more commonly means "trouble." And עָלָה . . . לְפָנַי is best translated idiomatically not "come . . . before me" but "come . . . to my attention." Eventually you conclude that the whole clause can very well mean "proclaim concerning it that their trouble has come to my attention."

The exegetical implications are significant. In contrast to the usual translation, your translation makes it clear why the hypernationalist Jonah fled from his assignment: God was sending him on a mission of concern, not a mission of denunciation. A careful reading of the rest of the book confirms this repeatedly (cf. esp. Jonah 4).

2.2.2. A modest, noninterpretive translation: Proverbs 22:6

חֲנֹךְ לַנַּעַר עַל־פִּי דַרְכּוֹ
גַּם כִּי־יַזְקִין לֹא־יָסוּר מִמֶּנָּה

This verse is usually translated about as follows: "Train a child in the way he should go, and when he is old he will not depart from it." But when you closely analyze the words' meaning ranges, you find no Hebrew equivalent for the English "should." This piques your interest. After all, the usual translation seems to promise quite a lot. Indeed, this rather popular verse has often been cited in support of the notion that parents can virtually guarantee that their children will turn out to be godly adults if raised properly. Most proverbs are of course generalizations, and generalizations have their exceptions. But you still have every right to "start fresh" in your own translation of this proverb, no matter how well known it may be. (Remember: The better known a wording in the Bible is, the more hesitant modern professional translators are to depart from it, even when they dislike it, for fear that people will not buy a Bible that has changed the wording of one of their "favorite verses.")

The process of translating afresh is not terribly complicated. It requires mainly a willingness to consider combinations of meanings slowly and carefully. Thus with regard to Proverbs 22:6, what you can easily determine by patiently consulting a lexicon is that עַל־פִּי means "according to" and that דֶּרֶךְ means simply "way," so that דַרְכּוֹ means either "his way" or "his own way." The first half of this poetic couplet actually says, then, "Train a child according to his (own) way." You still find nothing about "should" here. The real point of the verse, you rightly conclude, is that a child who is allowed selfishly to do what the child wants when young will have the same selfish tendencies as an adult.

Note: Excellent sources of alternative translations are the authors' translations in technical commentaries. A scholar who has studied a book intensively is usually best equipped to offer a nuanced translation. And for late-breaking information on more precise meanings of individual Hebrew words, check the annual listing of words discussed in such databases as *Old Testament Abstracts* (4.12.1), via either its book format or its computerized format.

2.3. Grammatical Data

Here is where all those hours spent learning your Hebrew grammar can finally pay off. The goal of grammar is accuracy. In any language, bad grammar may offend our tastes, but its greater danger is that it may block our comprehension. In the exegesis process, a failure to appreciate the grammar in an OT passage is not simply a failure to observe niceties of speech; it is a failure to be sure that you know exactly what was or was not said.

2.3.1. Identifying grammatical ambiguity: Judges 19:25

וַיַּחֲזֵק הָאִישׁ בְּפִילַגְשׁוֹ וַיֹּצֵא אֲלֵיהֶם

So the man seized his concubine, and brought her out to them.

Exegeting Judges 19, you become aware of a puzzling apparent inconsistency. The Levite seems rather inconsiderate (v. 28) of what he has put his concubine through in giving her over to a gang of rapists (vv. 22–25), and yet later he seems so furious at what they (predictably) have done to her that he calls all Israel to war over the matter (vv. 29–30; chap. 20). Carefully, with an eye toward precise grammar, you reread the relevant portions to determine if your initial impression has been accurate. Your special interest is in understanding exactly who the parties involved in verse 25 were.

You note that each of the characters in the story is referred to in more than one way. Specifically, the Levite is referred to as אִישׁ לֵוִי ("Levite," v. 1); אִישָׁהּ ("her husband," v. 3); חֲתָנוֹ ("his son-in-law," vv. 5, 9); and הָאִישׁ ("the man," vv. 7, 9, 17, 22, 28, etc.). The Ephraimite man in whose house he stayed at Gibeah is called אִישׁ זָקֵן ("an old man," v. 16); הָאִישׁ ("the man," vv. 16, 22, 23, 26); and הָאִישׁ הַזָּקֵן ("the old man," vv. 17, 20, etc.). You see from a quick comparison that either the Levite or the old man can be referred to as simply הָאִישׁ (the man). Who then is the actual grammatical referent for הָאִישׁ (the man) in verse 25? The concubine's identity is rather clear, but הָאִישׁ (the man) is apparently ambiguous. Deciding requires weighing the evidence on two fronts.

First, you observe that outside of verse 25, both the Levite and the old man may be called strictly הָאִישׁ (the man) or may be called הָאִישׁ (the man) with a modifier, as in הָאִישׁ הָאֹרֵחַ ("the man who was traveling," v. 17) or הָאִישׁ בַּעַל הַבַּיִת ("the man who owned the house," v. 22). Thus הָאִישׁ (the man) in verse 25 is truly ambiguous. The lack of a modifier makes it so.

Second, you note that in verses 22–25 it is clearly established that the owner of the house was in conversation with the rapists, but there is no indication that the Levite was. You then decide, rightly, that הָאִישׁ (the man) has as its grammatical referent the old man, not the Levite.

Grammatical analysis does have its limits. In the instance of Judges 19, a separate question remains: Would not the Levite know what the old man had done? Grammar can lead to that question but cannot answer it. Its solution is found both in the analysis of the structure of the passage (a typically laconic biblical narrative, the passage omits all but essential details and expects you to realize that the Levite was unaware of the old man's actions) and in the analysis of the historical context (as we know from archaeology, many Israelite houses had their living/sleeping quarters—where the Levite presumably was—in a back room, as far from the courtyard door as possible, so it would have been difficult for the guest to hear what was going on when the old man confronted the rapists).

2.3.2. Identifying grammatical specificity: Hosea 1:2

לֵךְ קַח־לְךָ אֵשֶׁת זְנוּנִים וְיַלְדֵי זְנוּנִים כִּי־זָנֹה תִזְנֶה הָאָרֶץ מֵאַחֲרֵי יְהוָה

Go, marry a woman of prostitution and have children
of prostitution because the land is completely
committing prostitution away from Yahweh.

Exegeting Hosea 1, you are immediately confronted with an interpretational question: Did God actually command Hosea to marry a prostitute? Many commentators have answered in the affirmative, often suggesting that Hosea's wife probably turned to prostitution sometime after their marriage; and Hosea, looking back on his past at a later point when he was seeking an analogy for Israel's unfaithfulness to Yahweh, recast the story of his marriage as if he had been commanded to marry a prostitute in the first place. However, these interpreters do not necessarily have Hebrew grammar on their side.

There are only three words for "prostitute" in Hebrew: קְדֵשָׁה (cult prostitute), זֹנָה (common prostitute), and כֶּלֶב (male prostitute). You observe the obvious: None of the three is used here. Instead, a special compound term appears: The word אִשָּׁה for "woman" or "wife" is used in what Hebrew grammarians call the "bound form" or, most commonly, the "construct form" in combination with a governing noun in the masculine plural, זְנוּנִים. Checking any Hebrew reference grammar (4.3.1), you are reminded that the masculine plural is one standard way in Hebrew for conveying abstraction—in this case, not "prostitute" but the concept "prostitution," thus in theological contexts, the opposite of "faithfulness." Moreover, you find that nouns in the "construct" are often related logically to their governing noun in the manner of "something characterized by," so that אֵשֶׁת זְנוּנִים would tend to mean "a woman characterized by [the abstract concept of] prostitution" rather than "a prostitute." You also observe that Hosea's children are called יַלְדֵי זְנוּנִים, "children of prostitution," in a precisely parallel Hebrew construction: "children characterized by [the abstract concept of] prostitution" rather than "children of a prostitute." You note as well that the verse goes on to say that the land (of Israel) זָנֹה תִזְנֶה, "is completely committing prostitution." Finally, the grammars tell you that the preposition employed at the end of the verse, מֵאַחֲרֵי, "away from," is a compound preposition literally meaning "away from after," thus here "in the other direction from going after [following]" Yahweh.

Thus the same thing is being said about Hosea's wife, about the children that are eventually born to him, and about the land of Israel in general—and in no case is the literal meaning apparently related to actually selling sex. But what, then, is being said? If neither the wife nor the children nor the population of Israel are being called literally "prostitutes," what is the charge against them? You must answer that question partly by reference to literary context and biblical context, though still with a keen eye to the Hebrew grammar involved. Looking at the way that the Hebrew root in question, *znh* (זנה), is used predominantly elsewhere in Hosea (and other prophetical contexts, notably Ezekiel), you find that it is employed mainly metaphorically, to convey the sense of "ultimate [religious] unfaithfulness" to Yahweh. Returning to Hosea 1:2, you conclude that the verse is conceptually parallel to Isaiah 64:6 or Psalm 14:2–3 (cf. Rom. 3:10–12). It makes the point, in a somewhat hyperbolic manner, that all Israel has abandoned Yahweh's covenant, so that even Hosea's wife and children—no matter whom he marries—will be tainted by the same unfaithfulness that "the land" in general displays.

2.3.3. *Analyzing orthography and morphology*

As 1.3.2 states, the analysis of Hebrew orthography or morphology is not a task that beginning students can easily undertake. But its value is often inestimable in connection with problem passages, especially where the decisions of the medieval Masoretes about how words were to be understood may be suspect.

Orthographic analysis removes an oddity: Genesis 49:10

לֹא־יָסוּר שֵׁבֶט מִיהוּדָה
וּמְחֹקֵק מִבֵּין רַגְלָיו
עַד כִּי־יָבֹא שִׁילֹה
וְלוֹ יִקְּהַת עַמִּים

In the third line, the Hebrew seems to say "until Shiloh comes" or "until he comes to Shiloh." Both meanings, you conclude, are odd, and your reading reveals a general dissatisfaction on the part of translators with the masoretic vocalization as it stands. In this case a convincing solution will require some ability to appreciate ancient Hebrew orthography (spelling style), which requires a knowledge of Hebrew beyond the beginner level (see 1.3.2).

The problem may involve vocalization, orthography, and even word division. The combination כִּי עַד (until) seems clear enough. But is there another way to construe שִׁילֹה יָבֹא? Since שִׁילֹה (Shiloh) is the really odd factor here, you decide to try to reanalyze it. Removing the vowels will remove the medieval Masoretes' possibly incorrect opinion as to vocalization. You now have שׁילה. Can the word be divided? Could a spacing problem have resulted in שׁילה? You divide שׁי from לה. Looking up שׁי, you find that its consonants are those of a normal Hebrew word (שַׁי) meaning "gifts(s), present(s), tribute(s)." But what about לה? Referring to Cross and Freedman's *Early Hebrew Orthography* (4.3.2), you learn that לה was how לוֹ (to him) was once spelled. Accordingly, שׁילה could be שַׁי לֹה, "tribute to him." Now you look closely at יָבֹא. Again, removing the masoretic accentuation so as to have a fresh look at vocalization, you get יבא. Cross and Freedman tell you that in early poems like Genesis 49, the original orthography was without vowels and thus quite ambiguous. So the consonants יבא could represent what was later vocalized as יָבֹא (comes) or יָבִיא

("brings," hiphil) or יוּבָא ("is brought," hophal), and so on. The last option catches your attention, because it fits the context so well.

You conclude (with some well-justified second-guessing of the Masoretes, whose vocalizations, after all, represent only their opinions about how words were to be construed long after a passage was originally written) that the "Shiloh" line of the poem should read as follows:

עַד כִּי־יוּבָא שַׁי לֹה

until tribute is brought to him

The fact that this meaning comports perfectly with the following parallel line ("And the obedience of the nations is his") confirms your conclusion.

A check of the relevant literature (step 2.12) provides welcome support: W. L. Moran proposed precisely this interpretation, by far the most convincing in the literature, in an article in *Biblica* 39 (1958): 405–25, titled "Genesis 49:10 and Its Use in Ezekiel 21:32."

Some of the same sort of skill necessary to produce a conclusion may be necessary to evaluate a conclusion confidently. Even if it might never have occurred to you to reconstrue Genesis 49:10 as above, choosing among the options that have occurred to others still requires some careful work. Thus your exegetical effort will reward you as an evaluator of scholarship, not just as a creator of scholarship. In other words, as your exegetical skills develop, you become a better reader—not just a better writer—of exegetical studies.

2.4. Lexical Data

Considerable subjectivity is involved in deciding which words and phrases are the most important ones in a passage. That is one reason why this step comes here in the process rather than earlier. You need to be as familiar with your passage as possible before choosing and ranking terms for close study. Let your own curiosity and the knowledge level of your audience guide you. Where necessary, see which words the commentators select to comment on. But be careful here. A commentator who has dwelt on a word in chapter 5 of a commentary may not be inclined to belabor it again in chapter 10. Trust your judgment as to what is important. For the frequency of occurrence of a given word in the OT, you can consult almost any computer concordance, or, for example, Even-Shoshan's concordance (4.4.2). For an idea of how much might be said about a term if one wanted to be relatively exhaustive in one's analysis, see, for example, *TDOT* or *TWOT* (4.4.2).

2.4.1. The value of looking at key words: 2 Chronicles 13

Following the instructions in 1.4, you go through the chapter, picking out terms that you think might call for an explanation. At first you choose freely, without concern for how many terms you will end up with. These are the terms you select:

verses		
3, 17	אֶלֶף	thousand
3, 17	אִישׁ בָּחוּר	able-bodied soldier
4	הַר צְמָרַיִם	Mount Zemaraim
4	כָּל־יִשְׂרָאֵל	all Israel
5	מַמְלָכָה	kingship
5	לְעוֹלָם	forever
5	בְּרִית מֶלַח	covenant of salt
6	עֶבֶד שְׁלֹמֹה	Solomon's servant
7	רֵקִים	worthless
7	בְּלִיַּעַל	good-for-nothing
7	רַךְ־לֵבָב	indecisive
8	לֵאלֹהִים	as gods
9	לְמַלֵּא יָדוֹ	to consecrate himself
9	לֹא אֱלֹהִים	no gods
10	בַּמְּלֶאכֶת	in the work
11	הַשֻּׁלְחָן הַטָּהוֹר	the clean table
15	וַיָּרִיעוּ	and they raised the cry
15, 20	נָגַף	routed/struck
18	אֱלֹהֵי אֲבוֹתֵיהֶם	God of their fathers
19	(בֵּית־אֵל) וְאֶת־בְּנוֹתֶיהָ	(Bethel) and its surrounding villages
22	מִדְרַשׁ הַנָּבִיא עִדּוֹ	commentary of the prophet Iddo

How many of these terms you want to or are able to discuss—and to some extent even which ones you will select initially—depends on the scope of your paper/project. You try to choose relatively few words for detailed analysis, realizing that terms needing no extensive discussion can be commented on in the translation notes or elsewhere in the exegesis. You choose five terms as requiring substantial discussion. They are the following:

אֶלֶף, "thousand" (vv. 3, 17)

Your reading has informed you that אֶלֶף probably means "military unit" rather than literally "1,000" here, and you need to explain the significance of this in your exegesis.

בְּרִית מֶלַח, "covenant of salt" (v. 5)

This unusual term, attested already in Numbers 18:19 and attested in concept although not exact wording in Leviticus 2:13 and Ezra 4:14, will certainly shed light on what Abijah thinks of the Davidic-lineage kingship.

לֹא אֱלֹהִים, "no gods" (v. 9)

Such a term is bound to be important for the understanding of polytheism/idolatry from the orthodox Judean perspective.

נָגַף, "rout, defeat, strike down," and so on (vv. 15, 20)

Most translations render the word differently in verse 15 from verse 20. Understanding its usage can help to identify the divine role in the events described.

מִדְרַשׁ הַנָּבִיא עִדּוֹ, "commentary of the prophet Iddo" (v. 22)

An understanding of this document would surely contribute to your appreciation of how the Chronicler compiled his history and the audience for whom he was writing.

From this group of five you decide to choose בְּרִית מֶלַח to analyze by a full word study. You must now follow the process described in 4.4.3 for both בְּרִית (covenant) and מֶלַח (salt). Referring also to the theological dictionaries (4.4.4) as well as the larger Bible dictionaries (*IDB*, *ISBE*, etc.; cf. 4.12.5), you learn that בְּרִית מֶלַח is a way of saying, in effect, "perpetual covenant" and perhaps even "perpetual royal covenant," because of the role of salt as a preserver/perpetuator (cf. Lev. 2:13) and because of the association of salt with royal covenant meals (cf. Ezra 4:14). Indeed, the richness of this term occasioned a book by H. C. Trumbull titled *The*

Covenant of Salt (New York: Charles Scribner's Sons, 1899), which, if available to you, would certainly be worth consulting carefully in the process of your word study.

2.5. Form

Knowing the form of a passage invariably pays exegetical dividends. If you can accurately categorize a piece of literature, you can accurately compare it to similar passages and thus appreciate both the ways in which it is typical and the ways in which it is unique. Moreover, the form of a piece of literature is always related in some way to its function.

The example below concentrates especially on this relationship of form and function. In the process it touches on aspects of the analysis of general literary type (1.5.1), specific literary type (1.5.2), subcategories (1.5.3), life setting (1.5.4), and relative completeness of form (1.5.5; 1.5.6).

2.5.1. Form as a key to function: Jonah 2:3–10 (Eng. 2–9)

In the course of analyzing the literary context of this Psalm of Jonah, you become aware that there is a question about its placement in the book. Some scholars have considered it an interpolation, inappropriate to its present context. Indeed, some have even suggested that its style is not consistent with the style of the rest of the book, ignoring the fact that style is virtually always a function of genre and form, so that a poetic psalm could hardly fail to reflect a different style from that of the rest of the book, which is narrative. However, to evaluate their arguments effectively and fully, you must determine what type of psalm it is: its form.

For this purpose you consult a book or commentary that categorizes psalms according to their forms. You happen to choose Bernhard W. Anderson's *Out of the Depths: The Psalms Speak for Us Today* (with Stephen Bishop, 3rd ed. [Louisville, KY: Westminster John Knox Press, 2000]) and from it conclude that the Psalm of Jonah is apparently a "thanksgiving psalm" because it has the five features that Anderson tells you make up most thanksgiving psalms. They are (a) an introduction that summarizes the psalmist's testimony (v. 3 [2]); (b) a main section describing the past affliction (vv. 4–7a [3–6a]); (c) an appeal for help (v. 8 [7]); (d) a description of the deliverance (v. 7b [6b]); (e) a conclusion in which God's grace is praised and the psalmist promises to demonstrate appreciation to God (vv. 9–10 [8–9]). Thanksgiving psalms, you note, are prayers of gratitude for rescue from a misery now past.

This sets you to thinking. You had always assumed—perhaps even been told—that Jonah's being swallowed by the fish was a *punishment*. But Jonah is praying a psalm that thanks God for deliverance! Rereading the story, you realize that Jonah's punishment actually came through the storm and being thrown overboard (Jonah 1:12–15). The fish therefore represents rescue from that punishment. Now some things begin to fall into place. The psalm serves the purposes of the story by vividly demonstrating Jonah's inconsistency. In it he eloquently expresses thanks to Yahweh for his own deliverance though he is fully deserving of death; he later resents Yahweh's deliverance of the Ninevites, however, and continues to wish death for them (chap. 4). Knowing the form of the psalm actually makes possible a fuller appreciation of Jonah's character.

A note on the life setting of Jonah 2:3–10 (2–9): Some scholars have theorized that thanksgiving psalms had their life setting in temple worship. An Israelite would bring an offering to the temple, recite (or listen to) a thanksgiving psalm while making the offering, and then depart, having pledged to return again to offer other sacrifices. The evidence, however, suggests that psalms were prayed on many occasions in the life of believers (cf. the Psalms' superscriptions, even though many are surely secondary; the use of psalms by the prophets; and the singing of psalms in nontemple contexts in the NT, as in Mark 14:26 or Acts 16:25; cf. Eph. 5:19; Col. 3:16). Accordingly, Jonah's use of a thanksgiving psalm was really quite typical. The life setting of such psalms could be any occasion of appreciation for deliverance from distress.

2.6. Structure

To understand the structure of a passage is to appreciate the flow of content designed into the passage by the mind of the author, consciously or even unconsciously. But beyond this, it is important to appreciate the fact that meaning is conveyed by more than just words and sentences. *How* the words and sentences relate to one another and *where* they occur within the passage can have a profound impact on its comprehension. Indeed, structure is often the main criterion for deciding whether a block of material is a single passage or a group of independent passages. A key word in structural analysis is "patterns." Patterns indicate emphases and relationships, and emphases and relationships prioritize meaning. The basic question you must answer in analyzing a passage's structure is, What can I learn from the way this is put together? Surprisingly often, by careful work one can learn more than meets the eye at first glance.

2.6.1. *Analyzing structure and unity: Amos 5:1–17*

While working on Amos 5, you realize that it is not immediately obvious whether verses 1–17 are a unified whole. You note that scholars have usually attributed virtually all this material to Amos, but some have suggested that these verses are a compendium of smaller units of discourse preached by Amos at various times and places. Following the directions of 1.6, you carefully outline the passage, looking for patterns, analyzing the poetic parallelism. You observe some interesting correspondences.

Verses 1–3 speak of lamentation (קִינָה) and predict doom for Israel. Verses 16–17 are similar, with their emphasis on wailing (מִסְפֵּד), mourning (אָבֵל), and so on. Indeed, verses 16–17 seem almost to describe the grief resulting from the destruction portrayed in verses 1–3. Moving to verses 4–6, you note that they have as their theme seeking (דִּרְשׁוּנִי) Yahweh and living (וִחְיוּ) by avoiding forbidden evil practices. Interestingly, verses 14–15 employ some of the same vocabulary and likewise contrast doing Yahweh's will with doing what is evil. Could there be other correspondences? In verse 7 the topic is injustice: things being the opposite of what they should be. Looking ahead, you find that verses 10–13 share this theme. There, in some detail, Yahweh excoriates the injustices that the Israelites are practicing in Amos's day. In verse 13, עֵת רָעָה (bad time) certainly sums up what verses 7 and 10–13 describe in common. Only verses 8 and 9 are left. How do they compare? You see that verse 8 describes the fact that Yahweh's power to create means that he also has the power to destroy. And verse 9 also speaks of that destruction, even of the strong (עָז). Finally, you note that in *BHS* the two words יְהוָה שְׁמוֹ at the end of verse 8 are placed on a line by themselves. Apparently the *BHS* editor of Amos (Elliger) is advising you that these two words stand out as having no parallel. Since these words, "Yahweh is his name," are about at the center of the passage, you decide to see if you might structure the passage around them symmetrically. Here is the result:

1–3
    4–6
        7
            8a–c
                8d יְהוָה שְׁמוֹ
            9
        10–13
    14–15
16–17

This you recognize as a large-scale chiasm, a purposeful concentric literary format. Judging that Amos intentionally structured his revelation in this manner, you reasonably conclude that the passage is unified.

Using the procedures described later, in step 2.12, you would find that J. de Waard largely confirms your analysis and provides a careful, detailed description of the structure of this passage in an article in *Vetus Testamentum* 27 (1977): 170–77, titled "The Chiastic Structure of Amos v 1–17." You could then use de Waard's article to refine and adjust your own conclusions where necessary. But you would not need to begin with de Waard's analysis to discover the basic structural features. That you can, with care, do for yourself. Moreover, having done the basic structural analysis yourself, you are in a far better position both to evaluate and to appreciate the contribution to your exegesis made by de Waard's article. In other words, the careful exegete is invariably a better "consumer" of what one finds suggested in the secondary literature on a passage than the person who turns first to the secondary literature without having done the necessary critical analysis by which the secondary literature can be assessed and exploited most effectively.

2.7. Historical Context

The historical situation out of which or to which a portion of Scripture was written must be understood for that portion of Scripture to be fully meaningful. Of course, some passages are less strictly "historical" than others. The Twenty-third Psalm, for example, addresses concerns that almost anyone, at any time or place, has been able to appreciate. And Psalm 117, with its simple injunction to praise God and its declaration of God's loyalty ("Praise the LORD, all nations . . . ; the faithfulness of the LORD endures forever") is about as panhistorical and pancultural as biblical literature could be.

But knowing the background, social setting, foreground, geographical setting, and date is normally essential to appreciating the significance of a passage. Most OT passages contain material that relates strongly to such considerations. The Bible is such a historically oriented revelation that ignoring historical context tends to assure misinterpretation. A basic principle of hermeneutics (the science of interpretation) is that a passage cannot mean what it could never have meant. In other words, you must know which events, situations, times, persons, and places your passage is referring to if you are not to remove your passage from the very context that gives it its true meaning. The illustration below is chosen as an example of a passage whose meaning cannot be adequately appreciated unless proper attention is paid to its historical background, social setting, foreground, geographical setting, and date.

2.7.1. Context clarifies a prophecy: Hosea 5:8–10

At first glance this brief prophetic oracle is puzzling. Why such emphasis on horns (שׁוֹפָר, חֲצֹצְרָה) and alarm (הָרִיעוּ)? Why the deep concern about a boundary marker (גְּבוּל)? And why does all this make Yahweh proclaim his wrath (עֶבְרָתִי)?

When you follow the suggestions in 1.7, "Historical Context," here is what you find. First, consulting the Scripture reference index in virtually any of the major histories of Israel (see 4.7.2), you find that Hosea 5:8–10 has a clear historical referent: the counterattack by Judah against (northern) Israel in the Syro-Ephraimite War of 734–733 BC. As you read beyond these sources in historically oriented commentaries and follow the geographical details via a good Bible atlas (4.7.6), you note the following (here only summarized):

Background. King Rezin of Aram-Damascus and King Pekah of Israel had approached King Ahaz of Judah to join them in a military coalition to throw off the Assyrian domination of Palestine, which had begun under Tiglath-Pileser III (745–728 BC). Ahaz, following the command of God through Isaiah, refused. Rezin and Pekah, fearing a traitor in their midst, then attacked Judah (734) to depose Ahaz. Ahaz promptly (and against God's command this time) appealed to Tiglath-Pileser, who soon attacked Aram-Damascus and Israel. Judah, taking advantage of the situation, then laid plans for a counterattack against Israel. It was at approximately this point that Hosea 5:8–10 was spoken (733).

Foreground. In their drive northward, the Judeans would naturally proceed by the central ridge road from Jerusalem (just south of the border of Benjaminite territory) to Gibeah, Ramah, and Bethel (called here derogatorily בֵּית אָוֶן, Beth-aven, "House of nothing," by Hosea). The counterattack was successful, and Judah captured not only most of the territory of Benjamin but also Bethel, on the southern border of Ephraim. Judah then controlled Bethel through the time of Josiah (640–609; cf. 2 Kings 23:4, 15–19).

Now you see the reason for God's wrath being poured out (אֶשְׁפּוֹךְ, v. 10). Judah is in the process of capturing a portion of northern territory, as someone who surreptitiously "moves a boundary stone" to take some of his neighbor's land (cf. Deut. 27:17). The horns and alarm are the warnings of war. Benjamin and Ephraim are the targets. The original attack of

Israel and Aram-Damascus on Judah in 734 was wrong. But Judah's vengeful counterattack in 733 was also wrong. Isaiah (7:1–9) had condemned the former. Hosea here condemns the latter.

2.8. Literary Context

The analysis of literary context has different interests from historical analysis. It is concerned not with the entire historical context from whatever sources it may be learned, but with the particular way that an inspired author or editor has placed a passage within an entire block of literature. Often the most important literary context for a passage will be the book in which the passage itself is found. How the passage fits within that book—what it contributes to the entire flow of that book and what the structure of that book contributes to it—constitutes a paramount interest of the literary context step in exegesis.

2.8.1. Examining literary function:
How a chapter fits a book—Lamentations 5

You read through Lamentations rapidly and begin to notice how the book is organized. Consulting an OT introduction (4.12.3) or a Bible dictionary article (4.12.5) on Lamentations, you confirm your initial observation: Each of the first four chapters is a separate lament poem organized to one degree or another on the format of an acrostic.

You find that in chapter 1 each verse contains three poetic couplets, and the first couplet of each verse starts with a successive letter of the Hebrew alphabet: אֵיכָה (1:1), בָּכוֹ (1:2), גָּלְתָה (1:3), and so on. There are twenty-two verses in chapter 1, corresponding to the twenty-two letters in the Hebrew alphabet. You find that chapter 2 is organized similarly. In chapter 3, however, you see a triple acrostic format. In groups of three, the sixty-six verses have at the outset of their couplets the same successive Hebrew letter: אֲנִי, אוֹתִי, אַךְ in 3:1, 2, 3; בְּלָה, בָּנָה, בְּמַחֲשַׁכִּים in 3:4, 5, 6; גָּדַר, גַּם, גָּדַר in 3:7, 8, 9; and so on. This third poem does not look to you any longer than the preceding two, and you therefore conclude that the different versification is not a real issue. It is the "intensity" of this poem that intrigues you: Will the poet get any more acrostic than this?

A glance at chapter 4 provides the answer. You are back to twenty-two verses again, the verses are only singly acrostic (אֵיכָה, 4:1; בְּנֵי, 4:2; גַּם, 4:3; etc.), and there are only two couplets per verse. Judging from the acrostic and couplet pattern, you see that the book is no longer gathering steam but winding down from the most intense point or climax in chapter 3.

2.8.2. Examining placement

Turning now to the fifth and final poem (Lam. 5), you find a most interesting situation. A single couplet is all that constitutes each verse. Furthermore, these couplets are not arranged acrostically any longer. Only the total number of couplets, as indicated by the verses (22), reflects an acrostic structure—and that only faintly. The relationship of chapter 5 to the rest of the book is now much clearer. It stands at the end of a progression that begins strongly (chaps. 1 and 2), peaks with intensity (chap. 3), and diminishes (chap. 4) to a whimper (chap. 5). Such a progression is one of the classic formats of literature technically called "tragedy."

2.8.3. Analyzing detail

Even the final verse (5:22) reflects Jerusalem's tragic state after the Babylonian conquest: Could it be that God has rejected his people, being angry with them עַד־מְאֹד, "completely"? This poignant statement of agonized uncertainty highlights the plight of the survivors.

2.8.4. Analyzing authorship

Regarding authorship, you conclude tentatively that since chapter 5 integrally relates to the rest of the book, it was probably written by the author of chapters 1–4. Consulting OT introductions, Bible dictionaries, and especially the introductory sections of commentaries on Lamentations, you find conflicting theories on the authorship of Lamentations and/or its various sections. Other steps of the exegesis process (especially historical context, form, structure, and lexical content) are relevant to the authorship question, so it cannot yet be answered definitively. But faced with conflicting scholarly opinions, you must make your own decision. When your own exegesis indicates unity of authorship, you need not avoid so declaring.

2.9. Biblical Context

Often steps 1.9.1, 1.9.2, and 1.9.3 will flow together. Seeing how the passage is used elsewhere in Scripture (if it is—and not all passages are) helps pinpoint the passage's relation to the rest of Scripture, which in turn leads to an appreciation of its import for understanding Scripture.

2.9.1. Seeing the broader context: Jeremiah 31:31–34

Your first concern is to find out if the passage is quoted or alluded to elsewhere in the Bible. Because actual quotation of one literary work in another literary work is very rare in the ancient Near East before the Roman era, you cannot expect to find one part of the OT quoted in another part. But reference by allusion may exist, and the New Testament (NT) certainly both quotes from and alludes to the Old. Here two aids will bring your exegesis a long way before you need to turn to commentaries: the "Index of Quotations" (sometimes called "Index of Citations and Allusions") in most Greek NTs, and the column or chain Scripture references in a reference Bible.

Starting with the NT index, you find the following entries for your passage:

Jer. 31:31	Matt. 26:28; Luke 22:20; 1 Cor. 11:25
31–34	2 Cor. 3:6; Heb. 8:8–12
33	2 Cor. 3:3; Heb. 10:16
33–34	Rom. 11:27; 1 Thess. 4:9
34	Acts 10:43; Heb. 10:17; 1 John 2:27

Looking each of these up in a Greek (or English) NT, you find that the first three (Matt. 26:28; Luke 22:20; 1 Cor. 11:25) all relate to the institution of the Lord's Supper, and all appear to represent genuine allusions to, though not necessarily quotations from, Jeremiah 31:31. From this you are made aware that, among other things, the Lord's Supper constitutes a reminder of the fulfillment of the kind of prophecy that Jeremiah made in 31:31. The fourth reference, 2 Corinthians 3:6, seems to allude to both Jeremiah 31:31 and 31:34; it gives the original prediction a certain depth of interpretation by emphasizing the enormous advantage of a spiritual relationship with God over a purely technical one wherein the keeping of written rules constitutes the essence of righteousness.

The Hebrews 8 reference is a full quote of the entire Jeremiah passage, which demonstrates its major significance (it is one of the longest OT citations in the NT). But beyond this, its use in Hebrews, a book devoted in part to showing the superiority of the New Covenant over the Old, especially emphasizes how the Jeremiah passage implicitly calls attention to the temporary nature of the Sinai covenant.

The use of Jeremiah 31:33 in 2 Corinthians 3:3 is another allusion—not a quotation—in which Paul stresses human participation in a living covenant, allowing you to see that he views the prophecy as having to do with a different, more responsive, and more vital way of relating to God. Hebrews 10:16 provides another actual quote, this time with the purpose of emphasizing how Jeremiah's prophecy envisions an era in which God's redemptive action will render unnecessary the Old Covenant's sacrificial order. That is a perspective you certainly want to take note of.

Parts of verses 33 and 34 of the prophecy appear in Romans 11:27, with reference to the restoration of the nation of Israel. That aspect of Jeremiah's words cannot be ignored (cf. Deut. 4:31). Paul is finding in the New Covenant the true fulfillment of the promises to Israel.

Examining next the listing 1 Thessalonians 4:9, you do not recognize any obvious allusion to any wording from Jeremiah 31:31–34. "Loving one another" seems to you more likely to be an allusion to Leviticus 19:18 or Deuteronomy 10:18–19 or Proverbs 17:17 or the like than to Jeremiah 31. Is the "Index of Quotations" wrong at this point? Quite possibly, yes(!). It is clearly a list you must use with caution.

Likewise, only in a most general sense can Acts 10:43 be considered to refer to Jeremiah 31. Forgiveness is a prophetic promise far broader than one text. Hebrews 10:17, however, is certainly a quote from part of Jeremiah 31:34, again with the emphasis on the possibility of sins being forgiven without continual Old Covenant sacrifices being made (cf. Heb. 10:16, above). But 1 John 2:27, the final listing, with its statement "You do not need anyone to teach you," seems to you not a reference to Jeremiah 31:34 at all. Again, the "Index of Quotations" is somewhat misleading, and you conclude that you may dismiss this reference as irrelevant.

Following a Bible column reference or chain reference yields similar results. Some references will be highly useful; some will be erroneous, based on a similarity in wording or topic but on close examination proving to be not an actual quotation or allusion at all. Sorting through the results generated by a computer concordance similarly requires selectivity on your part. Sensible exegetical work will help you distinguish the relevant from the irrelevant and will help you be prepared in advance to evaluate how well the commentators have addressed the issues raised by biblical usage.

But what about finding passages similar or relevant to the one you are working on when the "Index of Quotations" and the reference lists are silent, or when you want to go further than they do? To do this, you must rely on your own knowledge of the biblical context and whatever indications you can glean from books, articles, and commentaries that address your passage and/or its themes. But remember, your own judgment must prevail here. What someone else considers "related" may or may not be so. It is for you to decide.

Our example concerned a passage from the OT used in the NT. For many passages, the "uses" will be limited to other OT contexts. In not a few cases, parallel or relevant passages must be located exclusively on the basis of thematic or vocabulary connections that you must do your best to locate and evaluate. Topical concordances often help (if there is shared vocabulary), but otherwise only by reading the commentaries or articles on your passage, if they exist, will you become aware of how your passage ought to be understood in a wide context.

Note: Books like Elwell's *Topical Analysis of the Bible* or Davis's *Handbook of Basic Bible Texts* (4.9.2) are often helpful both here and in step 2.10.

2.10. Theology

If you are a Christian, the Old Testament is your theological heritage, too (Gal. 3:29). What you believe is informed by its content, corrected by its strictures, and stimulated by its teachings. Theology is a big and sometimes complicated enterprise, but it cannot be ignored. How a passage fits within the whole Christian belief system deserves careful attention. From the many individual passages of the Bible, we see the picture of what God has specifically revealed; from the whole orb of theology, we have proper perspective for appreciating the truths of the individual passage.

2.10.1. A special perspective on the doctrine of God: Hosea 6:1–3

This brief oracle is one of several promises of restoration distributed throughout Hosea. Among announcements of coming destruction and exile, now and again one finds reminders that Yahweh will never completely and finally destroy his people but will one day restore and bless a remnant rescued from exile.

Examining Hosea 6: 1–3, then, for its relation to Christian theology per se, you first note that its message is not limited to the Old Covenant. (In general, restoration promises encompass the New Covenant.) Its essence seems to be an invitation for a people to (re)accept God, since the language is plural and corporate, not singular and individual. The passage is thus eschatological from the OT perspective and also represents a partly realized eschatology from the NT perspective. Referring to one or more systematic theologies for a sense of the proper categories (4.10.2), you determine that it touches on the doctrine of sin, in that forgiveness is part of the promise; and it touches on the doctrine of the church, in that God's faithfulness to his people as a corporate entity is promised here (cf. Gal. 3:26–29; Eph. 2:11–22; etc.). But its most direct theological impact may well be in the area of the doctrine of God (theology proper). You note that the passage focuses throughout on the relation of God's people to him. He caused the punishments; he will heal (v. 1). He will revive and restore (v. 2). If acknowledged, he will show his faithfulness (v. 3). Thus God's consistency, his mercy as over against his judgment, his approachability, and so forth, are all aspects of the oracle.

You attempt to assess the passage's contribution to your understanding of theology as specifically as possible. In this case, the passage says nothing entirely unique in terms of its general themes (concepts), but it certainly uses somewhat unique language (words and wordings) to make its points. For example, you note in verse 1 that the description of God's punishment via the verbs טָרָף (tear apart) and יַךְ (attack), combined with immediate promises of healing (וְיִרְפָּאֵנוּ) and bandaging (וְיַחְבְּשֵׁנוּ), is a metaphorical description not precisely paralleled elsewhere in the Bible. The language of "two" and "three" days is also especially dramatic but not intended as a hint of the duration between the crucifixion and the resurrection, you rightly conclude. The idea that Yahweh shows his faithfulness via nature and is also as reliable as the more stable parts of creation (v. 3) is hardly without analogy in the Scriptures. But combinations of wordings such as נִרְדְּפָה לָדַעַת (let us pursue the knowledge of) and שַׁחַר (dawn), גֶּשֶׁם (rain) and מַלְקוֹשׁ (spring rain) provide an analogical description of God's dependability not precisely to be found in other contexts. You conclude, then, that the passage's most significant contribution to Christian theology is its strong reinforcement of the doctrine of God's faithfulness by particularly dramatic and even stunning wordings, including arresting metaphors and similes.

2.11. Application

Without application, exegesis is only an intellectual exercise. Every step of the process of exegesis should have as its goal right belief and right action. The Scripture fulfills its inspired purpose not merely in entertaining our brains but also in affecting our very living. The Bible is so varied that the applications of its various portions will be diverse. But that does not mean that any given application should not be the result of a rigorous, disciplined enterprise. The guidelines of step 2.11 are designed to help you keep your perception of the implications of a passage as faithful to its legitimate applicability as possible.

2.11.1. Samplings of an upright life: Job 31

Here Job concludes his "protestation of innocence," a speech form also found in such places as 1 Samuel 12:3–5 and Acts 20:25–35. He admits that if he had actually done various sorts of immoral acts, he would be well deserving of divine punishment. But he steadfastly denies having violated God's law and in the course of his denial describes how a decent, moral person ought, and ought not, to act. It is this perspective that interests you. From 1:8; 2:3; and 42:7–8 you are aware that Job's life has been something of a model of behavior, and you want to see what can be learned from his statements about his manner of life.

Analyzing the life issues (see 1.11.1) mentioned in the passage, you list six that seem clearly comparable to current life issues: sexual propriety (vv. 1–4, 9–12); honesty (vv. 5–8); just dealings with employees (vv. 13–15, 31); generosity toward the needy (vv. 16–23, 29–34); materialism/idolatry, two issues commonly linked in biblical thinking (vv. 24–28); and financial arrangements (vv. 38–40). Some of the six partly overlap with one another, but treating them separately at first tends to keep the issues clearly in focus.

Since Job 31 does not contain a direct command to the reader to do something, the nature (1.11.2) of the application is that it informs. This does not mean that the application is any less urgent or significant, however.

Does the passage speak mainly of faith or of action (1.11.3)? While some elements are related to faith (e.g., vv. 35–37), the major interest centers on Job's behavior, his action.

What about the audience (1.11.4)? Here the answer may vary depending on the specific issue. Everyone has a personal relationship to sexual propriety, so no person or group would be excluded from that life issue. Likewise honesty, generosity toward the needy, and financial arrangements concern everyone. But not everyone has employees. Most people are either employers or employees, but retired persons or children are usually neither. Furthermore, in the modern world many employers are not individuals but corporations. Recognizing these nuances helps to make your application as precise as possible.

Job 31 addresses several categories (1.11.5) of application. It is both personal and interpersonal, and it touches social, economic, religious, and financial concerns. Particularly interesting is the reference to idolatrous worship in verses 24–28 (i.e., worshiping the heavenly bodies as symbols of deities; cf. 2 Kings 21:3; 23:5, 11; Zeph. 1:5; etc.) in such a context. This might remind you that one important aspect of idolatry as a religious system is that it condones selfishness and materialism, whereas covenant religion does not.

The time focus (1.11.6), you decide, is relatively unlimited. The potential for sin in the areas mentioned by Job certainly continues at the present and will surely continue until the consummation of this age (multiple NT passages would support that conclusion).

Finally, you must try to set the limits of application (1.11.7). Your main concern would be to prevent misunderstanding on the part of your audience. The central application of Job 31 is that an upright life must be decent, honest, generous, fair, faithful, unselfish, and nonexploitive. The passage does not suggest, however, that legal oppression of orphans should be punished by amputation of an offender's arm (vv. 21–22), or that a closed front door is evidence of a homeowner's sinfulness (v. 32). Nor are the particular curses Job potentially calls down upon himself as proof of his decency indicated as appropriate or normal modern punishments. And metaphorical expressions such as "My door was always open" are not literal statements of fact. But if the audience for which you are doing your exegesis might not know some or any of this, whatever you can do to prevent misunderstanding of the passage will be a positive contribution to its applicability.

2.12. Secondary Literature

You can waste time and energy in exegesis if you miss articles, books, or commentaries relevant to your passage. Using the process outlined here, you can usually locate most of the relevant literature fairly rapidly. This process is not exhaustive, but it is a good way to cover a lot of ground rapidly.

1. Look up your passage in one or more of the electronic databases described in chapter 4, section 12. Follow the procedures described there for finding what has been written on your passage. As backup, you could also look up your passage in a print resource such as all three volumes of Langevin's *Biblical Bibliography* (4.12.1). Langevin will give you a list of most of the books and articles written on your passage from 1930 to 1983.

2. Look up your passage in the annual numbers of *Old Testament Abstracts* (4.12.1.) in either electronic or print form, for the years from 1978 to the present. The great advantage of *OTA* is that it not only gives you titles, but also gives you wisely worded summaries of what the article or book says.

That enables you to predict relatively accurately whether or not the book or article is likely to contain information useful to your exegesis.

3. If you have time, you may also choose to look up your passage in the *Elenchus bibliographicus biblicus* (4.12.1) for the years it covers. That can sometimes add an item or two to your list, especially before 1930, for which most of the electronic databases are silent. Hupper's *Index* (4.12.1) may also help you here. Remember: the old can be gold, and the new is not necessarily true just because it is new, so do not despise older works as if the new ones were automatically better.

4. From Longman and Dillard's *Introduction* (4.12.3) or Soggin's *Introduction* and/or Eissfeldt's older *Introduction* (4.1.2), or from one or more of the electronic databases, or to a lesser extent from Langevin's *Biblical Bibliography* (4.12.1), you can get a good list of commentaries on the book that includes your passage. For more recent commentaries, since the late 1970s, you will be able to check the annual listings in *Old Testament Abstracts* (4.12.1)—especially easy to do if you have access to the electronic version.

5. Quickly go through all the articles, books, and commentaries that are available to you, looking for the books and articles mentioned in them that might be relevant to your passage. (Bear in mind that things *relevant* to your passage may not have been written *directly on* your passage.) Add these to your list. Especially helpful here are volumes in series like Hermeneia and the Word Biblical Commentary because these series instruct their authors to compile relatively exhaustive bibliographical data both on the biblical book and on its individual passages, up to the date of the publication of the volume in question. It is always useful to see the bibliographical references that a seasoned scholar thinks are relevant to list in connection with a given pericope.

6. Even if you cannot read the foreign-language books, articles, and commentaries listed in chapter 4 or in the previous steps, you can still look through those available to you to see if they mention English-language articles and books relevant to your passage; add these to your list as well.

The process described here, while hardly exhaustive, will get you so far so fast that you will have at your disposal a substantial body of helpful literature against which to check the exegetical work you have done so far.

Chapter Three

Short Guide for Sermon Exegesis

T his short guide is intended to provide the pastor with a handy format to follow in doing exegetical work on a passage of Scripture for
the purpose of preaching competently on it. Each section of the guide
contains a suggestion of the approximate time one might wish to devote
to the issues raised in that section. The total time allotted is somewhat
arbitrarily set at about five hours, the minimum that a pastor ought normally to be able to give to the research aspect of sermon preparation.
Depending on the particular passage, the time available to you in any
given week, and the nature of your familiarity with exegetical resources,
you will find that you can make considerable adjustments in the time allotments. If you are new to exegetical preaching, you will need to increase
the time allotments substantially.

As you become increasingly familiar with the steps and methods, you
may arrive at a point where you can dispense with reference to the guide
itself. This is the intention of this primer—that it should get you started,
not that it should always be needed.

Comment

Most pastors who are theologically trained have been required to write at
least one exegesis paper during their seminary days. Many have written OT
exegesis papers based on the Hebrew text. But few have been shown how
to make the transition from the exegetical labor and skills required for a
full term paper to those required for a sermon. The term paper necessi-
tates substantial research and writing, is in many ways narrow and technical, and involves the writer in the production of a formal printout to be

evaluated by a single professor, with special attention to methodological competence and comprehensiveness, including notes and bibliography. The sermon is usually composed in ten hours or less (total—although pastors of the largest churches report spending in excess of twenty hours a week on their sermons), must avoid being excessively narrow or technical, does not require a formal manuscript, and is evaluated by a large and diverse group of listeners who are mostly not scholars and who are much less interested in methodological competence than in the practical results thereof.

Because the format and the audience are so radically different, is it any wonder that pastors find it hard to see the connection between what they were taught in seminary and what they are expected to do in their office and in the pulpit? Is it any wonder, too, that the average Sunday sermon is so often either devoid of exegetical insight or sprinkled with exegetical absurdities that countless congregations across the land long in vain for "simple preaching from the Bible"? The pastor, having long ago abandoned any hope that his or her weekly schedule would allow for all those hours and all that effort to produce the same sort of high-quality exegesis involved in writing the term paper, has nothing to put in its place. As a result, no real exegesis is done at all! The sermon becomes a long string of personal illuminations, anecdotes, truisms, platitudes, and whatever general insights the commentaries may provide.

Commentators are usually far removed from the specific comprehension level and practical concerns of the congregation hearing the sermon. This is a great shame, because the pastor stands in the ideal position to make the connection between the insights of scholarly research and the concerns of practical living, but cannot bring the one to bear upon the other. After all, how can the time be found week by week to devote oneself to the extensive research on which a truly exegetical sermon would be based? Both pastor and congregation suffer for want of a method to bridge the gap, a method that is, amazingly enough, almost never taught in the seminaries.

This short guide for sermon exegesis is both an abridged and a blended version of the full guide used for exegesis papers of chapter 1. Although the process of exegesis itself cannot be redefined, the fashion in which it is done can be adjusted considerably. Exegesis for sermon preparation cannot and, fortunately, need not be as exhaustive as that required for a term paper. The fact that it cannot be exhaustive does not mean that it cannot be adequate. The goal of the shorter guide is to help the pastor extract from the passage the essentials pertaining to sound hermeneutics (interpretation) and exposition (explanation and application). The final product, the sermon, can and must be based on research that is reverent and sound in scholarship. The sermon, as an act of obedience and worship, ought not to wrap shoddy scholarship in a cloak of fervency. Let your sermon be exciting, but let it be in every way faithful to God's revelation.

Note: The more familiar you are with the full process described in chapter 1, the more successful will be your use of the shorter process described here. It is not therefore advisable to skip over the one in order to try to profit immediately from the other.

3.1. Text and Translation (Allow about one hour.)

3.1.1. Read the passage repeatedly

Go over the passage out loud, in the Hebrew if possible. (Research shows that oral-aural memory is stored in the human brain differently from visual memory, so reading out loud will speed and enhance the process of becoming comfortable with the content of the passage.) Try to gain a feel for the passage as a unit conveying God's word to you and your congregation. Go over the passage out loud in English as well. (Use a modern translation, unless you and your congregation have determined to use an older one, such as the King James Version. In the latter case you must be doubly careful to pay close attention to step 3.1.4, below.) Try to become sufficiently familiar with the passage that you can keep its essentials in your head as you carry on through the next five steps. Be on the lookout for the possibility that you may need to adjust somewhat the limits of your passage, since the chapter and verse divisions as we have them are secondary to the composition of the original and are not always reliable guides to the boundaries of true logical units. Check by starting a few verses before the beginning of the passage and going a few verses past the end. Adjust the limits if necessary (shrink or expand the passage to coincide with more natural boundaries if your sense of the passage so requires). Once satisfied that the passage is properly delimited and that you have a preliminary feel for its content and the way its words and thoughts flow, proceed to step 3.1.2, below.

3.1.2. Check for significant textual issues

Refer to the textual annotations in the *Biblia Hebraica Stuttgartensia* (*BHS*, or *BH³* or *BHQ*) at the bottom of the Hebrew page. Look specifically for textual variations that would actually affect the meaning of the text for your congregation in the English translation. These are the major textual variants. There is not much point in concerning yourself with the minor variants—those that would not make much difference in the English translation. By referring to one or two of the major technical commentaries that address issues of text and translation (see 4.12.4), you can quickly check to see if you have correctly identified the major variants. Finally, you must evaluate the major variants to see whether any should be adopted, thus altering the "received text" (the Masoretic Text as printed in the Hebrew Bible). If you cannot make a decision—often the commentators cannot either—then you may wish to draw this to the attention of your congregation. In this regard, see also steps 3.1.4 and 3.1.5, below.

3.1.3. Make your own translation

Try this, even if your Hebrew is weak, dormant, or nonexistent. Whenever necessary, you can easily check yourself by referring to two or more of the respected modern versions. Avoid referring to the nonliteral paraphrases (even though some are called "versions" or "translations") since they will tend to confuse you without helping much. They are confusing because they do not usually represent a direct rendering of the Hebrew original and thus are hard to follow. They will not help much because they are useful primarily for skimming large blocks of material to get the gist— rather than for close, careful study where, to some degree, each word (and just the right word) is important. For translating help, you may also refer to an interlinear version (see 4.2.2) or any of the computer concordance versions such as *Accordance* and *BibleWorks* (4.4.2).

Making your own translation has several benefits. For one thing, it will help you recognize things about the passage that you would not notice in reading, even in the original. It is a little like the difference between how much you notice while walking down a street as opposed to what you can see while driving down it. Much of what you begin to observe as you prepare your translation will relate to steps 3.2–6. For example, you will probably become especially alert to the structure of the passage, its vocabulary, its grammatical features, and some aspects of its theology; all these are drawn naturally to your attention in the course of translating the words of the passage. Moreover, you are the expert on your congregation. You know its members' vocabulary and educational level(s), the extent of their biblical and theological awareness, and so forth. Indeed, you are the very person who is uniquely capable of producing a meaningful translation that you can draw upon in whole or in part during your sermon, to ensure that the congregation is really understanding the true force of the word of God as the passage presents it.

3.1.4. Compile a list of alternatives

If the passage does contain textual or translational difficulties, your congregation deserves to be informed about them. The congregation can benefit from knowing not just which option you have chosen in a given place in the passage, but what the various options are and why you have chosen one over the other(s). They can then follow some of your reasoning rather than accepting your conclusions merely "on faith." The best way to prepare this for the sermon is by way of a list of alternatives for both the textual and the translational possibilities. Only significant alternatives should be included in each list. You may expect your list to contain at most one or two textual issues, and a few translational issues. In the sermon itself, you can easily work these alternatives into the discussion of what the text says by such introductions as these: "Another way to read this verse would be . . ." or "In the original this part of the verse seems to be speaking of. . . ." A short summary of why you feel the evidence leads to your choice (or why you feel the evidence is not decisive) can be provided or not, depending on the demands of time.

3.1.5. Start a sermon use list

In the same manner as you compiled the list of alternatives mentioned in 3.1.4 above (and perhaps including that list), keep nearby a sheet of paper or an open computer window on which you can record the observations from your exegetical work on the passage that you feel might be worth mentioning in your sermon. This list should include points discovered from all of steps 3.1–6 and will provide an easy reference as you construct the sermon itself.

What to include? Include the very things that *you* would feel cheated about if you did not know them. They need not be limited to genuine life-changing observations, but they should not be insignificant or arcane either. If something actually helps you appreciate and understand the text in a way that would not otherwise be obvious, then put it down on the mention list.

Maximize at first. Include anything that you feel might deserve to be mentioned because your congregation might profit from knowing it. Later, when you actually write or outline your sermon, you may have to exclude some or most of the items on the mention list, by reason of the press of time and space. This will be especially so if you choose to make your sermon dramatic, artistic, stylized, or the like, thus departing more or less from a rigidly expository format. Moreover, in perspective you will undoubtedly see that certain items originally included for mention are not so crucial as you first thought. Or conversely, you may find that you have so much of significance to draw to your congregation's attention that you will need to schedule two sermons on the passage to exposit it properly.

Your sermon use list is not a sermon outline, any more than a stack of lumber is a house. The list is simply a tentative record of the exegetically derived observations that you initially think your congregation ought perhaps to hear and may indeed benefit from knowing.

3.2. Grammatical and Lexical Data (Allow about 50 minutes.)

3.2.1. Note any grammar that is unusual, ambiguous, or otherwise important

Your primary interest is to isolate grammatical features that might have some effect on the interpretation of the passage. Anything that can be explained, at least in some general way, is fair game for the congregation. But do not address yourself to minutiae. Find the major, significant anomalies, ambiguities, and cruxes (features crucial for interpretation), if any. Few passages contain many of these, so the task should not take long.

Ambiguities deserve special explanation. If a prophet reports that Yahweh has a word עַל־יְרוּשָׁלַ͏ִם, for example, your congregation will profit from knowing this can mean "about Jerusalem," "on behalf of Jerusalem," or "against Jerusalem." The translations must choose one of these options—they cannot include all three and thus cannot accurately represent the ambiguity in the passage, which in many cases is a purposeful, suspenseful ambiguity. The audience of the ancient prophet could not always tell whether Yahweh's word was good or bad until the prophet ended the suspense by further words. Cruxes certainly deserve special attention: If the interpretation of the passage (or a doctrine mentioned by the passage) depends on taking some grammatical feature a certain way (e.g., "You shall have no other gods *before me*"), this should be explained clearly. For example, only confusion can result if the hearer remains uncertain about the proper interpretation of this commandment in terms of whether "before me" refers to the spatial (in my presence) or the temporal (earlier than me) or the devotional (above me in importance) or whether the use of "gods"—a plural, after all—might imply actual polytheism. People need to know that אֱלֹהִים, "gods," had a range of meaning that included "false gods," "idols," "supernatural beings such as angels," and so forth.

3.2.2. Make a list of the key terms

As you go through the passage, write down all the English words (sometimes phrases) that you consider important. These may include verbs, adjectives, nouns, proper nouns, and so forth. Include anything that you are not sure that a majority of your congregation could define, as well as any terms they might want to know about. A typical passage of ten or fifteen verses might yield a dozen words or more. In the example at 2.4.1, the story of Abijah's speech and battle against Jeroboam in 2 Chronicles 13 yields more than twenty key words and phrases that the average congregation might either know relatively little about or might benefit from having exposited to them (Abijah, thousand, Mount Zemaraim, all Israel, covenant of salt, servant of Solomon, consecrate, no gods, burnt offerings, showbread, God of their fathers, etc.).

3.2.3. Pare down the list to manageable size

Because of the demands of time, you must be selective. Decide whether you can include five, ten, or perhaps more of the key terms in your inclusion list. Retain the terms that you are sure your congregation needs to learn about. (From the sample list above, this might include: "covenant of salt," "consecrate," "no gods," "God of their fathers," etc.) Eliminate what is not central to the needs of your sermon, as well as you can predict this. You may find that some important points of your sermon will suggest themselves in the process of deciding what to comment on and what to leave alone with minimal or no comment. From the sample passage above, for example, you might pick "A Covenant of Salt" or "What in the World Is a Covenant of Salt?" or "Do We Have a Covenant of Salt with God?" as your sermon title. That ought to arouse at least a little advance curiosity about the sermon.

3.2.4. Do a mini–word study (concept study) of at least one word or term

Any sensibly chosen passage will contain at least one important word or wording (concept) worthy of investigation beyond the confines of the passage. Force yourself to follow the weekly discipline of picking a word or term and sampling its usage and therefore its range(s) of meaning first in the section, then the book, then the division, then the OT, then the whole

Bible. Use the techniques for word (concept) study described in 4.4.3, but use your time wisely. Check the various contexts in English if you wish; know what to look for by seeking guidance from the lexicons and published word studies. But whatever you do, get beyond the immediate context of the passage. Let your congregation hear something about that word or wording as it is used throughout the Bible as best you can summarize the evidence in the short time you have. Again, remember that there is a difference between a word and a concept, and the actual concepts of the passage convey its message, not so much its individual words as isolated units of speech.

3.3. Form and Structure (Allow about half an hour.)

3.3.1. Identify the genre and the form

Your congregation deserves to know whether the passage is in prose or poetry (or some of both), and whether it is a narrative, a speech, a lament, a hymn, an oracle of woe, an apocalyptic vision, a wisdom saying, and so forth. These various types (genres) of literature have different identifying features and, more important, must be analyzed with respect to their individual characteristics lest the meaning be lost or obscured. For example, consider the preaching of Jonah, "Yet forty days, and Nineveh will be overthrown!" (Jonah 3:4). Your congregation will likely be puzzled as to why Jonah, the Nineveh hater, should have wanted to avoid preaching such an obviously negative message of doom unless you explain to them that the possibility of repentance and therefore forgiveness is *implicit* in this warning of delayed punishment: "yet forty days." The knowledge of the form and its characteristics leads to the knowledge that Jonah is actually, though reluctantly, preaching a message of hope to Nineveh. It is certainly not essential that you identify every form by its technical name, but you should try to be sure that you identify the overall type of literature—the genre (e.g., prophetic) and then the specific form used in the passage (e.g., the warning oracle), since in most cases such an identification will serve to enhance the appreciation and the interpretation of the passage.

3.3.2. Investigate the life setting of forms where appropriate

If any discernible links exist between the form(s) used in the passage and real-life situations, identify these for your congregation. The "watchman's song" used to describe the destruction of Babylon from the vantage point of a sentry (Isa. 21:1–10) has its greatest impact when the congregation is reminded that in ancient times the watchman or sentry on the city wall was often the first person to see something coming and thus to announce news of significant events. Since the prophet, too, is Yahweh's announcer of news or events, the imagery of Isaiah's oracle in chapter 21 is especially appropriate. A knowledge of the original life setting from which the form is borrowed for reuse is often crucial to grasping its significance. Explain these factors to your congregation, and the prophetic message can come across to them with much the same force with which it came across to Isaiah's original audience. You do not need to give a detailed form-critical analysis of the text to your congregation, but you should at least go by the principle that they ought to hear anything about the form(s) that would enhance their grasp of the message. To do less is to leave the congregation partly "out of the loop." Where possible, let your congregation in on anything that helps you follow the meaning.

3.3.3. Look for structural patterns

Outline the passage, seeking to discover its natural flow or progression. How does it start? How does it proceed? How does it come to an end? How does the structure relate to the meaning? Is the message of the passage (or the impact of the message) at least partly related to the structure? What are the stages of the "logic" of the passage, and what interpretational clues can you discern in its logic? In not a few instances, the outline of the passage can serve virtually as the outline of the sermon itself. In most others, the two ought certainly to interrelate in some way.

Then look specifically for meaningful patterns. Are there any repetitions of words, resumptions of ideas, sounds, parallelisms, central or pivotal words, associations of words, or other patterns that can help you get a handle on the structure? Look especially for evidence of repetitions and progressions that may help you understand what the passage is emphasizing. How exactly has the inspired writer ordered the words and phrases, and why? What is stressed thereby? What is brought full circle to completion? Is there anything especially beautiful or striking in the structure, especially if the passage is a poem? Remember that the structure not only contains the content but is also to some extent *part* of the content. Structures can be quite prominent (as in Gen. 1) or quite unobtrusive (as in some stories of Israelite kings), but they are usually significant.

3.3.4. Isolate unique features and evaluate their significance

Form criticism and genre criticism emphasize the typical and universal features that are common to all instances of a given form or broad category of literature. Structure criticism and rhetorical criticism, on the other hand, are concerned more with the unique and the specific in a particular passage. Both are necessary. You need to appreciate a passage for what it shares in common with similar passages, but also for what it alone contains that specially characterizes it, that makes it different. In terms of the general structure, and also in terms of the repetitions and progressive patterns, what do you find in the passage that gives it a distinct flavor— that describes the passage itself on its own terms and according to its own topics and concepts? What particular revelatory content is communicated within and beyond just the general form(s) and genre(s) which the passage contains or is part of?

3.4. Literary-Historical Context (Allow about one hour.)

3.4.1. Examine the background of the passage

There usually is considerable overlap between the literary context and the historical context of an OT passage. Nevertheless, it is helpful to try to identify whether some feature is *primarily* literary or *primarily* historical. Accordingly, you should first try to identify the general literary background of the passage. Refer to OT introductions (see 4.12.3) and commentaries (4.12.4) as necessary. If it is narrative, what preceded it in the narrative? If it is one of a group of stories, which stories came before, and how do they lead up to the passage? If it is a prophetic oracle, which oracles serve to introduce or orient the passage in any way? Try to isolate both the *immediate* background (preceding paragraphs or sections of the book in which the passage occurs) and the *general* background (the relevant OT literary materials from any earlier time in OT history).

Proceed in the same manner with the historical background, referring to the OT histories (see 4.7.2) as needed. Look first for the immediate background and then for the overall background. Be sure your congregation has a sense of what happened before—of what related events and forces God superintended that set the stage for the passage. Some passages do not have much of a discernible historical background. Psalm 23, for example, cannot easily be tied to any specific events in the psalmist's (or Israel's) past. This psalm, however, does have features that are important with regard to its setting (see 3.4.2, below).

You cannot expect to be exhaustive in your analysis of the literary-historical background of the passage in the modest time available to you for your sermon preparation. Therefore, you must be selective in two ways. First, concentrate on the highlights. Select the literary features and historical events that seem to be most clearly and obviously important for the congregation to be aware of. Eliminate from consideration aspects of the passage's literary and historical background that, if omitted, would not materially affect the ability of your congregation to understand or interpret the passage. In other words, you are searching for the essentials—the things that need to be pointed out in order to represent the background of the passage fairly. These must be *representative* rather than comprehensive. Second, summarize. In some cases, you may not be able to spare more than a minute or two of your sermon to discuss the background of a passage. Try, then, to construct a brief summary of the background information that sets the scene for the passage in its immediate and then its overall contexts according to the broad sweep of things.

3.4.2. Describe the literary-historical setting

To have described the background (3.4.1, above) and the foreground (3.4.3, below) of your passage is a major aspect of describing the context, but there is more. You should also be sure that your congregation has some sense of the literary setting in terms of placement and function as well as authorship, and of the historical setting in terms of social, geographical, and archaeological coordinates, as well as actual chronological coordinates (i.e., the date when the events of the passage took place).

Placement and function. Where does it fit in the section, book, division, OT, Bible? Is it introductory? Does it wind up something? Is it part of a group of similar passages? Is it pivotal in any way? What sort of a gap would its absence leave? It need not take long to discern this, and it need not take long in a sermon to pass what you have learned on to your congregation in summary form.

Authorship. Who wrote it? Is it clearly attributed to someone, or is it anonymous? Is there dispute about the authorship? Does (or would) knowing the authorship make any difference? If the author is known, what else did that author write? Is the passage typical or atypical of the author's work? Are there known characteristics of the author that help make the passage more comprehensible? To a listener, a passage of Scripture often seems more real if its author has been identified and the general character of his or her writing perhaps described just a bit.

Social setting (including economic and political setting). What in the life of Israel at this time would help your congregation to appreciate the passage? Does the passage touch on or reflect any social, economic, or political issues, customs, or events that should be mentioned? Under what personal, family, tribal, national, and international conditions and circumstances were the events or ideas of the passage produced?

Geographical setting. Where was it written? Where did the events take place? Do these make any difference in understanding the passage? Would the passage be different if it were written or its events had taken place elsewhere? How important is the geographical setting—marginally or centrally? If no setting is given, is this fact significant or merely incidental? Many preachers report that the results of this part of the process especially produce the sorts of remarks in a sermon that cause members of a congregation to say that they felt like they were "right there," able to imagine themselves in something of the same relationship to the biblical material that the original audience presumably was.

Archaeological setting. Consult the Scripture quotation index of one or more of the OT archaeologies (4.7.5), histories, and commentaries. Is anything specifically available from archaeological research that relates to the passage itself or to its relatively immediate context? If there is, does it provide a helpful perspective in any way?

Date. Wherever possible, give the absolute and relative dates for any event(s) or person(s) in the passage, or for the literary production (original publication) of the passage. Most churchgoers know few dates. They usually are not sure whether Ruth comes before or after David, or whether Esther comes before or after Abraham, or in what century to locate any of them. The more often you take the time to explain the dates related to a passage (it need not take long), the more clear the interrelationships of people, books, and events will become to your congregation. God's revelation to us is a historical one: do not neglect chronology.

3.4.3. Examine the foreground of the passage

What follows immediately, both literarily and historically? What comes next in the chapter(s) following? Is it something that relates closely to the passage or not? How does it relate, and what help, if any, does it give for understanding the passage? Are any events known to have taken place soon afterward that may shed light on the passage? Using the OT histories, check to see if there are aspects of Israelite or ancient Near Eastern history that are not covered (or not covered in detail) in the Bible that nevertheless may help to show the import of the passage. Does anything occur relatively soon afterward that might be significant for your congregation to know? Even though an event might not be a result of, or affected by, something mentioned in the passage, are any events similar or logically (even if not causally) related? Follow the same process with the longer-range literary and historical foreground. Try to describe what follows in the book, division, OT, and Bible that may be of genuine relevance to the passage. Do the same for the historical aspect. Do not hesitate to bring matters right up to or beyond current times, if legitimate. (For example, an OT prophecy about the kingdom of God might well include ancient Israel, the current church, and the heavenly, future kingdom.)

In general, you want to avoid talking to your congregation about the passage in isolation, as if there were no Scripture or history surrounding it. Doing so is unfair to the sweep of the historical revelation; it suggests to your congregation that the Bible is a collection of atomistic fragments not well connected one to another and without much relationship to the passage of time. That is surely not your conception of the Bible, and it should likewise not be the impression that you leave with your parishioners. Try to pay attention to the things (even in summary) that will help them realize that God has provided us with a Bible that can be appreciated for the whole as well as the parts, and that God controls history *now*, thus controlling our history with the same loyalty that he showed to his people in OT times.

3.5. Biblical and Theological Context (Allow about 50 minutes.)

3.5.1. Analyze use of the passage elsewhere in Scripture

Evaluate the cases where any part of the passage is quoted elsewhere in the Bible. How and why is it quoted? How is it interpreted by the quoter? What does that tell you about the proper interpretation of the passage? The significance of a passage is always elucidated by analysis of the way it is used in another context.

3.5.2. Analyze the passage's relation to the rest of Scripture

How does the passage function? What gaps does it fill in? What is it similar or dissimilar to? Is it one of many of similar types, or is it fairly unique? Does anything hinge on it elsewhere? Do other Scriptures help make it comprehensible? How? Where does it fit in the overall structure of biblical revelation? What values does it have for the student of the Bible? In what ways is it important for your congregation?

3.5.3. Analyze the passage's use in and relation to theology

To what theological doctrines does the passage add light? What are its theological concerns? Might the passage raise any questions or difficulties about some theological issue or stance that needs an explanation? How major or minor are the theological issues on which the passage touches? Where does the passage seem to fit within the full system of truth contained in Christian theology? How is the passage to be harmonized with the greater theological whole? Are its theological concerns more or less explicit (or implicit)? How can you use the passage to help make your congregation more theologically consistent or at least more theologically alert?

3.6. Application (Allow about one hour.)

3.6.1. List the life issues in the passage

Make a list of possible life issues mentioned explicitly, referred to implicitly, or logically to be inferred from the passage. There may be only one or two of these, or perhaps several. Be inclusive at first. Later you can eliminate those that, upon reflection, you judge to be either less significant or irrelevant.

3.6.2. Clarify the possible nature and area of application

Arrange your tentative list (mental or written) according to whether the passage or parts of it are in nature informative or directive, and then whether they deal with the area of faith or the area of action. Though these distinctions are both artificial and arbitrary to some degree, they are often helpful. They may lead to more precise and specific applications of the Scripture's teaching for your congregation, and they will help you avoid the vague, general applications that are sometimes no applications at all.

3.6.3. Identify the audience and categories of application

Are the life issues of the passage instructive primarily to individuals or primarily to corporate entities, or is there no differentiation? If to individuals, which? Christian or non-Christian? Clergy or lay? Parent or child? Strong or weak? Haughty or humble? If to corporate entities, which? Church? Nation? Clergy? Laity? A profession? A societal structure?

Are the life issues related to or confined to certain categories, such as interpersonal relationships, piety, finances, spirituality, social behavior, family life?

3.6.4. Establish the time focus and limits of the application

Decide whether the passage primarily calls for a recognition of something from the past, a present faith or action, or hope for the future; otherwise, perhaps a combination of times is envisioned. Then set the limits. Your congregation would be well served by suggestions of what would be extreme applications, lest they be inclined to take the passage and apply it in ways or areas that are not part of the intentionality of the Scripture. Is there an application that is primary while others are more or less secondary? Does the passage have double applicability as, for example, certain messianic passages do? If so, explain these to your congregation and suggest where *their* responsibilities to respond to the informing and directing nature(s) of the passage lie.

In suggesting applications, it is generally advisable to be cautious. Especially avoid the fallacy of exemplarism (the idea that because someone in the Bible does it, we also can or ought to do it). This is perhaps the most dangerous and irreverent of all approaches to application since virtually every sort of behavior, stupid and wise, malicious and saintly, is chronicled in the Bible. Yet this monkey-see-monkey-do sort of approach to applying the Scriptures is widely followed, largely because of the dearth of good pulpit teaching to the contrary. To be cautious involves staying with what is certain and shying away from the questionable (possible but uncertain) applications. You are not required to suggest to your congregation all the possible ways in which a passage might theoretically be applied. You *are* required to explain the application that is clearly and intentionally the concern of the passage. Unless you are convinced that it is the *intention* of the Scripture that a passage be applied in a certain way, no suggestion as to application can be confidently advanced. It would be far better to admit to your congregation that you have no idea how the passage could be applied to their lives than to invite them to pursue an application devoid of legitimate scriptural authority. In all likelihood, however—if your passage is sensibly chosen and your exegetical work properly done—in your sermon you will be in a position confidently and practically to suggest not only what the passage means but also what it should lead you and your congregation to believe and do.

3.7. Moving from Exegesis to Sermon

There are many ways to prepare sermons and to deliver them, as well as many different types of sermons and books about them. Still, some general advice can be given about creating a sermon that is exegetically sound.

3.7.1. Work from your sermon use list

Organize the various notes on your list into categories. See how many fit together. Do some groups seem especially weighty? For example, does much of the list seem to center on theological terms and themes? If so, perhaps your sermon ought to be especially theological. Does the list contain many elements that are part of a story? If so, might not the sermon as a whole or in part take a story form? Will you need to explain a good many lexical items? If so, perhaps a number of illustrations will be required, and so on. Generally the material on the sermon use list (3.1.5) should at least suggest what some of the major blocks for building the sermon will be, whether or not it suggests a particular format for the sermon. Remember, too, that you probably will not be able to include (or at least adequately cover) in the sermon everything you placed tentatively on the sermon use list. Discard what you must. A single sermon cannot do everything.

3.7.2. Do not use the twelve- or six-step exegesis outline as the sermon outline

You will surely not last long in the pastorate if your congregation hears every sermon begin with "Let us examine the textual problems of the passage." The six-point exegetical outline suggested above (3.1–3.6) provides an orderly and incremental format for covering the exegetical issues of a passage. It is not a sermon outline. You must organize and incorporate the results of your exegesis into the sermon according to an order that has as its primary concern to educate and challenge the congregation. It is up to you to decide what sort of a sermon—containing what elements and in what order—will best convey this to the listeners, and no one is in a better position to make such a decision than you are.

3.7.3. Differentiate between the speculative and the certain

Let your congregation know which exegetical "discoveries" are possible, which are probable, and which are definite. Suppose you are excited by the possibility that a particular poetic couplet in Micah seems to be adapted from Isaiah, but you would be irresponsible to present this as a given, since equally plausible cases can be built that Isaiah did the borrowing, or that both prophets drew upon a common repertoire of prophetic poetry, or that they were independently inspired with a similar message, and so forth. There may be no harm in alerting your congregation to any or all of these options as long as you identify them as speculative.

3.7.4. Differentiate between the central and the peripheral

The sermon should not give equally high priority to all exegetical issues. The fact that you may have spent a half hour trying to get straight a particularly tricky historical problem of Israelite-Assyrian chronology does not mean that 10 percent of the sermon should therefore be given to an explanation of it. You may well choose not to mention it at all. Try to decide what the congregation *needs* to know from the sermon passage, as opposed to what you needed to know to prepare the sermon. There is much they can do without. Your two best criteria for making this decision are the passage itself and your own reactions to it. What the passage treats as significant is probably what the sermon should treat as significant; what you feel is most helpful and important to you personally is probably what the congregation will find most helpful and important to them. Every passage properly identified is about something: it has a main subject. If your preaching is faithful to the passage, your congregation should be able to go away from church able to state what the "big idea" of the passage is. And by all means, that "big idea" should be something that helps them understand God and their relationship to him, or you did not think through the exegesis and its culmination in application as carefully as you should have. By the way, if you do a proper job with the supporting ideas, the big idea will be better clarified from the passage itself and fixed in people's minds; so do not assume that you can slight the smaller exegetical details and simply concentrate on the big idea and have a *biblical* sermon.

3.7.5. Trust the homiletical commentaries only so far

Most pastors rely far too heavily on the so-called homiletical commentaries (which emphasize suggestions for preaching) and not enough on their own scholarly exegesis. This can be counterproductive, since for the most part the homiletical commentaries are exegetically shallow. In addition, the commentator has no personal knowledge of you and your congregation and thus cannot possibly provide other than all-purpose observations and insights. The commentator can hardly speak to the controversies, the special strengths and weaknesses, the hot topics, the ethnic, familial, social, economic, political, educational, interpersonal, and other concerns that constitute the particular spiritual challenges for you and your congregation. The commentator has no idea how much or how little your congregation knows about a given topic or passage, how much ground you intend to cover in your sermon, or even the size of the units of the passage you have chosen to preach on. Accordingly, you are advised to refer to homiletical commentaries for the supplemental insights they may offer you after, not before, you have done the basic work yourself.

3.7.6. Remember that application is the ultimate concern of a sermon

A sermon is a presentation designed to apply the word of God to the lives of people. Without application, a talk is not a sermon; it may be a lecture, a lesson, or the like, but it is not a sermon. Be sure that the sermon you construct provides your people with an absolutely clear, practicable, and exegetically based application. This does not mean that most of the time given to the sermon must be spent on the application. The major proportion of time may actually be spent on matters that are not strictly applicational, as long as they help to lay the ground for the application. Indeed, you can hardly expect your congregation to accept your suggested application of a passage solely on your own authority. They need to be shown how the application is based on a proper comprehension of the passage's meaning; they will probably not take the application to heart unless this is clear to them. Likewise, you must not merely explain to them what it says while avoiding what it *demands*. The Bible is not an end in itself: it is a means to the end of loving God with one's whole heart and loving one's neighbor as oneself. That is what the Law and the Prophets are all about.

Reference to the secondary literature is always necessary. There are too many specialized issues and sources for interpreting those issues for the student (or the professional scholar, for that matter) to rely only on one's personal methodology. To properly interpret a portion of the book of Job, for example, one must have some understanding of the special ways in which Canaanite myths are used, reused (albeit sanitized), and otherwise employed in the service of the message of Yahweh's sovereignty over all creation. Likewise, some aspects of the special (old Edomite) dialect used in Job are simply beyond the ken of the seminary student or pastor whose only Semitic language is standard Hebrew. One must of necessity turn to the specialists for help and often even for an awareness of what the exegetical issues are.

No one's work may be accepted uncritically, however. Specialists display poor judgment and a willingness to accept unlikely conclusions as often as anyone else. They are capable of giving plausibility to their poor judgments and unlikely conclusions by surrounding them with large amounts of related data, erudite verbiage, and ponderous footnotes. Nevertheless, your own common sense and your right to remain unconvinced, until such time as you are shown facts and arguments that seem to you convincing, will serve you well. When facing difficult and specialized issues that require expertise beyond your own, your main concern is not to *originate* something, but to *evaluate* it. Look critically at what the specialists are saying, compare their logic and their data, and choose from among them what seems most convincing. No one can ever ask more of you.

Chapter Four

Exegesis Aids and Resources

T he helps and bibliographical referrals in this chapter are arranged
according to the outline for the full guide in chapter 1. With a few
necessary exceptions, the books recommended are limited to those available in English. The best books, in terms of relevancy as well as technical
expertise, are listed, regardless of theological slant. However, in the case
of OT and Christian theologies (4.10), some attention is paid to differing
theological viewpoints.

4.1. Textual Criticism

4.1.1. The need for textual criticism

Many pastors and students find textual criticism boring and cannot imagine that it could be more than marginally significant to biblical studies.
Boring it may sometimes be, but so are many important and necessary
scholarly tasks. However, the proper selection of textual readings may be
quite significant to the interpretation of a passage and therefore cannot
be avoided. Even the OT books that are relatively free from textual problems—the Pentateuch, Judges, Esther, Jonah, Amos, and so forth—still
present the reader with textual choices in virtually every chapter. And the
books well known for their frequent textual corruptions—Samuel–Kings,
Psalms, Job, Hosea, Ezekiel, Micah, Zechariah, and so forth—can often
require the exegete to make textual decisions affecting the interpretation
of a majority of the verses in a given passage! The task of textual criticism
may seem unappealing, even annoying; but it is unavoidable.

There is no single authoritative version of the OT text in existence.
The Hebrew text printed in the older BH^3, the current standard, *BHS* (see

4.1.5), and the forthcoming/underway *BHQ* is merely an edited arrangement of the Leningrad Codex, a manuscript from the early eleventh century AD, one manuscript among many from ancient and medieval times.

Because the formats of *BH³/BHS/BHQ* provide for the printing of this
manuscript in full with a selection of alternative readings (wordings)
given in the footnotes, the impression is given that the readings in the
footnotes are somehow irregularities, minor deviations from the norm or
standard given in the full, printed text. This is simply not so. The alternative readings (called variants) are themselves only a selection of the possible different readings from a great variety of ancient manuscripts of the
OT in various languages, each of which was considered both authoritative and "standard" by some community of faith at some time in the past.
The choice to print one particular eleventh-century manuscript by reason of its good state of preservation and relatively early date is not
wrong—but it can be misleading. If a slightly earlier medieval manuscript
had been in the same good state of preservation, it would have been chosen for printing, even though its readings might be different at many hundreds of places throughout the OT. In other words, the variants given in
the footnotes of the *BH* editions, along with the many other variants not
mentioned by the rather selective editors of those editions, should be
accorded fair consideration along with the Leningrad Codex. Many
times, perhaps even a majority of times, they are more likely to preserve
the original Hebrew wordings than the Leningrad Codex is. The variants
represent many other ancient copies of the OT that may also reflect the
original text. In any given instance (at any given point in the OT text),
any one of them could be right and all the others that differ could be
wrong. Each case must therefore be decided on its own merits even if, as
is well known, certain copies and versions are considered generally less
reliable than others.

There are many differences between the various versions and many
obvious corruptions (ungrammatical, illogical, or unintelligible wordings)
within given manuscript traditions or "recensions." Moreover, outnum-
bering the obvious corruptions are the "hidden" corruptions: those that
later copyists reworked into wordings that seem on their surface faultless
but are shown to be unoriginal when the full information from a variety
of versions is compared and analyzed.

Textual criticism can be fairly complicated, and because decisions about
original wordings are often subjective, you may be tempted to say, "I will
not make any decisions at all about the text. I will work exclusively from
the text in my *BHS* Hebrew Bible." In so doing, however, you will have

made thousands of decisions automatically. Everywhere in the OT, you will have chosen the masoretic readings of the Leningrad Codex, some of which are best, but some of which are the worst. You will commit yourself to trying to interpret garbled and incoherent sentences and verses—easily clarifiable by reference to the other versions. And you will, at least tacitly, insult the intelligence of the original human author, as well as the Holy Spirit's inspiration of the text, by accepting uncritically the sometimes nonsensical, sometimes too short, sometimes too long MT when fruitful, helpful alternative readings are available if you are willing to expend the necessary labor to look them up and evaluate them. By the way, doing textual criticism not only sharpens your knowledge of Hebrew, Greek, and any other relevant languages you may read; it also helps involve you in the basic exegetical decisions about the text. A "likely" reading is decided partly by appeal to the general nature, structure, vocabulary, and theological message of the text: the other steps of the exegesis process. So doing your textual criticism thoroughly will actually help you do the rest of your exegesis well. To decide against doing any textual criticism is to decide already that certain exegetical issues are beyond you—to give up the fight, as it were, before you start.

4.1.2. Explanations

If the whole concept of textual criticism is new to you, a good place to get a brief overview of the issues is either

Emanuel Tov, "Textual Criticism (OT)," in the *Anchor Bible Dictionary*, 4:393–412 (New York: Doubleday, 1992);

or

Bruce K. Waltke, "The Textual Criticism of the Old Testament," in the *Expositor's Bible Commentary*, 1:211–28 (Grand Rapids: Zondervan Publishing House, 1979).

A slightly less readable, but equally comprehensive introduction is found in

S. K. Soderlund, "Text and MSS of the OT," in the *International Standard Bible Encylclopedia*, 4:798–814 (Grand Rapids: Wm. B. Eerdmans, 1988).

To begin actually to learn the method, however, a clear step-by-step introduction to OT textual criticism is found in the following textbook:

Ellis R. Brotzman, *Old Testament Textual Criticism: A Practical Introduction* (Grand Rapids: Baker Academic, 1994).

A more erudite, technically excellent volume on the subject that is comprehensible to the beginner and yet valuable to someone who already knows the subject to some degree is

Emanuel Tov, *Textual Criticism of the Hebrew Bible*, 2nd ed. (Minneapolis: Augsburg Fortress Press, 2001).

Also helpful is

P. Kyle McCarter Jr., *Textual Criticism: Recovering the Text of the Hebrew Bible*, Guides to Biblical Scholarship (Philadelphia: Fortress Press, 1986).

A classic introduction to the subject is found in

Ernst Würthwein, *The Text of the Old Testament*, rev. ed. (Grand Rapids: Wm. B. Eerdmans, 1995).

This book emphasizes texts and versions but is not so useful for actually learning how to do textual criticism.

The following Web site contains links to books and articles that provide introductions to textual criticism:

Emanuel Tov, *Electronic Resources Relevant to the Textual Criticism of Hebrew Scripture*, http://rosetta.reltech.org/TC/vol08/Tov2003.html.

The Masorah is the medieval Jewish repository of text notes on the Hebrew Bible. Most of these Masorah notes are statistical (a typical note, for example, might say how many times a given word occurs in the masculine plural in Ezekiel) and therefore not terribly useful in modern times, when computer concordances can generate the same data—and more— even more quickly. Nevertheless, from time to time a student may wish to understand what a particular Masorah note—as printed, say, in the *BHS* (which has extensive masoretic notations)—is all about. The best introduction to how the Masorah works is

Page H. Kelley, Daniel S. Mynatt, and Timothy G. Crawford, The *Masorah of Biblia Hebraica Stuttgartensia* (Grand Rapids: Wm. B. Eerdmans, 1998).

The complete, classic reference work on the Masorah is

Christian D. Ginsburg, *The Massorah*, 4 vols. (repr., New York: Ktav Publishing House, 1975).

Very helpful for its definitions and explanations on texts and versions and their relevance to OT textual criticism (but not so much on the method of textual criticism itself) is

Frederick W. Danker, *Multipurpose Tools for Bible Study*, rev. ed. (Minneapolis: Fortress Press, 2003). A CD-ROM is included for ease of searching the book.

If you can find it, a convenient and remarkably thorough source of information on texts and versions, with attention to the individual books, is found in part 5 of Eissfeldt's *The Old Testament: An Introduction*. Its special value lies in the copious references to books and articles on the various topics up to 1965:

Otto Eissfeldt, *The Old Testament: An Introduction* (1965; repr., Oxford: Blackwell Publishers, 1978).

Also convenient, though considerably more general, is

Roland Kenneth Harrison, *Introduction to the Old Testament* (repr., Grand Rapids: Wm. B. Eerdmans, 2000).

It is fortunate that this work has been reprinted because in part 4 ("Old Testament Text and Canon") it contains not only a valuable survey of the history of Hebrew writing but also some judicious evaluations of the limits and fruits of textual criticism. Along with each book's introduction, Harrison provides a brief description of its textual characteristics and notable problems.

For easy access to clear and practical definitions of terms, alphabetically listed, see one of the following:

Richard N. Soulen and R. Kendall Soulen, *Handbook of Biblical Criticism*, 3rd ed., rev. (Louisville, KY: Westminster John Knox Press, 2003).

Harry J. Harm, "Glossary of Some Terms Used in Old Testament Studies," *Notes on Translation* 11, no. 4 (1997): 46–51.

Seeing how an expert does textual criticism is one of the best ways to try to understand the methods involved. One of the classic examples of careful textual criticism applied to a large section of the OT is worth learning from if you can find it (available, e.g., in one of the *Logos Bible Software* bundles):

S. R. Driver, *Notes on the Hebrew Text and the Topography of the Books of Samuel*, 3rd ed. (Oxford: Clarendon Press, 1913).

4.1.3. The versions

In addition to the Masoretic Text (MT)—one manuscript of which is printed in edited form as the basis of the *BH³*, *BHS*, *BHQ*—there are five other main ancient versions of the OT in four languages. I list them in descending order of importance:

The Greek OT. Usually called the Septuagint (LXX), but represented in *BH³/BHS/BHQ* by an old-style (Fraktur) letter *G*, this version represents a translation from the Hebrew in the third–second centuries BC. Its importance cannot be minimized. On the average, it is just as reliable and accurate a witness to the original wording of the OT (the "autograph") as the MT is. In many sections of the OT, it is more reliable than the MT; in others, less. Largely because the Greek language uses vowels and Hebrew does not, the LXX wordings were less ambiguous and the LXX was inherently less likely to be marred by textual corruptions than the Hebrew, which went on accumulating corruptions (as well as editorial expansions, etc.) for many centuries after the LXX was produced. When you undertake textual criticism (except in certain sections of the OT that books like those listed in 4.1.2 will help you identify), you can usually place the LXX side by side with the MT and treat them as equals. Where they differ, either may better reflect the original; no automatic decision about which to choose may be made, but rather you must analyze the data to see which preserves the original more faithfully.

The Qumran scrolls. These are also commonly called the Dead Sea Scrolls, though they are represented by a *Q* in the *BH* apparatus. In some cases, such as Isaiah and Habakkuk, large portions are preserved in a Hebrew text that is pre-Christian and thus many centuries earlier (and in some ways more reliable) than anything previously known. However, for most books only small fragments have been found. Chances are, therefore, that your passage will not have a corresponding Qumran text. If it does, however, you may generally treat the Qumran wording as potentially equal in reliability to the MT wording. During the Qumran era (roughly 100 BC–AD 70) many Hebrew words were spelled differently from how they were spelled in the earlier Persian period (whose spelling [orthographic] conventions were adopted by the rabbis for the Hebrew Bible as we know it). However, these spelling variations give only minor challenges when comparing Qumran to the MT.

The Syriac OT. Called the Peshitta, the Syriac OT is sometimes (but far less often than the LXX) a useful witness to the Hebrew text from which it was translated (and revised) several centuries after Christ. Frequently when it differs from the Hebrew MT, it does so in agreement with the

LXX. It is symbolized by a *P* in the *BH* apparatus. Its witness to the text is being increasingly more appreciated.

The Aramaic OT. Called the Targum and represented in the *BH* editions by a *T*, the Aramaic OT is occasionally important as an indication of the original Hebrew but is often marred by expansionism and a tendency to paraphrase excessively. Like the Syriac Peshitta, it is a relatively late (fourth-fifth century) witness.

The Latin OT. Jerome's translation of the Hebrew OT into Latin (AD 389 to 405), called the Vulgate (*V* in *BH* editions), is the only ancient Latin translation that has survived in full. Only rarely is it an independent witness to anything other than the MT, since it was produced from a version that we would call essentially an early or proto-MT. There are Old Latin versions partially available, too. These are discussed further in 4.1.4, below.

Fortunately, you are not entirely limited to the use of versions that are in a language you know. All the ancient versions have been translated into English (see 4.2.2); if carefully used, those English translations can give a fairly accurate sense of whether the given ancient non-English version supports or differs from the MT. Moreover, much insight on textual issues is to be found in the major "critical" (detailed, scholarly) commentaries that pay special attention to textual criticism (such as the Anchor Bible, Hermeneia, the Word Biblical Commentary, and the International Critical Commentary, currently under revision; see 4.12.4). Most of these are available via CD-ROM and/or are found within modules available with the major computerized Bible study aids (*Accordance, BibleWorks, Logos Bible Software,* etc.). Also, because the majority of crucial data for making intelligent textual decisions are located in the Hebrew and Greek, the languages most likely to be studied during one's seminary training are also the most valuable for textual criticism.

Perhaps the first place to turn for information on text-critical resources should be Emanuel Tov's Web site, which will link you both to information on print books and CD-ROM/online resources:

Emanuel Tov, *Electronic Resources Relevant to the Textual Criticism of Hebrew Scripture,*
    http://rosetta.reltech.org/TC/vol08/Tov2003.html.

4.1.4. Critical text editions

The LXX

After being produced, the LXX was copied and recopied hundreds of times, just as the Hebrew OT was. Over many centuries all this copying provided ample opportunity for different readings to develop, both as a result of accidental miscopyings (corruptions) and as expansions and other "editorial" work on the part of scribes. As a result, critical Greek texts have been required. These contain a single fully printed text, copious footnotes indicating the "inner-Greek" variants (variants that resulted during the process of hand-copying Greek texts without any regard for the original Hebrew), footnotes indicating the revision-produced variants (variants that were introduced by the conscious harmonizing of a given LXX copy to some Hebrew copy available to and trusted by the reviser), and footnotes giving information from versions in other languages.

Two major multivolume critical editions of the LXX now exist. Each series is incomplete, but the two together largely complement each other so that almost the entire OT is covered:

Alan E. Brooke, Norman McLean, and Henry St. J. Thackeray, eds., *The Old Testament in Greek* 3 vols. in 9 (Cambridge: Cambridge University Press, 1906–1940).

The following books are available in this series: Genesis through 2 Chronicles (following the English order), 1 Esdras, Ezra–Nehemiah, Esther, Judith, Tobit. In other words, what this series does *not* contain is the LXX of Job through Malachi (again following the English order).

The other series is

Septuaginta: Vetus Testamentum Graecum Auctoritate Societatis Litterarum Gottingensis Editum (Göttingen: Vandenhoeck & Ruprecht, 1931–).

The following books are included in this series:

Esther; 1–3 Maccabees; Psalms (*Psalmi cum Odis*); Wisdom of Solomon (*Sapientia Salomonis*); Sirach (*Sapientia Iesu Filii Sirach*); the Minor Prophets (*Duodecim Prophetae*); Isaiah (*Isaias*); Jeremiah (*Jeremias*); Baruch; Lamentations (*Threni*); The Letter of Jeremiah (*Epistula Jeremiae*); Ezekiel; Susanna; Daniel; Bel and the Dragon (*Bel et Draco*).

In other words, this series does *not* contain the books from Joshua through 2 Chronicles (in the English order) as well as Proverbs, Ecclesiastes, and Song of Songs.

For the three OT books (Proverbs, Ecclesiastes, Song of Songs) that are not covered by either the Cambridge Septuagint or the Göttingen Septuagint, you must use

Alfred Rahlfs, ed., *Septuginta*, 2 vols. (Stuttgart: Württembergische Bibelanstalt, 1935), new, corrected ed. (Peabody, MA: Hendrickson Publishers, 2006).

Rahlfs derives the LXX text from only three major codices, but its apparatus sometimes has variants from other manuscripts as well. It contains introductions in three languages, including English.

All three of the above use Latin as the basic means of communication, as do *BH³* and *BHS*. *BHQ* uses Latin and English, though not always both. Unlike the NT texts, none of the OT critical editions in either Hebrew or Greek produces an eclectic text (a text that is newly composed from the best possible choices from among all the variants). A partial exception is the Göttingen *Septuaginta*, which is marginally eclectic. The production of an eclectic text is thus up to you. Using the aids at your disposal, you are at least not likely to do worse than the existing MT (called sometimes the "received text"), and you may well improve upon it.

A very readable, remarkably comprehensive introduction to the Septuagint exists:

Karen H. Jobes and Moisés Silva, *Invitation to the Septuagint* (Grand Rapids: Baker Academic, 2000).

Jobes and Silva touch upon all the key issues, giving many examples and explaining the relationship of the Septuagint to the other ancient versions. Also helpful are:

Emanuel Tov, *The Text-Critical Use of the Septuagint in Biblical Research* (Winona Lake, IN: Eisenbrauns, 1981).
Jennifer Dines, *The Septuagint* (New York: T&T Clark International, 2004).
Natalio Fernández Marcos, *The Septuagint in Context: Introduction to the Greek Version of the Bible*, trans. W. G. E. Watson (Boston: Brill Academic Publishers, 2000).

If you need to pursue something about the Septuagint in even more detail, one or more of the following may point you to relevant works:

Sebastian P. Brock, Charles T. Fritsch, and Sidney Jellicoe, eds., *A Classified Bibliography of the Septuagint* (Leiden: E. J. Brill, 1973).
Emanuel Tov, *A Classified Bibliography of Lexical and Grammatical Studies on the Language of the Septuagint* (Jerusalem: Academon, 1980).
Cécile Dogniez, ed., *A Bibliography of the Septuagint: 1970–1993*, Vetus Testamentum Supplement 69 (Leiden: E. J. Brill, 1995).

The United Bible Societies LXX bibliography is updated periodically and as of this writing contains over 450 entries just from the 1990s:

http://www.ubs-translations.org/cgi-bin/dbman/db.cgi?db=lxxbib&uid=default.

Computer Assisted Tools for Septuagint/Scriptural Study, codirected by Robert Kraft and Emanuel Tov, can be found on the Web:

http://ccat.sas.upenn.edu/rs/rak/catss.html.

Theological and Academic Resources for the Septuagint can also be accessed:

http://www.kalvesmaki.com/.

This site has links to many online resources related to the Septuagint online, including a downloadable text. Related to it is

The Septuagint Online, http://www.kalvesmaki.com/LXX/Secondlit.htm.

Both pages are part of a site maintained and updated periodically by Joel Kalvesmaki.

As an example of the sorts of focused materials becoming available, consider the following, which parallels the LXX of the Psalms with the Hebrew Psalms and provides two different English translations for convenience:

John Kohlenberger, ed., *Comparative Psalter: Hebrew (Masoretic Text), Revised Standard Version Bible, The New English Translation of the Septuagint, Greek (Septuagint)* (Oxford: Oxford University Press, 2007).

Note: The URLs for these sites and others may change from time to time, but simply googling commonsense search phrases like "Septuagint bibliography" will likely keep you informed of where to find them.

The Dead Sea Scrolls

The various texts are published in a variety of sources. Most are so fragmentary as to be exegetically useless. For a good list of the publications up to 1990, see Fitzmyer, *The Dead Sea Scrolls* (4.12.6). A fine photographic reproduction of the two most nearly complete OT texts from Qumran (Isaiah and Habakkuk, the latter being included in an ancient commentary) is found in

John C. Trever, *Scrolls from Qumrân Cave I from Photographs* (Jerusalem: The Albright Institute of Archaeological Research and The Shrine of the Book, 1972).

Publications of the Qumran materials are found in an ongoing series, published by Oxford University's Clarendon Press, titled Discoveries in the Judaean Desert. Dozens of volumes have appeared in this series. Virtually any library or Internet search engine will find these for you if you simply use the series title, Discoveries in the Judaean Desert.

An example of a recent overview publication is

Emanuel Tov, ed., *The Texts from the Judaean Desert: Indices and an Introduction to the Discoveries in the Judaean Desert Series*, DJD 39 (Oxford: Clarendon, 2002).

The best way to keep abreast of what is happening in scrolls research is to check out the Web site of

The Orion Center for the Study of the Dead Sea Scrolls and Associated Literature, at Hebrew University in Jerusalem, http://orion.mscc.huji.ac.il/.

It contains various bibliographies, links, and news, all of which are kept currrent. Two of these are *The Dead Sea Scrolls Electronic Reference Library* and *The Dead Sea Scrolls Reader* series.

To see if a word in the passage you are working on is also used at Qumran, you can use the following:

Martin G. Abegg Jr., James E. Bowley, and Edward M. Cook, *The Dead Sea Scrolls Concordance*, vol. 3, *The Biblical Texts from Qumran and Other Sites* (Leiden and Boston: E. J. Brill, 2008).

On general issues related to the texts and many translated portions as well, see the following:

Lawrence H. Schiffman and James C. VanderKam, eds., *Encyclopedia of the Dead Sea Scrolls*, 2 vols. (New York: Oxford University Press, 2000).

The Samaritan Pentateuch

When working on text issues related to a passage from the Pentateuch, if you can get hold of both of the following editions of the Samaritan Pentateuch, you will have good coverage of that important ancient text tradition. Each has limitations in what it includes, and ideally they should be used together. It is not terribly common that a Samartian reading involves or solves a problem, but when it does, these books may be needed:

August Von Gall, ed., *Der hebräische Pentateuch der Samaritaner: Genesis–Deuteronomy*, 5 vols, in 1 (Giessen, 1918; repr., Berlin: Walter de Gruyter, 1966).
Abraham Tal, ed., *The Samaritan Pentateuch: Edited According to MS 6 of the Shekem Synagogue* (Tel-Aviv: Chaim Rosenberg School, 1994).

The Peshitta

A critical edition of the text is gradually underway and now covers quite a few portions of the OT:

The Old Testament in Syriac, ed. the Peshitta Institute of Leiden (Leiden: Brill Academic Publishers, 1972–).

The most widely available full copy is an uncritical edition, usually obtainable from Bible societies:

Vetus Testamentum Syriace et Neosyriace (Urmia, Iran, 1852; repr., London: Trinitarian Bible Society, 1954).

For a relatively comprehensive, current bibliography on the Peshitta (as well as the Targums), see

http://www.targum.info/biblio/reviews.htm.

The Peshitta is also found as a searchable text in modules of the leading Bible software programs (*Accordance, BibleWorks, Logos Bible Software*, et al.), and at several Web sites as well (google "Peshitta online").

The Targum(s)

There are many Targums. Various ancient translators rendered various parts of the OT from Hebrew into Aramaic, and each of these is called a Targum (translation). The only OT books that do not have Targums are Daniel and Ezra–Nehemiah, because those books already are partly in Aramaic. A standard edition continues to be

Alexander Sperber, ed., *The Bible in Aramaic*, 4 vols. (Leiden: E. J. Brill, 1959–1973).

The newer multivolume *Aramaic Bible* project already covers the OT Targums with translations and notes. Any library or Internet search engine can locate

The Aramaic Bible, 19 vols. (Collegeville, MN: Liturgical Press, 1987–2007).

There are also public-domain Targum texts online (google "Targum online") and within modules of the major computer Bible software programs.

The Vulgate and Vetus Latina

There are various Latin versions of the Bible from ancient times—some complete, some partial. If your passage involves significant variants from the Latin, the following three articles will help explain the resources available to you as you try to understand the ancient Latin translations and their relative value:

P.-M. Bogaert, "Bulletin de la Bible latine. VII. Première série," *Revue Bénédictine* 105 (1995): 200–238; "Bulletin de la Bible latine. VII. Deuxième série," *Revue Bénédictine* 106 (1996): 386–412; "Bulletin de la Bible latine. VII. Troisième série," *Revue Bénédictine* 108 (1998): 359–386.

A critical edition of the Old Latin (OL, also called *Vetus Latina* or VL) text of the Bible is underway in what is known as the Beuron edition, produced by the Vetus Latina Institut of St. Martin's Abbey in Beuron, Germany, but it has appeared so far only in Genesis, Ruth, and Isaiah among the agreed-upon OT canonical books, and Wisdom of Solomon and Sirach (Ecclesiasticus) among the so-called Apocrypha:

Vetus latina: Die Reste der altlateinischen Bibel nach Petrus Sabatier neu gesammelt und in Verbindung mit der Heidelberger Akademie der Wissenschaften herausgegeben von der Erzabtei Beuron, various editors (Freiburg: Herder, 1949–).

For a good overall introduction to the Old Latin, Vulgate, and other Latin versions, see

L. F. Hartman, B. M. Peebles, and M. Stevenson, "Vulgate," *New Catholic Encyclopedia,* 14:591–600, 2nd ed. (Detroit: Thomson Gale; Washington, DC: Catholic University of America, 2003).

A critical edition of the Vulgate, with attempts made to provide the original text as far as is possible, is

R. Weber et al., eds., *Biblia sacra: Iuxta Vulgatam versionem,* 4th ed. (Stuttgart: Deutsche Bibelgesellschaft, 1994).

For both the Vulgate and its predecessor, the *Vetus Latina* (Old Latin), there are editions, based in the latter case on the few portions that still survive, such as

Roger Gryson, *Manuscrits vieux latins* (Freiburg: Herder, 1999).

There are also inexpensive editions of the Vulgate available. Two common ones are

Alberto Colunga and Laurentio Turrado, eds., *Biblia Vulgata* (Madrid: Biblioteca de Autores Cristianos, 1953; repr., 1965).
Biblia sacra: Iuxta Vulgatam versionem, 4th ed. (Stuttgart: Deutsche Bibelgesellschaft, 1994).

4.1.5. The footnotes and other helps in BH³, BHS (for BHQ, see below)

In the older *BH³* (the Kittel edition) are two separate paragraphs of foot-notes. The upper paragraph contains information on variants thought by the editors to be of relatively minor importance. They are indicated in the text by small Greek letters. The lower paragraph, indicated by small Latin letters, contains what the editors thought was most significant, including suggestions for actual correction of the MT toward a more likely origi-nal. Sometimes the editor does nothing more than record the evidence from the various versions and manuscripts, leaving any decision about changing the text up to the reader. At other times the editor will actually suggest how the MT should be corrected or at least report what a com-mentator has suggested by way of a change (emendation). The explana-tions are given in Latin abbreviations. A convenient English key to the abbreviations and to the signs and major versions is found in a valuable little pamphlet:

Prescott H. Williams Jr., *An English Key to the Symbols and Latin Words and Abbreviations of Bib-lia Hebraica* (Stuttgart: Württembergische Bibelanstalt, 1969).

In the newer *BHS* (the Stuttgart edition), which most people now use, there are also two separate paragraphs, but they have different purposes. The upper paragraph, set in very small type, contains notations related to the masoretic apparatus printed in the margins (see 4.1.6). The lower paragraph combines and updates the kinds of notations grouped into two separate paragraphs by the *BH³* editors. In general, the *BHS* textual notes are superior to those of *BH³* but are still neither exhaustive nor always definitive. They tend to be partial, selective, and occasionally even mis-leading and so must be used with proper caution. In other words, they are a good starting point but may not provide all the information you need to analyze the state of the text fully.

For *BHS* the standard key to the Latin used in the notes has been

Hans Peter Rüger, *An English Key to the Latin Words and Abbreviations and the Symbols of Biblia Hebraica Stuttgartensia* (New York: American Bible Society, 1990).

This same key, with minor modifications, is printed in its entirety as an appendix to Brotzman's *Old Testament Textual Criticism* (4.1.2, above). Rüger's key is also found within the following:

William R. Scott, Harold Scanlin, and Hans Peter Rüger, *A Simplified Guide to BHS: Critical Apparatus, Masora, Accents, Unusual Letters & Other Markings*, 4th ed. (N. Richland Hills, TX: D&F Scott Publishing, 2007).

This is the newest edition of a popular and widely used manual for understanding both masoretic tradition and the critical apparatus of *BHS*. Its index is useful, too.

Also very useful and even more detailed in some aspects of using the *BHS* is

Reinhard Wonneberger, *Understanding BHS: A Manual for the Users of Biblia Hebraica Stuttgartensia*, 2nd ed. (Rome: Pontifical Biblical Institute Press, 1990).

Wonneberger's book explains the apparatus in *BHS* and provides some helpful critiques of it and of the theory that it is based on.

The critical apparatus in both *BH³* and *BHS* will help you see at a glance some of the evidence for certain obvious textual issues, but they are no substitute for your own comprehensive word-by-word check of the versions in a full exegetical analysis of a passage.

4.1.6. *The Hebrew University Bible Project*, Biblia Hebraica Quinta, HaKeter, *and the Oxford Hebrew Bible Project*

The Hebrew University Bible Project

Begun in Jerusalem in 1965, this project intended to produce a massive, multivolume critical edition of the Hebrew OT based on the Aleppo Codex, which dates to about AD 900–925 (i.e., perhaps as much as a century earlier than the Leningrad Codex). Unfortunately, the Aleppo Codex is incomplete, lacking almost the entire Pentateuch as well as some or all of Song of Songs, Ecclesiastes, Lamentations, Esther, Daniel, and Ezra. Envisioned as an alternative to the *BHS*, the Hebrew Bible Project made only partial progress. In the three fascicles published (Isaiah, Jeremiah, Ezekiel), four critical apparatuses are used. One of them cites the major ancient versions, one the Qumran and rabbinic evidence for the text, one the corresponding medieval masoretic evidence, and one comments on spelling, vowel pointing, accents, and so on. Ezekiel, the most recent volume, appeared in 2004, and it is not known whether the project will continue.

Moshe H. Goshen-Gottstein et al., eds., *The Hebrew University Bible* (Jerusalem: Magnes Press, 1975–).

Quinta

Just as *BHS* has now almost completely replaced the use of the older *BH³*, a new edition of the Hebrew Bible is under way. This new edition is called

Biblia Hebraica Quinta (BHQ; BHS was actually *BH*[4]), and it is based on the same excellent manuscript as that of its predecessors, the Leningrad Codex of AD 1008. One big change with the *Quinta* is its apparatus (notes and commentary), which distinguishes text issues based on external evidence (other versions) from issues based on internal evidence (in the MT tradition itself) and addresses questions of the MT's literary development over time. In most cases the textual commentary explains how textual choices were made. The first fascicle (*The Megilloth: Ruth, Song of Songs, Ecclesiastes, Lamentations, Esther*) includes a general introduction to the whole project. The *BHQ* includes much more data from and emphasis on the Dead Sea Scrolls and the Syriac Peshitta, with corresponding diminution of emphasis on the LXX and Latin Vulgate variants. The wisdom of this tilt is debatable, but *BHQ* may well eventually replace the *BHS* as the standard critical edition of the ancient Hebrew text of the OT.

A. Schenker, Y. A. P. Goldman, A. van der Kooij, G. J. Norton, S. Pisano, J. de Waard, and R. D. Weis, eds., *Biblia Hebraica Quinta*, fascicle 18, *General Introduction and Megilloth* (Stuttgart: Deutsche Bibelgesellschaft, 2004).

HaKeter

Miqraot Gedolot HaKeter aims to provide a new critical edition of the OT in Hebrew. It is based mainly on the Aleppo Codex, with supplementation from other manuscripts as necessary, and also includes both Masorahs with case-by-case explanations. It pays special attention to Aramaic, and when it refers to Targums, it relies on Targum Onkelos or the Targum to the Prophets via a new, superior critical text. It also includes text information from such rabbis as Rashi, Kimchi, Ibn Ezra, and others.

HaKeter began with a General Introduction and Joshua–Judges in 1992, and now includes Genesis, 1–2 Samuel, 1–2 Kings, Isaiah, Ezekiel, and Psalms. The completion of *HaKeter* may come even before that of the *BHQ*.

The Oxford Hebrew Bible Project

The OHB Project has only recently begun. In a manner somewhat similar to that of *BHQ*, it hopes to reach an international user audience. The OHB Project claims to take the most innovative approach of all the newer text-critical projects by incorporating as much as possible of the latest and best research now in progress. It is expected to print in parallel format the texts of some recensions of portions of the Hebrew Bible, and hopes to be more eclectic and less dependent on any one text tradition than the other projects are.

4.1.7. The Masorah

Printed in the margins of both *BH*[3] and *BHS* are groups of notations— written in Aramaic and mostly abbreviated—made by the Masoretes. Some notations may suggest possible improvements upon the text, but most indicate observations useful for the accurate preservation and copying of the text. In the ancient masoretic manuscripts, many of these notes were placed in the margins. These were called the "Masorah parva," the "little Masorah." Longer notations were placed at the beginning or the end of the manuscripts. These were called the "Masorah magna," the "large Masorah." For most purposes of exegesis, scholars pay little attention to the Masorah itself because its truly significant observations are already incorporated into *BH*[3]/*BHS*/*BHQ* or can be duplicated by quick reference to a concordance. Moreover, such observations have been rendered unnecessary by the development of the printing press. In other words, it is quite common to ignore the Masorah in doing exegesis.

A fine guide to the masoretic scribal notes in the *BHS* is

Page H. Kelley, Daniel S. Mynatt, and Timothy G. Crawford, *The Masorah of Biblia Hebraica Stuttgartensia: Introduction and Annotated Glossary* (Grand Rapids: Wm. B. Eerdmans, 1998).

4.1.8. Other masoretic indicators

The Masoretes produced a dots-and-dashes vowel pointing system so that their students, for whom Hebrew was by then a dead language, could pronounce the words properly (according to the postbiblical pronunciation that had evolved by the sixth to ninth centuries AD), mainly for the purpose of chanting the text in synagogue worship. In addition, they developed special symbols to indicate word accents, verse divisions, and sections of verses, again mainly for the purpose of group chanting in worship. They also included notations for such things as Scripture portions used in the yearly cycle of synagogue readings. None of these markings or notations, including the vowel-pointing system, represents anything more than the opinion of the Masoretes according to their own early medieval, and often conflicting, traditions. In other words, you must be ready to disregard pointings, verse divisions, and other markings whenever your exegetical judgment suggests that they are unreliable. See also 4.1.2.

4.2. Translation

4.2.1. Translation theory

A good translation not only renders the words of the original into their best English equivalents, it also reflects the style, the spirit, and even the impact of the original wherever possible. You are the best judge of what constitutes a faithful translation. Your familiarity with the passage in the original, and with the audience for whom you write or preach, allows you to choose your words to maximize the accuracy of the translation. Remember that accuracy does not require wooden literalism. The words of different languages do not correspond to one another on a one-for-one basis, yet the concepts must correspond. Your translation should leave the same impression with you when you read it as does the original. A translation that meets this criterion can be considered faithful to the original.

Three fine books on Bible translation remain valuable:

Eugene A. Nida and Charles R. Taber, *The Theory and Practice of Translation* (1969; repr; Leiden: E. J. Brill, fourth impression, 2003).

John Beekman and John Callow, *Translating the Word of God* (Grand Rapids: Zondervan Publishing House, 1974).

Sakae Kubo and Walter Specht, *So Many Versions?* (Grand Rapids: Zondervan Publishing House, 1975).

The following more recent works focus on the debate about types of translations and translation theory, and all are of use and importance:

Eugene Nida and Jan de Waard, *From One Language to Another: Functional Equivalence in Bible Translation* (Nashville: Thomas Nelson, 1986).

Eugene Nida, "The Sociolinguistics of Translating Canonical Religious Texts," in *Traduction, Terminologie, Rédaction* 7, no. 1 (July 1994): 191–217.

Stanley E. Porter and Richard S. Hess, eds., *Translating the Bible: Problems and Prospects* (Sheffield: Sheffield Academic Press, 1999).

Glen G. Scorgie, Mark L. Strauss, and Steven M. Voth, eds., *The Challenge of Bible Translation: Communicating God's Word to the World* (Grand Rapids: Zondervan Publishing House, 2003).

4.2.2. Translation aids

Even if your knowledge of Hebrew, Greek, and other languages has deteriorated (or was never adequate), you can still work profitably with the original languages by using several English-oriented texts. Do not hesitate to use these. There is no shame in saving time and frustration, and no value in guessing your way through material you simply cannot read.

The fastest and most versatile basic translation aids come in the form of computer software, the two most powerful being *Accordance* and *Bible-Works*, followed by *Logos Bible Software* (see 4.4.2). These programs provide instant lexical and grammatical data for any word you point your cursor at. They also can in seconds assemble for you all the various contexts where a given word is used throughout the rest of Scripture so that you can examine for yourself the range of its usages. Moreover, they can instantly provide a complete list of translated contexts in any of the modern translations whose modules you have purchased so that you can readily examine how various modern translators have dealt with your word or wording in various parts of their translations. All this is enormously useful, but it does not automatically render useless the book references listed below. A book can be selective and focused at various points according to the author's judgment in a way that the mechanical processes of a computer concordance do not allow, and a book can also follow a particular format or variety of formats for the presenting of its data (including the unique way that authors may have chosen to show the intersection of their specific advice to you within the context of a helpfully formatted text). Moreover, a book can show judiciously selected combinations of contexts that may prove more helpful to you in some instances than the automatic complete screen formats generated by the computer concordances.

For the Hebrew OT several complete interlinear editions are available. Each contains an acceptable translation printed in interlinear fashion, as well as separately in paragraph form alongside the main text. Interlinears can be useful for skimming through larger passages:

Jay P. Green Sr., ed., *Interlinear Bible: Hebrew, Greek, English* (Lafayette, IN: Sovereign Grace Publishers, 1997).

Jay P. Green Sr., ed., *Interlinear Bible: Hebrew, Greek, English*, large edition (Lafayette, IN: Sovereign Grace Publishers, 2000).

John R. Kohlenberger III, ed., *NIV Interlinear Hebrew-English Old Testament* (Grand Rapids: Zondervan Publishing House, 1987).

Also available for part of the OT is a similar interlinear edition, somewhat less useful because it is more wooden in style:

Joseph Magil, *The Englishman's Linear Hebrew-English Old Testament* (Grand Rapids: Zondervan Publishing House, 1974).

An excellent translation of the LXX is available:

Albert Pietersma and Benjamin Wright, eds., *New English Translation of the Septuagint* (Oxford: Oxford University Press, 2007).

For the LXX no book-form interlinear is available, but a convenient side-by-side Greek and English publication does exist:

Lancelot Charles Lee Brenton, *The Septuagint Version of the Old Testament with an English Translation* (London: Samuel Bagster & Sons, 1844; repr., Grand Rapids: Zondervan Publishing House, 1971).

Several Web sites have interlinear LXX-English Bibles that provide the convenience of rapid-search speed. Simply google "interlinear Septuagint." See also ApostolicBible.com for a CD-ROM version that can be purchased or accessed online.

The Web site "The Septuagint Online" has a variety of suggestions for LXX text and translation links:

http://www.kalvesmaki.com/LXX/Texts.htm.

A translation of the Syriac Peshitta into English has been made. Usually reliable, it serves to tell you when the Peshitta is different from the MT and other versions, even if you do not know Syriac well:

George M. Lamsa, *The Holy Bible from Ancient Eastern Manuscripts* (Philadelphia: A. J. Holman Co., 1957).

Various portions of the Aramaic Targums are available in English translation. Among these are

J. W. Etheridge, *The Targums of Onkelos and Jonathan ben Uzziel on the Pentateuch*, 2 vols. (London: Longman, Green, Longman & Roberts, 1862–65; repr., New York: Ktav Publishing House, 1969).
Bernard Grossfeld, ed., *The Targum to the Five Megilloth* (New York: Hermon Press, 1973).

Some Targum translations into English are available online. Google "Targum translation" or "Targum online." See also

http://www.library.upenn.edu/cajs/etexts.html.

The Latin Vulgate is also translated into English:

Ronald Knox, *The Old Testament: Newly Translated from the Vulgate Latin*, 2 vols. (New York: Sheed & Ward, 1950).

And a reasonable translation is available online at

http://www.latinvulgate.com/.

Analytical lexicons list words directly as they occur in the biblical text and then provide the parsing. They can be useful as time-savers or if you have no access to a computer program to do the same thing, but they are not be to relied on for meanings or other technical data. Use the formal lexicons for that purpose. For Hebrew and Aramaic there is

Benjamin Davidson, *The Analytical Hebrew and Chaldee Lexicon* (London: Samuel Bagster & Sons, 1848), 2nd ed. (1850; repr., Grand Rapids: Zondervan Publishing House, 1970).

For LXX Greek words, Bagster's analytical lexicon of the NT is often adequate even though its vocabulary is limited to words found in the NT:

Harold K. Moulton, ed., *The Analytical Greek Lexicon Revised* (originally published as *The Analytical Greek Lexicon*, London: Samuel Bagster & Sons, 1852; rev. ed., 1908; new rev., Grand Rapids: Zondervan Publishing House, 1978).

The newer Bible software programs are faster and easier to use than these books, so if you own or have access to *Accordance*, *BibleWorks*, *Logos Bible Software*, or another such program you will find them faster and more productive than analytical concordances in book form.

To make it easier to use the still-popular Brown, Driver, and Briggs *Hebrew Lexicon* (see 4.4.1), an index was produced that lists the Hebrew words mostly in the order in which they occur in the chapters and verses of each book, with reference given to the appropriate entry in BDB. Such an aid is necessary only if your Hebrew is weak enough to make parsing a problem:

Bruce Einspahr, *Index to Brown, Driver and Briggs Hebrew Lexicon* (Chicago: Moody Press, 1982).

You must use a reliable lexicon for careful exegesis. But if you are reading a passage in Hebrew for the first time, or trying to read through several passages quickly—and your Hebrew vocabulary is limited—you may find the following books to be time-savers:

John Joseph Owens, *Analytical Key to the Old Testament* (Grand Rapids: Baker Book House, 1989; also packaged in *Logos Bible Software*, for example).
Terry A. Armstrong, *A Reader's Hebrew-English Lexicon of the Old Testament* (Grand Rapids: Zondervan Publishing House, 1989).
A. Philip Brown II and Bryan W. Smith, *A Reader's Hebrew Bible* (Grand Rapids: Zondervan Publishing House, 2008).

4.3. Grammar

4.3.1. Reference grammars

Properly used, reference grammars are a ready source of exegetically relevant information. The grammars often collect many or all of the instances of a certain type of grammatical phenomenon. When you refer to the grammar for information on such a phenomenon, you are thus provided with a list of parallels and an explanation of how the phenomenon functions in the OT. That can be just the sort of information you need to help you make certain exegetical decisions.

If you need to refresh your knowledge of Hebrew by using a basic grammar, the following are excellent:

Gary D. Pratico and Miles Van Pelt, *Basics of Biblical Hebrew* (Grand Rapids: Zondervan Publishing House, 2001).

Duane Garrett, *A Modern Grammar for Classical Hebrew* (Nashville: Broadman & Holman, 2002).

Choon Leong Seow, *A Grammar for Biblical Hebrew*, rev. ed. (Nashville: Abingdon Press, 1995).

Thomas O. Lambdin, *Introduction to Biblical Hebrew* (New York: Charles Scribner's Sons, 1971).

Allen P. Ross, *Introducing Biblical Hebrew* (Tappan, NJ: Fleming H. Revell, 2001).

Arthur Walker-Jones, *Hebrew for Biblical Interpretation* (Atlanta: Society of Biblical Literature, 2003).

For Hebrew the classic reference grammar has been

H. F. W. Gesenius, *Hebrew Grammar*, rev. E. Kautzsch, ed. and trans. A. E. Cowley, 2nd English ed. (Oxford: Clarendon Press, 1910).

Some newer grammars offer a fine array of sophisticated insight into the grammatical structures and nuances of Hebrew. The first one, by Williams, is easier to use than the others and is particularly comprehensive because it is keyed to all of them, although all are useful and erudite:

Ronald J. Williams, *Williams' Hebrew Syntax*, 3rd ed., revised and expanded by John C. Beckman (Toronto: University of Toronto Press, 2007).

Paul Joüon and T. Muraoka, *A Grammar of Biblical Hebrew*, rev. ed., 2 vols. (Rome: Pontifical Biblical Institute, 2006).

Bruce K. Waltke and M. O'Connor, *An Introduction to Biblical Hebrew Syntax* (Winona Lake, IN: Eisenbrauns, 1990).

B. T. Arnold and J. H. Choi, *A Guide to Biblical Hebrew Syntax* (Cambridge: Cambridge University Press, 2003).

C. H. J. van der Merwe, J. A. Naudé, and J. H. Kroeze, *A Biblical Hebrew Reference Grammar* (Sheffield: Sheffield Academic Press, 2002).

Helpful both for its collection of instances of special grammatical features from throughout the Hebrew Bible, and for its solutions for many problematic grammatical issues, is

Alexander Sperber, *A Historical Grammar of Biblical Hebrew* (Leiden: E. J. Brill, 1966).

For Aramaic grammatical features, you will probably find almost everything you need in one of these:

Frederick E. Greenspahn, *An Introduction to Aramaic.* 2nd ed. (Atlanta: Society of Biblical Literature, 2003).
Alger F. Johns, *A Short Grammar of Biblical Aramaic* (Berrien Springs, MI: Andrews University Press, 1982).
Franz Rosenthal and D. M. Gurtner, *A Grammar of Biblical Aramaic: With an Index of Biblical Citations,* 7th ed., rev. (Wiesbaden: Harrassowitz, 2006).
William B. Stevenson, *Grammar of Palestinian Jewish Aramaic* (repr., Eugene, OR: Wipf & Stock Publishers, 2000).

If you wish to refer to data relevant to the Aramaic grammar from the entire Old Aramaic period (earliest texts through the end of the Persian Empire in 333 BC), a technical and very comprehensive source is

Stanislav Segert, *Altaramäische Grammatik* (Leipzig: Verlag Enzyklopädie, VEB, 1990).

Attention to Targumic Aramaic is found in

David Marcus, *A Manual of Babylonian Jewish Aramaic* (Washington, DC: University Press of America, 1981).
Yitzchak Frank, *Grammar for Gemara and Targum Onkelos* (New York: Ariel Institute/ Feldheim Publishers, 2003).

Two useful grammars for the Septuagint are available, though the first tends to concentrate on morphology:

Henry St. J. Thackeray, *A Grammar of the Old Testament in Greek according to the Septuagint* (Cambridge: Cambridge University Press, 1909).
F. C. Conybeare and St. George Stock, *Grammar of Septuagint Greek: With Selected Readings, Vocabularies, and Updated Indexes* (repr., Peabody, MA: Hendrickson Publishers, 2002).

If you do exegesis of passages of poetry, especially the Psalms or Job, you may find in the secondary literature frequent reference to two languages, Ugaritic and Phoenician, which are quite similar to Hebrew. Even if you have not studied these languages formally, you may be able to understand something of their relevance and helpfulness on specific points by consulting the following grammars:

William M. Schniedewind and Joel H. Hunt, *A Primer on Ugaritic: Language, Culture, and Literature* (Cambridge: Cambridge University Press, 2007).

Stanislav Segert, *Basic Grammar of the Ugaritic Language: With Selected Texts and Glossary* (Berkeley: University of California Press, 1985).

Daniel Sivan, *A Grammar of the Ugaritic Language* (Leiden: Brill Academic Publishers, 1997).

Cyrus H. Gordon, *Ugaritic Textbook*, rev. repr. (Rome: Pontifical Biblical Institute, 1998).

Zellig S. Harris, *A Grammar of the Phoenician Language* (New Haven, CT: American Oriental Society, 1936).

Stanislav Segert, *A Grammar of Phoenician and Punic* (Munich: C. H. Beck, 1976).

Charles R. Krahmalkov, *A Phoenician-Punic Grammar* (Leiden: Brill Academic Publishers, 2001).

For Syriac, a language necessary for competence in OT textual criticism, three recent works may be commended:

Wheeler M. Thackston, *Introduction to Syriac: An Elementary Grammar with Readings from Syriac Literature* (Bethesda, MD: IBEX Publishers, 2000).

Takamitsu Muraoka, *Classical Syriac: A Basic Grammar* (Wiesbaden: Harrassowitz, 1997).

Michael P. Weitzman, *The Syriac Version of the Old Testament: An Introduction* (Cambridge: Cambridge University Press, 1999).

For Akkadian, the language of hundreds of thousands of documents from Babylon and Assyria, many of which directly bear on biblical knowledge, an excellent grammar is

John Huehnergard, *A Grammar of Akkadian*, rev. ed. (Winona Lake, IN: Eisenbrauns, 2005). A key to its excercises has also been published by Wm. B. Eerdmans. John Huehnergard, *Key to a Grammar of Akkadian*, 2nd ed. (Cambridge: Harvard Semitic Museum; Winona Lake, IN: Eisenbrauns, 2005).

Consider also:

Richard Caplice, *Introduction to Akkadian*, 3rd ed. (Chicago: Loyola Press, 1988).

4.3.2. Other technical sources

It is sometimes helpful to be able to refer to a comparative grammar, one that considers Hebrew forms and features in the context of those of other Semitic languages. The following are all useful in this regard:

Patrick R. Bennett, *Comparative Semitic Linguistics: A Manual* (Winona Lake, IN: Eisenbrauns, 1998).

E. Lipiński, *Semitic Languages: Outline of a Comparative Grammar*, 2nd ed. (Leuven: Peeters, 2001).

Gideon Goldenberg, *Studies in Semitic Linguistics: Selected Writings* (Jerusalem: Magnes Press, 1998).

De Lacy O'Leary, *Comparative Grammar of the Semitic Languages* (London: Routledge, 2001).

William Wright, *Lectures on the Comparative Grammar of the Semitic Languages* (1890; repr., Piscataway, NJ: Gorgias Press, 2002).

To understand Hebrew in the more immediate context of the Canaanite language family, see the following:

Zellig S. Harris, *Development of the Canaanite Dialects* (New Haven, CT: American Oriental Society, 1939; repr., New York: Kraus Reprint Co., 1976).

William L. Moran, "The Hebrew Language in Its Northwest Semitic Background," in *The Bible and the Ancient Near East*, ed. G. Ernest Wright, 54–72 (Garden City, NY: Doubleday, 1961).

Anson F. Rainey, *Canaanite in the Amarna Tablets: A Linguistic Analysis of the Mixed Dialect Used by Scribes from Canaan* (Leiden: Brill Academic Publishers, 1996).

Orthography (spelling analysis) is a technical study within the field of grammar that can occasionally help the exegete unravel aspects of a difficult text. The classic study compares Hebrew with Phoenician, Aramaic, and Moabite during the OT period, based on the evidence of the inscriptions dating to OT times:

Frank Moore Cross Jr. and David Noel Freedman, *Early Hebrew Orthography* (New Haven, CT: American Oriental Society, 1952).

This has been helpfully updated in various aspects by

David Noel Freedman, A. Dean Forbes, and Francis I. Andersen, *Studies in Hebrew and Aramaic Orthography* (Winona Lake, IN: Eisenbrauns, 1992).

4.4. Lexical Analysis

4.4.1. Lexicons

A lexicon is a dictionary. The fact that the term "lexicon" has been used instead of the term "dictionary" by biblical and classical scholars is simply a quirk of linguistic history, well deserving of a word study of its own.

The lexicons are valuable sources of information about the words they list. Lexicons often devote lengthy articles (mini-word studies or, better, concept studies) to the words that are especially interesting or significant theologically, and also to words that have any unusual or crucial features.

It is a mistake to launch upon a word study or even to comment at length about the usage of a word in Scripture without first consulting the relevant lexicons.

The Hebrew lexicon to use (if possible) is

Ludwig Koehler and Walter Baumgartner, rev. Walter Baumgartner and Johann J. Stamm, *Hebrew and Aramaic Lexicon of the Old Testament*, 5 vols. (Leiden: Brill Academic Publishers, 1994–2000).

This lexicon is the world's standard. It is available on CD-ROM and is also packaged as a module with the leading Bible software. It is a massive and expensive work, and therefore it is also wise to consider a fine abridgment, one that preserves virtually all the essential information of its comprehensive parent:

William L. Holladay, *A Concise Hebrew and Aramaic Lexicon of the Old Testament*, new ed. (Leiden: Brill, 2000).

Currently nearing completion is a most welcome, massive lexicon project, which includes not only all biblical Hebrew but also Qumran, Hebrew inscriptions, and Ben Sira:

David J. A. Clines, ed., *The Dictionary of Classical Hebrew*, 8 vols. (Sheffield: Sheffield Academic Press, 1994–).

Much less reliable, though still widely used (mainly because its copyright protection is gone and therefore it is cheaply available and sometimes bundled with or linked to various Bible software programs), is

Francis Brown, S. R. Driver, and Charles A. Briggs, *A Hebrew and English Lexicon of the Old Testament* (Oxford: Clarendon Press, 1907; repr., 1962, 1966, 1978, 1999, etc.).

The BDB is also available as a module of Bible software programs. It is still somewhat useful because of the sheer volume of its fine articles, but it is relatively outdated because it lacks cognate information from Ugaritic and other recent finds. Moreover, many of its suggested etymologies (histories of word origins and their relation to Semitic word roots) are often unacceptable.

For biblical Aramaic, the standard Hebrew lexicons all have an Aramaic section. For Aramaic outside the Bible, especially in the Targums, a traditional source in English has been

Marcus Jastrow, *A Dictionary of the Targumim, the Talmud Babli and Yerushalmi, and the Midrashic Literature*, 2nd ed., 2 vols. (New York: Choreb, 1926; repr., New York: Pardes Publishing House, 1950). The entire work is now available online: Google "Jastrow Dictionary."

To Jastrow's work may now be added the newer volumes:

Michael Sokoloff, *A Dictionary of Jewish Palestinian Aramaic of the Byzantine Period* (Baltimore: Johns Hopkins University Press, 1990).

Michael Sokoloff, *A Dictionary of Jewish Babylonian Aramaic of the Talmudic and Geonic Periods* (Ramat Gan, Israel: Bar Ilan University Press, 1990); 2nd ed. (with Baltimore: Johns Hopkins University Press, 2002).

If you can read Latin, an excellent Aramaic lexicon is yours to use:

Ernesto Vogt, *Lexicon Linguae Aramaicae Veteris Testamenti Documentis Antiquis Illustratum* (Rome: Pontifical Biblical Institute, 1971).

But the default source, even though it may take a few moments for you to learn the transliteration and search system, is the *Comprehensive Aramaic Lexicon*, which contains entries covering virtually all the Aramaic known from the ancient world and is searchable freely online:

Comprehensive Aramaic Lexicon (*CAL*) (Cincinnati: Hebrew Union College–Jewish Institute of Religion), http://cal1.cn.huc.edu/.

For the Septuagint, nothing excels the combination of the following works:

Takamitsu Muraoka, *A Greek-English Lexicon of the Septuagint* (Leuven: Peeters, 2002).

Johann Lust, Erik Eynikel, and Katrin Hauspie, eds., *Greek-English Lexicon of the Septuagint*, rev. ed., 2 vols. (New York: American Bible Society, 2004).

Consider also the following:

W. Bauer, W. F. Arndt, F. W. Gingrich, and F. W. Danker, *A Greek-English Lexicon of the New Testament and Other Early Christian Literature*, 2nd ed. (Chicago: University of Chicago Press, 1979) or 3rd ed. (2000).

Also often useful, but occasionally plagued by misleading Septuagint definitions, is

Henry O. Liddell and Robert Scott, *A Greek-English Lexicon*, rev. Henry Stuart Jones and Roderick McKenzie, 9th ed. (Oxford: Clarendon Press, 1940), revised and augmented throughout (1996).

See as well

E. A. Barber et al., eds., *A Greek-English Lexicon: Supplement* (Oxford: Oxford University Press, 1968).

For working from the Syriac Peshitta, use

R. Payne Smith, *A Compendious Syriac Dictionary*, ed. J. Payne Smith (Oxford: Clarendon Press, 1903; repr., 1957; repr., Eugene, OR: Wipf & Stock, 1999).

The two following massive Latin dictionaries are excellent for the Vulgate and other Latin texts:

Charlton T. Lewis and Charles Short, *A Latin Dictionary*, also titled *A New Latin Dictionary*, first published as *Harper's Latin Dictionary* (New York: American Book Co., 1879; repr., Oxford: Oxford University Press, 1979).
P. G. W. Glare, ed., *The Oxford Latin Dictionary* (Oxford: Oxford University Press, 1982).

Handy is

James Morwood, ed., *The Oxford Latin Desk Dictionary* (Oxford: Oxford University Press, 2005).

Since much lexical information about OT Hebrew has come from Assyrian/Babylonian and Ugaritic sources, from time to time you may find it necessary to consult the lexicons for these languages.

For Assyrian/Babylonian, use wherever possible the multivolume *CAD*:

Ignace Gelb, Benno Landsberger, A. Leo Oppenheim, Erika Reiner, et al., eds., *The Chicago Assyrian Dictionary*, 21 vols. (Chicago: Oriental Institute of the University of Chicago, 1956–).

For those who can read German, von Soden's dictionary is still useful:

Wolfram von Soden, *Akkadisches Handwörterbuch*, 3 vols. (Wiesbaden: Harrassowitz, 1965–81).

An affordable paperback is

Jeremy Black et al., eds., *A Concise Dictionary of Akkadian* (Wiesbaden: Harrassowitz, 2000).

For Ugaritic words, one comprehensive lexicon is in German:

Joseph Aisleitner, *Wörterbuch der ugaritischen Sprache*, 4th ed. (Berlin: Akademie-Verlag, 1974).

And another is in English:

Gregorio del Olmo Lete and Joaquin Sanmartín, trans. Wilfred G. E. Watson, *A Dictionary of the Ugaritic Language in the Alphabetic Tradition*, rev. ed. (Leiden: Brill Academic Publishers, 2003).

A Phoenician-Punic lexicon is also available:

Richard Tomback, *A Comparative Semitic Lexicon of the Phoenician and Punic Languages* (Missoula, MT: Scholars Press, 1978).

4.4.2. Concordances

A concordance lists the places where a given word occurs throughout the Bible (or some other literary collection). Concordances can help you determine the usage, distribution, and contextualizations of any given word (see 4.4.3) and are thus valuable tools for lexical analysis. It is almost impossible to do word (concept) studies without concordances, and almost impossible to do thorough exegesis without word (concept) studies.

Computer concordances are much faster and much more powerful than book concordances. Any of the various computer concordances can give information quickly, many allow original-language searches, and some are available for free via various Web sites. Two stand out for their true exegetical sophistication (the rich number of ways that Hebrew, Greek, and Aramaic grammatical and lexical information can be ascertained, combined, and/or assembled for exegetical use).

The two best are these:

Accordance (Macintosh), from OakTree Software, accordancebible.com.
BibleWorks (Windows), from Hermeneutika, bibleworks.com.

Logos Bible Software is also relatively sophisticated, though not quite as technically adept as the two above (www.logos.com). It has a greater library of secondary literature than either of them, however.

Book concordances remain useful. Their strength can be the fact that they are the result of judicious choices made by scholars of what to include and what to exclude, so that even though they are far less comprehensive than and not nearly as versatile as the computer concordances, they provide at a glance some of the key sorts of information most exegetes are looking for. Any of the following may prove useful to you:

John R. Kohlenberger III and James A. Swanson, *The Hebrew-English Concordance to the Old Testament* (Grand Rapids: Zondervan Publishing House, 1998).

Abraham S. Evans, ed., *A New Concordance of the Old Testament Using the Hebrew and Aramaic Text* (Grand Rapids: Baker Book House, 1989).

Robert L. Thomas, ed., *New American Standard Exhaustive Concordance of the Bible with Hebrew-Aramaic and Greek Dictionaries* (Nashville: Broadman & Holman, 1990).

Eliezer Katz, *Topical Concordance of the Old Testament Using the Hebrew and Aramaic Text* (Grand Rapids: Baker Book House, 1992).

An older standard and still useful book concordance for the Hebrew OT is Mandelkern's. Written in Latin and Hebrew only, it lists words in a somewhat complicated order (partly by context within a given book rather than by successive references), but these drawbacks are minor:

Solomon Mandelkern, *Veteris Testamenti concordantiae Hebraicae atque Chaldaicae*, 8th ed. (repr., Brooklyn, NY: P. Shalom Publications, 1988).

Mandelkern's concordance is becoming difficult to find, however. Largely replacing it is

Abraham Even-Shoshan, ed., *A New Concordance of the Old Testament*, 2nd ed., introduction by John H. Sailhamer (Jerusalem: Kiryat Sefer Publishing House; Grand Rapids: Baker Book House, 1989).

Somewhat easier to use, though less complete, is another concordance:

Gerhard Lisowsky, *Konkordanz zum hebräischen Alten Testament* (Stuttgart: Württembergische Bibelanstalt, 1958).

For King James–Hebrew connections the standard concordance is:

George V. Wigram, *The Englishman's Hebrew and Chaldee Concordance of the Old Testament*, 3rd ed. (London: Samuel Bagster & Sons, 1874; repr., Peabody, MA: Hendrickson Publishers, 1996).

For the Aramaic Targums there are also concordances:

J. C. de Moor et al., eds., *A Bilingual Concordance to the Targum of the Prophets*, 17 vols. (Leiden: E. J. Brill, 1995–2005).

Chaim J. Kasovsky, *Otsar Leshon Targum Onkelos* (Jerusalem: Magnes Press, 1986).

For the Septuagint, a complete book concordance exists. In analyzing the text of a passage, you must analyze the Septuagint wording. The only way to know whether the Septuagint wordings are unique, unusual, or common is to consult the concordance, which gives the Hebrew word equivalents for the Greek word chosen by the Septuagint translators:

Edwin Hatch and Henry A. Redpath, *A Concordance to the Septuagint and the Other Greek Versions of the Old Testament*, 3rd ed., 2 vols., including R. A. Kraft and E. Tov, "Introductory Essay," and Takamitsu Muraoka, "Hebrew/Aramaic Index to the Septuagint: Keyed to the Hatch-Redpath Concordance" (Grand Rapids: Baker Book House, 1998).

A brief but very useful (and inexpensive) one-volume Septuagint concordance is also available:

George Morrish, *A Concordance of the Septuagint* (London: Samuel Bagster & Sons, 1887; repr., Grand Rapids: Zondervan Publishing House, 1976).

The granddaddy of sources for Greek words, phrases, and larger units of speech is the

Thesaurus linguae graecae (*TLG E*), www.tlg.uci.edu.

The online version of this amazingly comprehensive database contains almost a hundred million words, practically everything known from the ancient world to have been written in Greek. Parts of it require a subscription to search, but other parts are free, including an abridged version of the basic lexical database.

See also

A Handy Concordance of the Septuagint: Giving Various Readings from Codices Vaticanus, Alexandrinus, Sinaiticus, and Ephraemi (London: Samuel Bagster, 1887; repr., Eugene, OR: Wipf & Stock, 2008).

Bernard Alwyn Taylor, *The Analytical Lexicon to the Septuagint: A Complete Parsing Guide* (Grand Rapids: Zondervan Publishing House, 1994).

For the Dead Sea Scrolls, a fine new concordance exists:

Martin G. Abegg Jr., James Bowley, and Edward Cook, eds., *Dead Sea Scrolls Concordance*, 3 vols. Vol. 1: *The Non-Biblical Texts from Qumran* (Leiden: Brill Academic Publishers, 2006).

Searching online is possible at a number of sites, including septuagint .org, which is one of many that has a searchable text of the Rahlfs edition. Google the following for information on Tov's Hebrew/Greek matchup electronic concordance, which has a good number of text-critical annotations: "The Parallel Aligned Hebrew-Aramaic and Greek Texts of Jewish

Scripture." For the books of the Apocrypha, there is a book concordance keyed to English words but listing the Greek equivalents:

Lester T. Whitelocke, ed., *An Analytical Concordance of the Books of the Apocrypha*, 2 vols. (Washington, DC: University Press of America, 1978).

A strictly English-language equivalent is

A Concordance to the Apocrypha/Deuterocanonical Books of the Revised Standard Version (Grand Rapids: Wm. B. Eerdmans; London: Collins Liturgical Publications, 1983).

4.4.3. Word studies (concept studies)

A word (concept) study is a thorough analysis of the range of meaning(s) of a word or wording designed to arrive at its specific meaning in a given passage: what concept the word or wording connotes and, as appropriate, what other words or wordings may connote the same essential concept. There are various ways to approach this sort of study, but the following outline may serve as a basic guide. A word study seeks to establish how the word or wording under investigation is used (1) in general, (2) in various contexts, and (3) in the passage itself. The steps to establish this are generally the following:

1. Using a concordance—electronic or printed—find where all the OT occurrences of the word or wording are. If the word or wording is common, think in terms of groups of occurrences; if it is rare, you may be able to examine every usage in detail. Because of the magnitude of the enterprise, you may find it advisable to set more narrow limits (e.g., "the meaning of זנה [prostitution/prostitute] in Hosea").

2. Using other aids such as lexicons and concordances, take cognizance of the non-OT usages of the word or wording (in inscriptions, rabbinic literature, etc.).

3. Using lexicons and concordances, take note of any cognates in other languages you know well enough to work with. Try also to identify any synonyms of the word or wording, because a given concept can be connoted by different wordings, and it is ultimately the *concept* behind the word or wordings in your passage that you want to be sure you understand.

4. Examine the biblical usage, trying to establish the various ranges of meaning that the word or wording and its cognates seem to have. Bear in mind here as well that a concept can be connoted by various words or wordings, and there may be a number of synonyms or closely related terms that will come to your attention and ultimately inform your judg-

ment as you seek to connect your word or wording with its actual meaning (concept) in your passage. Part of the reason for this is that what we call "definition" is established not merely by trying to say what a word means, but also by being sure to try to say what it does not mean. (Example: Is the word "man" to be understood in a given context as man as opposed to woman, or man as opposed to child, or man as opposed to animal, or man as opposed to supernatural being, or man as opposed to coward, etc.?)

5. Examine the distribution of the word or wording. Much can be learned about the meaning this way. Is the word or wording used only or mostly by the prophets, for example? That might tell you a great deal about its meaning. Is it used only or mostly in legal formulas? In certain kinds of wisdom expressions? And so on. Look for patterns wherever possible.

6. Establish the key usages—those that are unambiguous enough to really pin down the meaning (concept) in a definite way.

7. Center on the function of the word or wording in the passage itself. Bring all you have learned in the study so far to bear on the passage, relating the specific use and meaning in the passage to the ranges of use and meaning known from elsewhere.

8. Offer a paraphrase, synonyms, a summary statement, or all of these to your reader or congregation as a means of defining the word or wording. That is, give your own "dictionary" definition of the word, not just in its general use or uses, but according to its use in the passage itself. Again, remember that the concept is the ultimate goal, and the word or wording functions not in itself alone but always in the role of pointing to a concept.

On the theory behind word studies, see

Moisés Silva, *Biblical Words and Their Meaning: An Introduction to Lexical Semantics*, rev. ed. (Grand Rapids: Zondervan Publishing House, 1994).

James Barr, *The Semantics of Biblical Language* (London: Oxford University Press, 1961; repr., Eugene, OR: Wipf & Stock, 2004).

Arthur Gibson, *Biblical Semantic Logic: A Preliminary Analysis* (Sheffield: Sheffield Academic Press, 2002).

4.4.4. Theological dictionaries

The theological dictionaries provide the reader with the results of careful word/concept studies. Obviously they must concern themselves with the broad, general usage of words and wordings throughout the OT and cannot usually focus on individual passages. But they are nevertheless invaluable as time-saving, informative exegetical resources written by seasoned scholars. It is important not to accept blindly the conclusions of any theological dictionary article, however. A given writer's view can be slanted. Sometimes an older work is better on a given word or wording than a newer work; sometimes it is the other way around. Because theological dictionaries are anthologies of articles written by many individuals of varying skill, perspective, and energy, the quality of some articles will be superb and that of other articles may be mediocre. It is always best to follow with a critical eye the arguments and the evidence contained in the article devoted to the word or wording you are investigating.

The *TDOT* is usually thorough, erudite, and invaluable as a reference tool:

G. Johannes Botterweck, Helmer Ringgren, and Heinz-Josef Fabry, eds., *Theological Dictionary of the Old Testament*, trans. J. T. Willis, G. W. Bromiley, and D. E. Green, 15 vols. (Grand Rapids: Wm. B. Eerdmans, 1974–2006).

Extensive coverage of words and themes is also found in *NIDOTTE*:

Willem A. VanGemeren, ed., *New International Dictionary of Old Testament Theology and Exegesis*, 5 vols. (Grand Rapids: Zondervan Publishing House, 1997), also on CD-ROM (2001) and as a module within some of the Bible software programs.

Also see *TLOT*:

Ernst Jenni and Claus Westermann, eds., *Theological Lexicon of the Old Testament*, trans. M. E. Biddle, 3 vols. (Peabody, MA: Hendrickson Publishers, 1997).

The *TWOT* is a very useful two-volume theological dictionary containing careful analysis of Hebrew words. Its articles are briefer than the corresponding articles in *TDOT* or *TLOT* or *NIDOTTE* but by the same token are often more readable:

R. Laird Harris, Gleason Archer, and Bruce K. Waltke, eds., *Theological Wordbook of the Old Testament*, 2 vols. (Chicago: Moody Publishers, 2003).

There is still also much to be learned from

Johannes B. Bauer, ed., *Encyclopedia of Biblical Theology*, 3 vols. (London: Sheed & Ward, 1970; repr., New York: Crossroad, 1981).

The older *TDNT* provides useful background information on OT terms with equivalents in the NT:

Gerhard Kittel and Gerhard Friedrich, eds., *Theological Dictionary of the New Testament*, trans. G. W. Bromiley, 10 vols. (Grand Rapids: Wm. B. Eerdmans, 1964–76; repr., 1993).

Note: You can also use with great profit the major Bible dictionaries, which contain detailed articles on hundreds of key words and concepts, often written by scholars who have studied these concepts extensively. In other words, the best article on "faith" might *not* be found in a theological dictionary, but might easily be found in, say, the *International Standard Bible Encyclopedia* or the *Anchor Bible Dictionary*.

4.4.5. Inscriptions

Reading and analyzing inscriptions is a specialty that requires linguistic and philological training beyond the interests of most students and pastors. Nevertheless, a detailed word (concept) study may well take you to the inscriptional evidence. There are many fine analytical collections of inscriptions that may contain vocabulary related to that of an OT passage—in various languages, with varying contents. While many of the important inscriptions are translated in Pritchard's *ANET* and works similar to it (see 4.8.1), their vocabulary is not analyzed there. In their titles the following works contain descriptions of their respective contents:

George Albert Cooke, *A Text-Book of North-Semitic Inscriptions: Moabite, Hebrew, Phoenician, Aramaic, Nabataean, Palmyrene, Jewish* (Oxford: Clarendon Press, 1903; repr., Whitefish, MT: Kessinger Publishing, 2007).

Jacob Hoftijzer et al., *Dictionary of the North-West Semitic Inscriptions*, 2 vols. (Leiden: Brill Academic Publishers, 1994).

Graham I. Davies et al., An*cient Hebrew Inscriptions: Corpus and Concordance*, 2 vols. (Cambridge: Cambridge University Press, 1991–2004; repr., 2007).

John C. L. Gibson, *Textbook of Syrian Semitic Inscriptions*, vol. 1, *Hebrew and Moabite Inscriptions*; vol. 2, *Aramaic Inscriptions*; vol. 3, *Phoenician Inscriptions Including Inscriptions in the Mixed Dialect of Arslan Tash* (Oxford: Oxford University Press, 1971, 1975, 1982).

Walter Aufrecht and John C. Hurd, *A Synoptic Concordance of Aramaic Inscriptions* (Wooster, OH: Biblical Research Associates; Missoula, MT: Scholars Press, 1975).

James M. Lindenberger, *Ancient Aramaic and Hebrew Letters*, 2nd ed. (Atlanta: Society of Biblical Literature, 2003).

F. W. Dobbs-Allsopp, J. J. M. Roberts, C. L. Seow, and R. E. Whitaker, *Hebrew Inscriptions: Texts from the Biblical Period of the Monarchy with Concordance* (New Haven: Yale University Press, 2004).

Another useful source is in German:

H. Donner and W. Röllig, *Kanaanäische und aramäische Inschriften*, 5th ed. (Wiesbaden: Harrassowitz, 2002–).

Several Bible software programs also include inscription texts. Check the respective Web sites for listings of modules (see 4.12.7).

4.5. Form

4.5.1. Form criticism

The concern of form criticism is the isolation and analysis of specific literary types contained in a passage. From such an analysis the exegete can often discern something about the way the passage has been composed, its themes, its central interests, or even the type of situation in which it may have been employed (depending on the form) in ancient Israel. All of these bits of information may theoretically be deduced even if the context of the passage itself does not contain them because study of all the various manifestations of the specific form throughout the Bible (and other ancient literature where it exists) allows certain generalizations to be applied to each usage.

Form criticism has often come under attack as a method that gathers too little meaning from passages and neglects other valid critical techniques. Form criticism has also earned something of a bad name since some scholars have applied it in an all-encompassing manner and with an overconfidence in the insights it can provide. For example, some form-critical enthusiasts have used the technique to arrive at (what they regard as) firm conclusions about the dating, authorship, genuineness, originality, contextual propriety, historical validity, and so forth of biblical passages, which the method in reality simply cannot support. It is more widely understood now that ancient writers (including the prophets, on whose books form critics especially focus) often borrowed forms from the ancient world in a tentative manner and reworked them. Their own inspired creativity was everywhere evident, and they were hardly slaves to a set of rules to which the forms (and parts of forms) they used could always be conformed. Ancient biblical writers and speakers thus took what they wanted from the existing forms (the typical) and produced new combinations or constructions (the unique).

Two helpful sources for understanding form criticism are available. A good introduction to the method is that of Tucker, who treats it systematically according to the four elements of structure, genre, setting, and intention:

Gene M. Tucker, *Form Criticism of the Old Testament,* Guides to Biblical Scholarship (Philadelphia: Fortress Press, 1971).

Hayes's collection of six essays explains the history of, as well as current trends in, form criticism. For understanding the goals and presuppositions of form criticism, as well as how it applies in various OT passages, see

John H. Hayes, ed., *Old Testament Form Criticism* (San Antonio, TX: Trinity University Press, 1974).

On the specific relationship of form criticism to history, with examples, see

Martin J. Buss, *Biblical Form Criticism in Its Context*, JSOTSup 274 (Sheffield: Sheffield Academic Press, 1999).

A classic, originally German-language introduction to OT form criticism, with examples of the method applied, is

Klaus Koch, *The Growth of the Biblical Tradition: The Form-Critical Method* (New York: Charles Scribner's Sons, 1969).

Best of all, a comprehensive series includes among its multiple volumes a discussion of all the individual literary forms in the OT, unit by unit. The volume in this series that covers your particular passage can profitably be consulted for specific advice, for a seasoned form critic's judgment on the pericope you are trying to exegete.

Rolf Knierim and Gene Tucker, eds., Forms of the Old Testament Literature (Grand Rapids: Wm. B. Eerdmans, 1981–).

4.5.2. The relationship of form to structure

There is no way to discover a literary form or to identify it properly without first identifying the various ingredients of which it is composed (its content) and the way those ingredients are arranged in relation to one another and in relation to the larger context (the structure). In other words, the exegete faces the danger of putting the cart before the horse by jumping too quickly to the conclusion that a passage contains, or is composed in the manner of, form X, simply on the basis of some key words that form X usually contains, or some other stylistic features normally associated with form X. One can actually go so far as to ignore the majority of the evidence for form typology and mistakenly categorize a form. Alternatively, one can place so much emphasis on a strictly form-critical methodology that many exegetically significant features not contained in the results of the form-critical analysis are simply forgotten.

First, then, be sure that you try to understand each element or ingredient of the passage's content and understand at least tentatively how those elements/ingredients are structured before identifying a form. The proper identification of the form(s) may subsequently help you refine your identification of the ingredients and the structure, but do not let the known typical features of the form dominate the way you analyze the specific features of the passage. Rather, it is just the other way around: The specific features of the passage tell you how much or how little any forms that happen to be present influence the passage, if at all—and to what extent the form is pure, adapted, broken, or incomplete.

4.6. Structure

4.6.1. Definitions

Five similar terms are used in OT studies with varying degrees of frequency and with at least two very different meanings. Three of these terms—"structuralism," "structural exegesis," and "structural analysis"— usually are employed to refer to a kind of linguistic analysis that is applied to biblical studies. Structuralism (the most common of these terms) is concerned largely with certain special, rather technically defined relationships between or within the words in a sentence. The structuralist seeks to understand the rules by which language functions, on the theory that those rules can lead to a deeper understanding of the structure (and meaning) of the components of sentences and of sentences themselves. The following books explain structuralism and provide some examples of its possible use in biblical sentences:

Roland Barthes et al., *Structural Analysis and Biblical Exegesis: Interpretational Essays* (Pittsburgh: Pickwick Press, 1974).
Jean Calloud, *Structural Analysis of Narrative* (Philadelphia: Fortress Press; Missoula, MT: Scholars Press, 1976).
Daniel Patte, *The Religious Dimensions of Biblical Texts: Greimas's Structural Semiotics and Biblical Exegesis* (Atlanta: Society of Biblical Literature, 1990).
Daniel Patte, *Structural Exegesis for New Testament Critics* (Valley Forge, PA: Trinity Press International, 1996).

Best for the beginner to learn from, however, is

Daniel Patte, *What Is Structural Exegesis?* Guides to Biblical Scholarship (Philadelphia: Fortress Press, 1976).

Two other terms—"structural criticism" and "structural studies"—are usually employed to describe the way larger units of text (passages) are composed of their various elements of content. The latter two terms, in other words, refer generally to the content structure of a passage, whereas the former three terms refer mostly to concern for the linguistic patterns in individual sentences.

Structuralism (the specialized linguistic analysis) is technical and narrowly applied; it is also less interested in the historical, cultural, or theological except in a secondary way. Thus it is not likely that you will find occasion to use it widely in any given exegesis. Like "linguistic analysis" in philosophy, the results are occasionally stellar, but too often meager. Nevertheless, the diligent student may find the task well worth the effort in particular passages.

For an understanding of the broader method of structural studies, how passages are put together from their constituent elements, how their structure may be deduced and outlined, and the significance for exegesis, there are two books filled with helpful examples:

David A. Dorsey, *The Literary Structure of the Old Testament: A Commentary on Genesis–Malachi* (Grand Rapids: Baker Academic, 2004).
Robert C. Culley, *Studies in the Structure of Hebrew Narrative* (Philadelphia: Fortress Press; Missoula, MT: Scholars Press, 1976).

The broader method of structural studies is far more likely to be of constant value to exegetes, as is the broader discipline of rhetorical criticism, whose methods may generally be considered to encompass structural studies as well.

4.6.2. Rhetorical criticism, discourse analaysis, textlinguistics

Rhetorical criticism

Rhetorical criticism looks at how a literary unit (usually a passage) is put together. Form criticism tends to emphasize the typical and general; rhetorical criticism concentrates on the genius of a passage, what is personal, specific, unique, or original. The rhetorical critic seeks to understand the inspired writer's logic, style, and purpose—but especially style. To do this, emphasis must be placed on (a) the patterns found within the literary unit; (b) the individual stylistic devices that contribute to the overall impact of the whole unit; and (c) the relationship of the parts to the whole. Rhetorical criticism is most often synchronic (concerned with the passage as it stands now) rather than diachronic (concerned with the theoretical history of how the passage might have been transmitted, mutated, reshaped, or edited before reaching its present form).

As usually practiced, rhetorical criticism emphasizes the structure of the canonical text, yet uses the most modern, reliable techniques to implement this emphasis. For the original statement of the need to go beyond the limits of form criticism to rhetorical criticism, see:

James Muilenburg, "Form Criticism and Beyond," *Journal of Biblical Literature* 88 (1969): 1–18.

For a more comprehensive analysis, with examples and bibliographical helps, see any or all of the following:

Stanley E. Porter and Dennis L. Stamps, eds., *Rhetorical Criticism and the Bible*, JSNT Supplement Series 195 (Sheffield: Sheffield Academic Press, 2002).
Roland Meynet, *Rhetorical Analysis: An Introduction to Biblical Rhetoric* (Sheffield: Sheffield Academic Press, 1999).
L. J. de Regt, J. de Waard, and J. P. Fokkelman, eds., *Literary Structure and Rhetorical Strategies in the Hebrew Bible* (Winona Lake, IN: Eisenbrauns, 1996).
Duane F. Watson and Alan J. Hauser, *Rhetorical Criticism of the Bible: A Comprehensive Bibliography with Notes on History and Method* (Leiden: E. J. Brill, 1994).
Dale Patrick and Allen Scult, *Rhetoric and Biblical Interpretation*, JSOTSup 82 (Sheffield: Almond Press, 1990).

Examples of rhetorical criticism applied to various biblical passages are found in

James W. Watts, *Reading Law: The Rhetorical Shaping of the Pentateuch* (Sheffield: Sheffield Academic Press, 1999).
Phyllis Trible, *Rhetorical Criticism: Context, Method, and the Book of Jonah* (Minneapolis: Fortress Press, 1994).
Pieter van der Lugt, *Rhetorical Criticism and the Poetry of the Book of Job* (Leiden: E. J. Brill, 1995).
Jared J. Jackson and Martin Kessler, eds., *Rhetorical Criticism: Essays in Honor of James Muilenburg* (Pittsburgh: Pickwick Press, 1974).

Part of analyzing a passage's rhetoric involves identifying its figures of speech. For this task, consult the classic

E. W. Bullinger, *Figures of Speech Used in the Bible* (London: Eyre & Spottiswoode, 1898; repr., Grand Rapids: Baker Books, 2003).

Discourse analysis, textlinguistics

Though some scholars prefer the term "discourse analysis" and some "textlinguistics," most scholars mean the same thing by them: an analysis of the way sections of text bigger than a clause (usually an entire passage or section of a book) are put together, including their various linguistic patterns, and how the information gleaned thereby helps the reader capture the meaning.

Some good introductions to the method exist:

Walter R. Bodine, *Text-Linguistics and Biblical Hebrew* (from an article in the *Journal of the American Oriental Society*, 2005), electronic version, downloadable from Amazon.com.

Walter R. Bodine, ed., *Discourse Analysis of Biblical Literature: What It Is and What It Offers* (Atlanta: Society of Biblical Literature, 1995).

Ernst R. Wendland, *Translating the Literature of Scripture*, Publications in Translation and Textlinguistics 1 (Dallas: SIL International Publications, 2004).

David Allan Dawson, *Text-Linguistics and Biblical Hebrew*, JSOTSup Series 177 (Sheffield: Sheffield Academic Press, 1994).

4.6.3. Formula criticism

Certain groups of words (sometimes individual words) tend to appear in different passages in similar ways. When a word group functions consistently to express a given essential idea, yet in a variety of contexts, it is called a formula. Poetry seems to have many more formulas than does prose. Some examples (in translation) of common, well-known formulas are "Thus says the LORD," "says the LORD of hosts," "How long will you . . . ?" "In that day," "In the latter days," "Great is the LORD and greatly to be praised." Such formulas appear in a variety of passages. Understanding how formulas function, how they represent building blocks within literary units, how they relate to the meter of a passage, and so forth is the goal of formula criticism. Because formula criticism emphasizes the comparison of formula contexts, it is especially relevant to biblical context (step 4.9) and to structure (step 4.6). Two books explain the process and its implications for exegesis:

Robert C. Culley, *Oral Formulaic Language in the Biblical Psalms* (Toronto: University of Toronto Press, 1967).

William R. Watters, *Formula Criticism and the Poetry of the Old Testament* (Berlin: Walter de Gruyter, 1976).

4.6.4. Poetry analysis (poetics)

Poetics is a vast study. Nevertheless, a proper feel for the poetry of the OT is not so hard to come by that it should be avoided. With a reasonable investment of time, the student of the OT can move rather quickly from relative ignorance to relative competence in analyzing poetry. It is especially important to be able to recognize the types of parallelism and the metrical structure that characterize a given passage of poetry, and good sources are available for each.

For an introduction to both issues, see

Norman K. Gottwald, "Poetry, Hebrew," in *The Interpreter's Dictionary of the Bible*, 3:829–38 (Nashville: Abingdon Press, 1962).
S. E. Gillingham, *The Poems and Psalms of the Hebrew Bible* (Oxford: Oxford University Press, 1994).
Wilfred G. E. Watson, *Classical Hebrew Poetry: A Guide to Its Techniques* (repr., Edinburgh: T&T Clark, 2005).

For additional coverage, see

Frank Moore Cross and David Noel Freedman, *Studies in Ancient Yahwistic Poetry* (Missoula, MT: Scholars Press, 1975; new ed., Grand Rapids: Wm. B. Eerdmans, 1997).
David L. Petersen and Kent H. Richards, *Interpreting Hebrew Poetry* (Minneapolis: Fortress Press, 1992).
James L. Kugel, *The Idea of Biblical Poetry: Parallelism and Its History* (New Haven: Yale University Press, 1981; repr., Baltimore: Johns Hopkins University Press, 1998).

Also see the old but still useful classic:

George Buchanan Gray, *The Forms of Hebrew Poetry*, with Prolegomenon by David Noel Freedman (New York: Ktav Publishing House, 1972).

To analyze certain types of poetic parallelism effectively, you need to learn how fixed pairs of words function in OT poems. The best (and clearest) introduction to this analysis, with hundreds of easy-to-follow examples, is

Stanley Gevirtz, *Patterns in the Early Poetry of Israel* (Chicago: University of Chicago Press, 1963).

On Hebrew meter, see

Douglas K. Stuart, *Studies in Early Hebrew Meter* (Missoula, MT: Scholars Press for the Harvard Semitic Museum, 1976).
Donald R. Vance, *The Question of Meter in Biblical Hebrew Poetry* (Lewiston, NY: Edwin Mellen Press, 2001).

The situation regarding meter is difficult for the student since conflicting theories of metrical composition persist. Nevertheless, whichever of the four most common approaches (stress meter, semantic parallelism meter, alternating meter, syllabic meter) is used, if it is used consistently, it will provide the student with an objective means of discerning and evaluating the relative length of lines of poetry and also the way that lines may be grouped together into couplets and triplets (often called bicola and tricola), or large units (sometimes called strophes).

Two important books on Hebrew style are sufficiently technical and complex in their analyses that the more advanced Hebrew student is best suited to make routine use of them. They are

Stephen Geller, *Parallelism in Early Biblical Poetry*, Harvard Semitic Monographs 20 (Missoula, MT: Scholars Press, 1979).

Michael O'Connor, *Hebrew Verse Structure* (Winona Lake, IN: Eisenbrauns, 1980).

4.7. Historical Context

4.7.1. General chronology

Comprehensive overviews of the chronology of the ancient Near East, including Israel, may be found in any of the following:

William W. Hallo and William K. Simpson, *The Ancient Near East: A History*, 2nd ed. (Fort Worth: Harcourt Brace College Publishers, 1998).

Amélie Kuhrt, *The Ancient Near East: 3000–330 BC*, 2 vols. (London: Routledge, 1995).

Jack Sasson, ed., *Civilization of the Ancient Near East*, repr., 4 vols. in 2 (Peabody, MA: Hendrickson Publishers, 2000).

Donald B. Redford, *Egypt, Canaan, and Israel in Ancient Times* (Princeton, NJ: Princeton University Press, 1992).

Marc Van De Mieroop, *History of the Ancient Near East, ca. 3000–323 B.C.* (Malden, MA: Blackwell Publishers, 2004), 2nd ed. (2007).

A convenient, shorter treatment of chronological issues specifically involving Israel is

Jack Finegan, *Handbook of Biblical Chronology* (Peabody, MA: Hendrickson Publishers, 1998).

The difficult problem of synchronizing the biblical chronologies of the Israelite and Judean kings is well handled by Thiele, whose ingenious solutions have increasingly gained acceptance:

Edwin R. Thiele, *The Mysterious Numbers of the Hebrew Kings*, new rev. ed. (Grand Rapids: Kregel Academic, 1994).

Two alternative approaches with different analyses of some of the more controversial chronological puzzles have also been written:

Gershon Galil, *The Chronology of the Kings of Israel and Judah* (Leiden: E. J. Brill, 1996).
J. H. Hayes and P. K. Hooker, *A New Chronology for the Kings of Israel and Judah* (Atlanta: John Knox Press, 1988).

4.7.2. Israelite history

Most histories are written to be studied in their entirety rather than consulted here and there for information about specific times or events. Several major Israelite histories exist, however, that are fairly well suited to both purposes. The first listed, by Kaiser, is especially convenient to use because of its indices for subject, author, and Scripture reference, as well as for its extensive glossary and bibliography.

Walter C. Kaiser Jr., *A History of Israel: From the Bronze Age to the Jewish Wars* (Nashville: Broadman & Holman, 1998).
Iain W. Provan, V. Philips Long, and Tremper Longman III, *A Biblical History of Israel* (Louisville, KY: Westminster John Knox Press, 2003).
Eugene H. Merrill, *Kingdom of Priests: A History of Old Testament Israel* (Grand Rapids: Baker Academic, 2008).
Leon J. Wood, *A Survey of Israel's History* (Grand Rapids: Zondervan Publishing House, 1986).
J. Maxwell Miller and John H. Hayes, *A History of Ancient Israel and Judah*, 2nd ed. (Louisville, KY: Westminster John Knox Press, 2006).
John Bright, *A History of Israel*, 4th ed. (Louisville, KY: Westminster John Knox Press, 2000).

Combining both history and a survey of the OT books themselves is the classic work by

Samuel J. Schultz, *The Old Testament Speaks: A Complete Survey of Old Testament History and Literature*, 5th ed. (San Francisco: HarperSanFrancisco, 2000).

See also

Paul R. House and Eric Mitchell, *Old Testament Survey* (Nashville: Broadman & Holman, 2007).
Bill T. Arnold and Bryan E. Beyer, *Encountering the Old Testament: A Christian Survey*, 2nd ed. (Grand Rapids: Baker Academic, 2008).

Especially helpful for the way it follows very closely the OT ordering and subject matter rather than being more generally a "secular" history of Israel is the classic

Charles F. Pfeiffer, *Old Testament History* (Grand Rapids: Baker Book House, 1973).

Somewhat more specialized in focus are

Patrick D. Miller, *The Religion of Ancient Israel* (Louisville, KY: Westminster John Knox Press, 2000).
Rainer Albertz, *A History of Israelite Religion in the Old Testament Period*, 2 vols. (Louisville, KY: Westminster John Knox Press, 1994).
Rainer Kessler and Linda M. Maloney, *The Social History of Ancient Israel: An Introduction* (Minneapolis: Fortress Press, 2008).

Readable and erudite is

Hershel Shanks, ed., *Ancient Israel: From Abraham to the Roman Destruction of the Temple* (Washington, DC: Biblical Archaeology Society, 1999).

The many volumes of the prestigious Cambridge Ancient History series include several that cover issues directly relevant to OT history. For example,

John Boardman et al., eds., *The Assyrian and Babylonian Empires and Other States of the Near East, from the Eighth to the Sixth Centuries* (Cambridge: Cambridge University Press, 1991).
John Boardman et al., eds., *Persia, Greece, and the Western Mediterranean c. 525–479 B.C.* (Cambridge: Cambridge University Press, 1988).

4.7.3. Israelite and ancient Near Eastern culture

For understanding the Bible in its immediate sociological context, nothing excels the classic

Roland de Vaux, *Ancient Israel: Its Life and Institutions* (New York: McGraw-Hill, 1961; repr., Grand Rapids: Wm. B. Eerdmans; Livonia, MI: Dove Booksellers, 1997).

Two other volumes with a similar purpose are

Daniel C. Snell, *Life in the Ancient Near East, 3100–332 B.C.E.* (New Haven: Yale University Press, 1998).
Michael D. Coogan, ed., *The Oxford History of the Biblical World* (Oxford: Oxford University Press, 2001).

These books are paralleled by and in some cases supplemented by

J. David Pleins, *The Social Visions of the Hebrew Bible* (Louisville, KY: Westminster John Knox Press, 2001).

Victor H. Matthews and Don C. Benjamin, *The Social World of Ancient Israel* (Peabody, MA: Hendrickson Publishers, 1995).

John H. Walton, Victor H. Matthews, and Mark W. Chavalas, *The IVP Bible Background Commentary: Old Testament* (Downers Grove, IL: InterVarsity Press, 2000).

John W. Walton, *Ancient Israelite Literature in Its Cultural Context* (Grand Rapids: Zondervan Publishing House, 1989).

Wolfram von Soden, *The Ancient Orient: An Introduction to the Study of the Ancient Near East*, trans. Donald G. Schley (Grand Rapids: Wm. B. Eerdmans, 1994).

Philip J. King and Lawrence E. Stager, *Life in Biblical Israel* (Louisville, KY: Westminster John Knox Press, 2002).

More narrowly focused but comparable in their usefulness relative to the cultural subcategories they address are the following four books:

Moshe Weinfeld, *Social Justice in Ancient Israel and in the Ancient Near East* (Minneapolis: Fortress Press, 1995).

H. J. Boecker, *Law and the Administration of Justice in the Old Testament and Ancient East* (Minneapolis: Augsburg, 1980).

Herbert G. Livingstone, *The Pentateuch in Its Cultural Environment*, 2nd ed. (Grand Rapids: Baker Book House, 1987).

Norman K. Gottwald, *The Politics of Ancient Israel* (Louisville, KY: Westminster John Knox Press, 2000).

4.7.4. Other parts of the ancient Near East

From among the many fine historical works on various peoples and cultures in the biblical world, several major works may be recommended for their comprehensiveness and reliability.

For a general presentation of the data on ethnic and national groups mentioned in the OT as Israel's neighbors or conquerors, see either of the following two volumes:

Alfred J. Hoerth, Gerald L. Mattingly, and Edwin Yamauchi, eds., *Peoples of the Old Testament World* (Grand Rapids: Baker Book House, 1998).

Donald J. Wiseman, ed., *Peoples of Old Testament Times* (Oxford: Oxford University Press, 1973).

On the ways of thinking among the various cultures of the ancient Near East and how they compare to biblical revelation, see

John H. Walton, *Ancient Near Eastern Thought and the Old Testament: Introducing the Conceptual World of the Hebrew Bible* (Grand Rapids: Baker Academic, 2006).

Henri Frankfort, *Kingship and the Gods: A Study of Ancient Near Eastern Religion as the Integration of Society and Nature* (Chicago: University of Chicago Press for the Oriental Institute, 1948), Phoenix ed. (1978).

Wolfram von Soden, *The Ancient Orient: An Introduction to the Study of the Ancient Near East*, trans. Donald G. Schley (Grand Rapids: Wm. B. Eerdmans, 1994).

On Egyptian history and civilization more than one excellent work is available:

Cyril Aldred, *The Egyptians*, 3rd ed., revised and updated by Aidan Dodson (London: Thames & Hudson, 1998).
Alan Gardiner, *Egypt of the Pharaohs* (Oxford: Oxford University Press, 1961).
Donald Redford, ed., *The Oxford Encyclopedia of Ancient Egypt*, 3rd ed., 3 vols. (Oxford: Oxford University Press, 2000).
David P. Silverman, *Ancient Egypt* (Oxford: Oxford University Press, 2003).
Ian Shaw, *The Oxford History of Ancient Egypt*, new ed. (Oxford: Oxford University Press, 2003).
Barry J. Kemp, *Ancient Egypt: Anatomy of a Civilization*, 2nd ed. (London: Routledge, 2006).
Toby Wilkinson, ed., *Egyptian World* (London: Routledge, 2007).
Kathryn Ann Bard, ed., *Encyclopedia of the Archaeology of Ancient Egypt* (London: Routledge, 1999).

Some fine volumes have been written that address the parallels and connections between OT and Egyptian history and culture:

John D. Currid, *Ancient Egypt and the Old Testament* (Grand Rapids: Baker Book House, 1999).
Donald B. Redford, *Egypt, Canaan, and Israel in Ancient Times* (Princeton, NJ: Princeton University Press, 1993).

Specifically for the culture and religion of the Egyptians, including a sensitive analysis of the Egyptian mythopoeic (myth-making) religious mind, read

Henri Frankfort, *Ancient Egyptian Religion: An Interpertation* (1948; repr., Mineola, NY: Dover Publications, 2000).

Significant relations between the Israelites and the Assyrians and Babylonians were more or less constant during the years from 745 BC to 540 BC, the time of the production of the vast majority of the prophetical books of the OT as well as the subject of much of the content of Kings and Chronicles. For Assyrian and Babylonian history, see:

H. W. F. Saggs, *The Greatness That Was Babylon: A Survey of the Ancient Civilization of the Tigris-Euphrates Valley* (1962; repr., New York: St. Martin's Press, 1988).
H. W. F. Saggs, *The Might That Was Assyria* (1984; repr., New York: St. Martin's Press, 1990).
George Roux, *Ancient Iraq*, 3rd ed. (London: Viking Penguin, 1992).
Gwendolyn Leick, *The Babylonians: An Introduction* (London: Routledge, 2003).

Very helpful specifically for its insights into the time of Nebuchadnez-zar the Great, who brought Judah to its end, is

Donald J. Wiseman, *Nebuchadrezzar and Babylon* (repr., Oxford: Oxford University Press, 1991).

A reliable general survey of the literature, life, religion, and civil insti-tutions of the ancient Sumerians, Babylonians, and Assyrians is found in

A. Leo Oppenheim, *Ancient Mesopotamia*, rev. ed. (Chicago: University of Chicago Press, 1976).

Increased interest in Sumerian history and culture has resulted from the extraordinary new finds at Syrian Ebla. Good introductions to Sumer-ian literature are available, and the first two contain descriptions of some Sumerian documents with biblical parallels:

Samuel N. Kramer, *The Sumerians* (Chicago: University of Chicago Press, 1990).
C. Leonard Woolley, *The Sumerians* (1928; repr., New York: W. W. Norton & Co., 1978).
Enrico Ascalone, *Mesopotamia: Assyrians, Sumerians, Babylonians* (Berkeley: University of Cal-ifornia Press, 2007).
Samuel Noah Kramer, *Sumerian Mythology: A Study of Spiritual and Literary Achievement in the Third Millennium B.C.* (1944; repr., Forgotten Books, 2007, www.forgottenbooks.org).

See also

The Electronic Text Corpus of Sumerian Literature (*ETCSL*, etcsl.orinst.ox.ac.uk).

Maintained at Oxford, this database allows you to read and search online almost four hundred major ancient Sumerian documents both in translit-eration and with English translations. It also includes bibliographical information for each document.

The *ETANA* (*Electronic Tools and Ancient Near Eastern Archives*), sup-ported by a consortium of scholars and scholarly institutions, is an online project to publish original ancient documents and modern studies related to the history and culture of the ancient Near East. It has only a few dozen documents available for searching online so far, but it aims to be the most comprehensive place on the Web for such materials:

etana.org/coretexts.shtml.

The Hittites exerted considerable early influence on Bible lands, even though they are not specifically mentioned in the Bible. (The "Hittites" of the Bible are the Sons of Heth, a Canaanite subgroup.) The standard introduction to their history and civilization is

O. R. Gurney, *The Hittites*, 2nd ed. (London: Penguin Books, 1954).

For Persia, some fine histories are available. The first of these is of special note because of its conscious focus on OT connections:

Edwin M. Yamauchi, *Persia and the Bible* (Grand Rapids: Baker Book House, 1996).
Josef Wiesehöfer, *Ancient Persia: From 550 BC to 650 AD* (New York: St. Martin's Press, 1996).
Pierre Briant, *From Cyrus to Alexander: A History of the Persian Empire* (Winona Lake, IN: Eisenbrauns, 2002).

Olmstead's classic history of Persia (with helpful indexes) is still valuable, if you can find it:

A. T. Olmstead, *History of the Persian Empire* (1948; repr., Chicago: University of Chicago Press, 1959).

See also the more recent works:

J. E Curtis and N. Tallis, eds., *Forgotten Empire: The World of Ancient Persia* (Berkeley: University of California Press, 2005).
Lindsay Allen, *The Persian Empire* (Chicago: University of Chicago Press, 2005).
Amélie Kuhrt, ed., *Persian Empire: A Corpus of Sources from the Achaemenid Period* (London: Routledge, 2007).

For matters related to the Ugaritic civilization, the Phoenicians, the Canaanites, and the Philistines, see the relevant volumes from the following:

Marguerite Yon, *The City of Ugarit at Ras Shamra* (Winona Lake, IN: Eisenbrauns, 2000).
Jacob H. Katzenstein, *The History of Tyre*, 2nd rev. ed. (Jerusalem: Ben Gurion University of the Negev Press, 1997).
Jonathan N. Tubb, *Canaanites: Peoples of the Past* (Norman: University of Oklahoma Press, 1998).
Trude Dothan and Moshe Dothan, *People of the Sea: The Search for the Philistines* (New York: Macmillan Publishing Co., 1992).
Othniel Margalith, *Sea Peoples in the Bible* (Wiesbaden: Harrassowitz, 1994).
William M. Schniedewind and Joel H. Hunt, *A Primer on Ugaritic: Language, Culture, and Literature* (Cambridge: Cambridge University Press, 2007).
Gregorio del Olmo Lete, *Canaanite Religion: According to the Liturgical Texts of Ugarit* (repr., Winona Lake, IN: Eisenbrauns, 2004).
John C. L. Gibson, *Canaanite Myths and Legends*, 2nd ed. (London: T&T Clark, 2004).
Ann E. Killebrew, *Biblical Peoples and Ethnicity: An Archaeological Study of Egyptians, Canaanites, Philistines, and Early Israel, 1300–1100 B.C.E.* (Leiden: Brill Academic Publishers, 2005).
George Rawlinson, *Phoenicia: History of a Civilization* (1889; repr., London: I. B. Tauris, 2005).

4.7.5. Archaeology

Several introductions to the field of Palestinian archaeology are widely used, and a variety of valuable sources are also available for specific knowledge about individual areas and sites. Unfortunately, many archaeologists either do not publish their excavation results at all or publish them in such a narrow, technical way that the average OT student cannot make reasonable use of them in exegesis, except as the excavation reports themselves draw attention to biblical texts. Among the most useful of recent works on biblical archaeology are the following. Any of them may prove useful, depending on the nature of your passage.

James K. Hoffmeier, *The Archaeology of the Bible* (Oxford: Lion, 2008).

Alfred Hoerth and John McRay, *Bible Archaeology: An Exploration of the History and Culture of Early Civilizations* (Grand Rapids: Baker Books, 2005).

Kenneth A. Kitchen *The Bible in Its World: The Bible and Archaeology Today* (1977; repr., Eugene OR: Wipf & Stock, 2004).

John D. Currid, *Doing Archaeology in the Land of the Bible: A Basic Guide* (Grand Rapids: Baker Books, 1999).

Amnon Ben-Tor, *The Archaeology of Ancient Israel*, trans. R. Greenberg (New Haven: Yale University Press, 1992).

Brian Fagan, ed., *The Oxford Companion to Archaeology* (Oxford: Oxford University Press, 1996).

Alfred J. Hoerth, *Archaeology of the Old Testament* (Grand Rapids: Baker Books, 1998).

Amihai Mazar, *Archaeology of the Land of the Bible*, vol. 1, Anchor Bible Reference Library (New York: Doubleday, 1992).

Ephraim Stern, *Archaeology of the Land of the Bible*, vol. 2, *The Assyrian, Babylonian, and Persian Periods (732–332 B.C.E.)*, Anchor Bible Reference Library (New York: Doubleday, 2001).

William F. Albright, *Archaeology and the Religion of Israel*, new introduction by Theodore J. Lewis (Louisville, KY: Westminster John Knox Press, 2006).

The following excellent dictionaries of archaeology are each quite comprehensive. They are among the sources you would be well advised always to check.

Eric M. Meyers, ed., *The Oxford Encyclopedia of Archaeology in the Near East*, 5 vols. (Oxford: Oxford University Press, 1997).

Ephraim Stern, ed., *The New Encyclopedia of Archaeological Excavations in the Holy Land*, 4 vols. (Jerusalem: Israel Exploration Society and Carta; New York: Simon & Schuster, 1993).

Concentrating on urban archaeology are

Volkmar Fritz, *The City in Ancient Israel* (Sheffield: Sheffield Academic Press, 1995).

LaMoine DeVries, *Cities of the Biblical World* (Peabody, MA: Hendrickson Publishers, 1997).

The following may prove useful to you in terms of specialized interests:

Thomas E. Levy, ed., *The Archaeology of Society in the Holy Land*, 2nd ed. (London: Leicester University Press, 1998).

Still valuable, from the pens of great Palestinian archaeologists, are

William F. Albright, *The Archaeology of Palestine*, rev. ed. (London: Penguin Books, 1954; repr., Gloucester, MA: Peter Smith, 1971).
Yohanan Aharoni, *The Archaeology of the Land of Israel* (Philadelphia: Westminster Press, 1982).
G. Ernest Wright, *Biblical Archaeology*, rev. ed. (Philadelphia: Westminster Press, 1963).
Kathleen Kenyon, *Archaeology in the Holy Land*, 4th ed. (New York: W. W. Norton & Co., 1979).
Kathleen Kenyon, *The Bible and Recent Archaeology* (Atlanta: John Knox Press, 1978).
Michael Avi-Yonah, ed., *Encyclopedia of Archaeological Excavations in the Holy Land*, 4 vols. (Englewood Cliffs, NJ: Prentice-Hall, 1975).

Emphasizing inscriptional evidence is

P. Kyle McCarter Jr., *Ancient Inscriptions: Voices from the Biblical World* (Washington, DC: Biblical Archaeology Society, 1996).

A fine example of archaeology applied to the interpretation of prophetical books is

Philip J. King, *Amos, Hosea, Micah: An Archaeological Commentary* (Philadelphia: Westminster Press, 1988).

For a collection of maps, illustrations, and generally reliable commentary on the relationship of archaeological discoveries to OT history, particularly as related to specific books and even passages, consult

Gaalyahu Cornfeld, *Archaeology of the Bible: Book by Book*, with David Noel Freedman as consulting ed. (New York: Harper & Row, 1976).
Gonzalo Báez-Camargo, *Archaeological Commentary on the Bible* (Garden City, NY: Doubleday, 1984).

Helpful for its more than eight hundred individual articles on archaeological topics is

E. M. Blaiklock and R. K. Harrison, eds., *The New International Dictionary of Biblical Archaeology* (Grand Rapids: Zondervan Publishing House, 1983).

See also the now somewhat dated

Robert F. Heizer et al., *Archaeology: A Bibliographical Guide to the Basic Literature* (New York: Garland Publishing, 1980).

A large number of individual articles on key subjects and findings related to the OT were gathered together in

Edward F. Campbell Jr., David Noel Freedman, and G. Ernest Wright, eds., *The Biblical Archaeologist Reader*, 3 vols. (Garden City, NY: Doubleday/Anchor Books, 1961–1970).

For evaluations of archaeology that look back at what it has produced and forward to where it is going (and some of its limitations), see

James K. Hoffmeier and Alan Millard, eds., *The Future of Biblical Archaeology: Reassessing Methodologies and Assumptions* (Grand Rapids: Wm. B. Eerdmans, 2004).

Good results can also be obtained by googling "Bible archaeology," "archaeology online," "Bible history online," and so forth.

4.7.6. Geographies and atlases

One of the best geographies of the Bible is

Leslie J. Hoppe, *A Guide to the Lands of the Bible* (Collegeville, MN: Liturgical Press, 1999).

Two older, yet still authoritative studies on Holy Land geography (weather, agriculture, topography, etc.) may be used with much profit:

Denis Baly, *The Geography of the Bible*, rev. ed. (New York: Harper & Row, 1974).
Yohanan Aharoni, *The Land of the Bible: A Historical Geography*, trans. and ed. Anson F. Rainey, rev. ed. (Philadelphia: Westminster Press, 1979).

The best atlas for OT studies is also the easiest to use and the most helpful in exegetical tasks. It is chock-full of maps, charts, diagrams, and other illustrations, accompanied by clear explanatory notes. The many biblical passages to which the atlas is relevant are contained in a separate index, as well as with each illustration:

Yohanan Aharoni et al., *Carta Bible Atlas*, 4th ed. (Jerusalem: Carta; Philadelphia: Coronet Books, 2002).

Several others are also useful and accurate, notably including

R. Steven Notley and Anson F. Rainey, *Carta's New Century Handbook and Atlas of the Bible* (Jerusalem: Carta, 2007).

J. J. Bimson et al., eds., *The New Bible Atlas* (1985; repr., Downers Grove, IL: InterVarsity Press, 1996).

Thomas V. Brisco, ed., *Holman Bible Atlas: A Complete Guide to the Expansive Geography of Biblical History* (Nashville: Broadman & Holman, 1999).

Carl G. Rasmussen, ed., *The Zondervan NIV Atlas of the Bible* (Grand Rapids: Zondervan Publishing House, 1989).

Adrian Curtis, ed., *Oxford Bible Atlas*, 4th ed. (New York: Oxford University Press, 2007).

Barry J. Beitzel, ed., *Biblica: The Bible Atlas: A Social and Historical Journey through the Lands of the Bible* (Hauppauge, NY: Barron's Educational Series, 2007).

4.7.7. Historical criticism

As it is most narrowly defined, historical criticism is concerned with the historical settings of biblical texts, including the establishing of names, dates, and times for events mentioned or attended to in a given passage. The aim of this sort of historical criticism is to arrive at a useful understanding of the relevant historical factors, in a form that elucidates them fully. Thus the historian goes well beyond the limits of the passage itself in establishing the historical factors and trends, more or less independently of the way they happen to be presented in the Bible.

However, historical criticism is a term also used to mean what is otherwise called the historical-critical method. This method has as its basic assumption the idea that "objective" biblical-historical study must treat the Bible like any other book, putting aside such "subjective" ideas as inspiration, authority, and divine causation. For obvious reasons, the historical-critical method is a subject of great debate as to its own "objectivity."

A lucid introduction to the special issues involved and the methodological assumptions is

Edgar Krentz, *The Historical-Critical Method* (1975; repr., Eugene, OR: Wipf & Stock, 2002).

See also

Joseph A. Fitzmyer, *The Interpretation of Scripture: In Defense of the Historical-Critical Method* (New York: Paulist Press, 2008).

A properly motivated but inadequately documented attack on the historical-critical method may be found in

Gerhard Maier, *The End of the Historical-Critical Method* (St. Louis: Concordia Publishing House, 1977).

Very helpful as a corrective to the kind of unchecked skepticism that has characterized some OT historical studies in the name of objectivity is

Kenneth A. Kitchen, *On the Reliability of the Old Testament* (Grand Rapids: Wm. B. Eerdmans, 2006).

For a perspective on the challenges and difficulties encountered in the historical study of the OT, sometimes with controversial conclusions about the evidence and what can be inferred from it, see these:

V. Philips Long, *Israel's Past in Present Research: Essays on Ancient Israelite Historiography* (Winona Lake, IN: Eisenbrauns, 1999).
J. Maxwell Miller, *The Old Testament and the Historian*, Guides to Biblical Scholarship (Philadelphia: Fortress Press, 1976).
Jon D. Levenson, *The Hebrew Bible, the Old Testament, and Historical Criticism* (Louisville, KY: Westminster John Knox Press, 1993).
Niels Peter Lemche, *Prelude to Israel's Past: Background and Beginnings of Israelite History and Identity* (Peabody, MA: Hendrickson Publishers, 1998).
John Van Seters, *In Search of History: Historiography in the Ancient World and the Origins of Biblical History* (repr., Winona Lake, IN: Eisenbrauns, 1997).

4.7.8. Tradition criticism

The study of the history of oral traditions as they functioned to preserve the literature and especially the history of ancient Israel before formalization in writing is called tradition criticism.

For a useful overview, see one of the following:

Douglas A. Knight, "Tradition History," in *The Anchor Bible Dictionary*, 6:633–38 (New York: Doubleday, 1992).
J. H. Hayes and C. R. Holladay, "Tradition Criticism," chap. 7 in *Biblical Exegesis: A Beginner's Handbook*, 3rd ed. (Louisville, KY: Westminster John Knox Press, 2007).
Stanley E. Porter, ed., *Dictionary of Biblical Criticism and Interpretation* (London: Routledge, 2006).

Some widely used introductions to this somewhat theoretical field are

Jan Vansina, *Oral Tradition as History* (Madison: University of Wisconsin Press, 1990).
Douglas A. Knight, *Rediscovering the Traditions of Israel*, 3rd ed. (Atlanta: Society of Biblical Literature, 2006).
Walter Rast, *Tradition History and the Old Testament*, Guides to Biblical Scholarship (Philadelphia: Fortress Press, 1972).

4.8. Literary Analysis

4.8.1. Parallel literature

The Bible is a unique book; there is nothing like it. There are, however, many individual literary works preserved from the ancient world that are remarkably similar to parts of the Bible. To ignore these valuable parallels where they exist is to impoverish an exegesis. Fortunately, the majority of the known parallels have been collected for easy reference.

The standard translation of (usually complete) texts parallel to the OT is found in the following large volume, which is recommended even though very expensive:

James B. Pritchard, ed., *Ancient Near Eastern Texts Relating to the Old Testament*, 3rd ed. with supplement (Princeton, NJ: Princeton University Press, 1969).

Two abridgments are found in

James B. Pritchard, ed., *The Ancient Near East: An Anthology of Texts and Pictures* (Princeton, NJ: Princeton University Press, 1958); *The Ancient Near East*, vol. 2, *A New Anthology of Texts and Pictures* (Princeton, NJ: Princeton University Press, 1975).

Both the full edition and the abridgments contain indexes of Scripture references for easy correlation to biblical passages. (The companion volumes for pictures are listed in 4.12.6.)

Much of the time, your interest will probably be focused toward parallel literature from the ancient Near East that is specifically religious in nature. Any of the following contain more comprehensive introductions and generally more helpful notes than Pritchard's volume, and all are virtually as complete with regard to important religious documents that parallel OT materials:

William W. Hallo and K. L. Younger, eds., *The Context of Scripture*, 3 vols. (Leiden: Brill Academic Publishers, 1997–2002), also found in Bible software packages.

Victor H. Matthews and Don C. Benjamin, *Old Testament Parallels: Laws and Stories from the Ancient Near East*, 3rd ed. (New York: Paulist Press, 2007).

John H. Walton, *Ancient Israelite Literature in Its Cultural Context: A Survey of Parallels between Biblical and Ancient Near Eastern Texts* (Grand Rapids: Zondervan Publishing House, 1994).

Walter Beyerlin, ed., *Near Eastern Religious Texts Relating to the Old Testament* (Philadelphia: Westminster Press, 1978).

Kenton L. Sparks, *Ancient Texts for the Study of the Hebrew Bible: A Guide to the Background Literature* (Peabody, MA: Hendrickson Publishers, 2005).

Bill T. Arnold and Bryan E. Beyer, eds., *Readings from the Ancient Near East: Primary Sources for Old Testament Study* (Grand Rapids: Baker Academic, 2002).

The Society of Biblical Literature is publishing an ongoing series of texts from various provenances in the ancient Near East:

SBL Writings from the Ancient World = SBLWAW (Atlanta: Society of Biblical Literature, 1990–).

So far the following volumes have appeared, with translators/editors noted:

Ancient Aramaic and Hebrew Letters, 2nd ed., by James M. Lindenberger (2003).
Ancient Egyptian Pyramid Texts, by James P. Allen (2005).
Biographical Texts from Ramessid Egypt, by Elizabeth Frood, edited by John Baines (2007).
Epics of Sumerian Kings, by Herman Vanstiphout (2003).
Hittite Myths, by Harry A. Hoffner (1998).
Hittite Diplomatic Texts, 2nd ed., by Gary M. Beckman (1996).
Hittite Prayers, by Itamar Singer (2002).
Hymns, Prayers, and Songs: An Anthology of Ancient Egyptian Lyric Poetry, by John L. Foster (1995).
Inscriptions from Egypt's Third Intermediate Period, by R. K. Ritner (2008).
Law Collections from Mesopotamia and Asia Minor, 2nd ed., by Martha T. Roth (1995).
Letters from Ancient Egypt, by Edward F. Wente (1990).
Letters from Early Mesopotamia, by Piotr Michalowski (1993).
Mesopotamian Chronicles, by Jean-Jacques Glassner (2004).
Prophets and Prophecy in the Ancient Near East, by Marti Nissinen, with C. L. Seow and Robert K. Ritner (2003).
Ritual and Cult at Ugarit, by Dennis Pardee (2002).
Texts from the Amarna Period in Ancient Egypt, by William J. Murnane (1995).
Texts from the Pyramid Age, by Nigel C. Strudwick (2005).
Ugaritic Narrative Poetry, translated by Simon B. Parker, Mark S. Smith, Edward L. Greenstein, Theodore L. Lewis, and David Marcus (1997).

For the important individual semantic parallels from the Late Bronze Age tablets found at Ugarit, there is a very useful collection built around words, terms, and concepts that occur in both Ugaritic and Hebrew. These include animals, plants, numerals, names, professions, social institutions, literary phrases, literary genres, and so forth:

Loren Fisher, ed., *Ras Shamra Parallels: The Texts from Ugarit and the Hebrew Bible*, 2 vols., Analecta Orientalia 49–50 (Rome: Pontifical Biblical Institute, 1972–76).

Each entry has a translation of the Ugaritic passage, textual notes, a bibliography, and an evaluation of the Ugaritic-Hebrew connections.

You can learn much about the beliefs of the Canaanites of Ugarit by reading for yourself their major myths. An excellent translation of these is by Coogan:

Michael Coogan, *Stories from Ancient Canaan* (Philadelphia: Westminster Press, 1978).

More narrowly focused is

Nicolas Wyatt, *Religious Texts from Ugarit* (Sheffield: Sheffield Academic Press, 1998).

For parallels from Akkadian and Sumerian sources, see

Robert William Rogers, trans. and ed., *Cuneiform Parallels to the Old Testament*, Ancient Texts and Translations (1912; repr., Eugene, OR: Wipf & Stock, 2005).

4.8.2. Genre criticism

The criticism or analysis of genres (literary types) is usually limited to larger literary units and styles such as law, history, and wisdom. Often, however, individual scholars may use "genre" interchangeably with "form," so that there is no distinction between form criticism (see 4.5.1) and genre criticism, and thus no distinction between larger literary types (genres) and smaller, specific individual types (forms). Even though the distinction between the two types may be considered somewhat arbitrary, and even though it is a subjective decision as to whether a given literary type is general and large enough to be a genre or small and specific enough to be a form, the distinction is still useful, and it is recommended that you follow it. Thus, for example, "narrative" is considered a whole genre, but a "census narrative" would be considered an individual form; "wisdom" is a whole genre, but a "numerical wisdom enumeration" would be considered a specific form; elegiac poetry might be frequent enough in the OT to be called a genre, whereas a "battle aftermath lament" such as 2 Samuel 1:19–27 would be specific enough to be considered a "form." As a rule, you should confine use of the term "genre" to literary types that are represented fairly widely by varying subtypes; the subtypes themselves are the forms.

The best, easiest-to-follow overall introduction to genres (and forms as well) remains part 1 of Eissfeldt's *The Old Testament: An Introduction* (4.1.2).

A more detailed analysis, with examples, of the method of genre criticism is found in

D. Brent Sandy and Ronald L. Giese, eds., *Cracking Old Testament Codes: A Guide to Interpreting Literary Genres of the Old Testament* (Nashville: Broadman & Holman, 1995).

4.8.3. Redaction criticism

Redaction criticism concerns itself with how the various units that make up a section or book of the OT were put together in their intermediate or final form. It therefore requires analysis of the work of the (anonymous) editors of the section or book, and it is accordingly a very speculative kind of criticism since nothing is directly known about editorial activity or the editors themselves.

A useful introduction to the subject was written by Perrin, though it concentrates largely on the NT rather than the OT:

Norman Perrin, *What Is Redaction Criticism?* Guides to Biblical Scholarship (Philadelphia: Fortress Press, 1969).

For OT materials, a brief introduction to the method is found in

John H. Hayes and Carl R. Holladay, "Redaction Criticism," chap. 8 in *Biblical Exegesis: A Beginner's Handbook*, 3rd ed. (Louisville, KY: Westminster John Knox Press, 2007).
John Barton, *The Nature of Biblical Criticism* (Louisville, KY: Westminster John Knox Press, 2007).

An example of redaction criticism undertaken with a view to applying its results to biblical theology is

Simon J. De Vries, *From Old Revelation to New: A Tradition-Historical and Redaction-Critical Study of Temporal Transitions in Prophetic Prediction* (Grand Rapids: Wm. B. Eerdmans, 1995).

4.8.4. Literary criticism

The term "literary criticism" is used in several ways. For many years, literary criticism meant little more than source criticism (see 4.8.5). Occasionally it meant roughly what the term "historical criticism" is now used to describe (see 4.7.7). Increasingly, however, the term is used in its most basic meaning to refer to the process of analyzing and understanding parts of the Bible as literature, examining technique, style, and other features in order to gain an appreciation for the intention and results of a given portion as a literary composition.

For a brief overview of this type of criticism, you can read

John H. Hayes and Carl R. Holladay, "Literary Criticism," chap. 5 in *Biblical Exegesis: A Beginner's Handbook*, 3rd ed. (Louisville, KY: Westminster John Knox Press, 2007).

A longer introduction offers somewhat controversial examples of the method applied:

David Robertson, *The Old Testament and the Literary Critic*, Guides to Biblical Scholarship (Philadelphia: Fortress Press, 1977).

For more extensive examples of and arguments for the method, with an emphasis on source criticism within the definition of literary criticism, see

Norman C. Habel, *Literary Criticism of the Old Testament* (Philadelphia: Fortress Press, 1997).
J. Cheryl Exum and David J. A. Clines, eds., *The New Literary Criticism and the Hebrew Bible* (Valley Forge, PA: Trinity Press International, 1994).

Three of the best books on the topic give special attention to the kinds of results useful to pastors and teachers in doing exegesis:

David A. Dorsey, *The Literary Structure of the Old Testament: A Commentary on Genesis–Malachi* (Grand Rapids: Baker Academic, 2004).
Paul R. House, ed., *Beyond Form Criticism: Essays in Old Testament Literary Criticism* (Winona Lake, IN: Eisenbrauns, 1992).
Leland Ryken and Tremper Longman III, eds., *A Complete Literary Guide to the Bible* (Grand Rapids: Zondervan Publishing House, 1993).

4.8.5. Source criticism

Applicable mostly in the case of the Pentateuch, and to a lesser extent the historical books, source criticism tried to discern the various written documents that the final editor (of the Pentateuch, for example) drew from in producing the finished work. This criticism is now often considered outdated since the human "sources" of the OT are far more complex and more difficult to recover or isolate than a few written documents would be. Even so, the general features of the documentary hypothesis of Graf and Wellhausen, which posits four main sources for the Pentateuch (J, E, D, P) and suggests approximate dates for each, are still accepted by many OT scholars. An introduction to source criticism (under its alternate appellation, literary criticism) is found in

Norman C. Habel, *Literary Criticism of the Old Testament*, Guides to Biblical Scholarship (Philadelphia: Fortress Press, 1971).

4.8.6. Dating

For many years, the tendency among OT scholars was to date portions of Scripture on the basis of theories about the evolution of Israelite religion rather than on any intrinsic, objective criteria. The law was therefore dated late because it supposedly evidenced "developed" features, whereas the more "primitive" stories about Yahweh's leadership of the exodus, for example, could be dated early. Such hypothetical constructions are now largely out of favor, but great diversity still exists concerning the dating of various OT books and sections thereof. Dating books on the basis of linguistic features has always been inherently more objective in intent, but it has suffered from a lack of specific knowledge. For poetry, there are some tentative approaches that appear to offer hope. If your passage is poetry, you may be able to suggest a date for it—even if the context gives no clue—by consulting:

David A. Robertson, *Linguistic Evidence in Dating Early Hebrew Poetry* (Missoula, MT: Scholars Press, 1973).

Robertson provides a preliminary typology for dating poetry according to mostly morphological features.

Also still helpful is chapter 1 of

W. F. Albright, *Yahweh and the Gods of Canaan* (Garden City, NY: Doubleday, 1968).

Taking account of advances in the field is

Ian Young, Robert Rezetko, and Martin Ehrensvärd, *Linguistic Dating of Biblical Texts: An Introduction to Approaches and Problems* (Oakville, CT: Equinox Publishing, 2008).

In the case of some poetry, and virtually all prose, there is very little agreed-upon evidence that allows for specific dating on the basis of linguistic features. In a few cases you must rely primarily on the claims of the text itself and nonlinguistic features. Orthographic (spelling) features may be indicative of date. In most cases, however, the orthography of the Hebrew OT is of no help. This is because early and late texts alike are written in the orthography of the Persian period (540–333 BC), since the texts from early times were conjoined and copied widely during the Restoration. Thus a single orthography was applied through the entire OT in both Hebrew and Aramaic. Only the small portions that partially escape this leveling process (such as some of the earliest poems) can be dated by the orthographic evidence. For how it is done, see

David Noel Freedman, A. Dean Forbes, and Francis I. Andersen, *Studies in Hebrew and Aramaic Orthography* (Winona Lake, IN: Eisenbrauns, 1992).

Or see the older but still valuable

Frank Moore Cross Jr. and David Noel Freedman, *Early Hebrew Orthography* (New Haven, CT: American Oriental Society, 1952).

4.9. Biblical Context

4.9.1. Chain-reference lists

Some Bible editions (usually so-called study Bibles) contain what is colloquially called a "chain" reference list. In a separate column, or at the end of each verse, references are listed to passages elsewhere in the Bible that are in some way similar to or connected with that verse. None of these reference lists is entirely reliable or consistent, and many suggest connections that are far-fetched or unreasonable. Nevertheless, these lists can often lead you quickly to parallel or related passages containing similar concepts but not necessarily containing the same words found in the passage you are working on, and thus not to be found by the use of a concordance. Several Bible editions contain notably ample reference lists, as indicated by the following sampling:

The Thompson Chain-Reference Bible, in various English versions (Indianapolis: Kirkbride Bible Co., 2007).
Harper Study Bible, rev. ed. (San Francisco: HarperSanFrancisco, 2006).
NASB Zondervan Study Bible (Grand Rapids: Zondervan Publishing House, 2006).
The Catholic Study Bible (New York: Oxford University Press, 2006).
Archaeological Study Bible (Grand Rapids: Zondervan Publishing House, 2006).

4.9.2. Topical concordances

Most students are familiar with word concordances (see 4.4.2, above). A word concordance can serve both to facilitate "word studies" and to guide the student to biblical context data. For the latter purpose, such concordances are used as a quick means of searching the OT (and NT) for (1) parallel passages containing the word and (2) parallel passages containing related topics or concepts found by reference to their characteristic vocabulary.

In addition to word concordances, however, there are topical concordances, which group together biblical passages related to one another by a common topic or theme (concept). They can be immensely valuable in suggesting to you other passages related to the one you are working on. In a sense, the topical concordances do what the chain-reference lists (see above) do, only in much more detail and usually with a substantial amount of text from the related passages printed out for immediate analysis.

For a convenient grouping of the complete text of Scripture passages relating to given doctrines (arranged by the classical categories, i.e., God, Christ, salvation, etc.), see

Walter A. Elwell, *Topical Analysis of the Bible* (Grand Rapids: Baker Book House, 1991).
John J. Davis, *Handbook of Basic Bible Texts* (Grand Rapids: Zondervan Publishing House, 1984).

The following are samples of many others also in this category:

Orville J. Nave, *Nave's Topical Bible* (Chicago: Moody Press, 1974).
Charles R. Joy, *Harper's Topical Concordance*, rev. and enlarged ed. (San Francisco: Harper & Row, 1976).
Edward Viening, ed., *The Zondervan Topical Bible* (Grand Rapids: Zondervan Publishing House, 1969).
Steve Bond, ed., *Holman Concise Topical Concordance* (Nashville: Holman Bible Publishers, 1999).

Topical concordances may also be accessed online at such sites as

Crosswalk.com.
Biblestudytools.net.
Studylight.org.
Biblegateway.com.

4.9.3. Commentaries and biblical context

One of the tasks of a commentator is to bring to the attention of the reader the manner in which a passage relates to the book in which it is found, and to the wider biblical context as well. The insights of a commentator usually go beyond what you can happen upon by using chain references and concordances. Therefore, it pays to consult several exegetically oriented commentaries, both classical and modern, looking specifically for indications of intrabiblical relationships. For specific bibliographical information on exegetical commentary series, see 4.12.4, below.

4.9.4. Apocrypha and Pseudepigrapha

Ancient Judaism produced certain religious works that purported to be revelatory and were modeled on biblical writings. A fair number of these have survived, partly because they were accorded at least semiscriptural status by one group or another in the early centuries AD. They are called the Apocrypha ("obscure works") and the Pseudepigrapha ("works falsely attributed to a given author"). Though almost exclusively post-OT in date, and though rejected from canonicity by Jewish and Christian councils (with the notable exception of the sixteenth-century Catholic formalization of the Apocrypha as canonical), these books are very closely related to parts of the OT and useful to OT exegesis. Even by those of us who regard them as neither inspired nor doctrinally reliable, they are useful for philological, topical, historical, and stylistic comparisons. In the sense of genre, they are "biblical" in their type and thus suitable for comparative purposes. When possible, therefore, pay attention to these noncanonical writings for the data they contain.

The classic publication of the Apocrypha and Pseudepigrapha, reprinted often, was that of Charles:

R. H. Charles, ed., *The Apocrypha and Pseudepigrapha of the Old Testament*, vol. 1, *Apocrypha*; vol. 2, *Pseudepigrapha* (Oxford: Clarendon Press, 1913; repr., Berkeley, CA: Apocryphile Press, 2004).

The best English translation of the pseudepigraphic books is now to be found in

James H. Charlesworth, ed., *The Old Testament Pseudepigrapha*, 2 vols. (Garden City, NY: Doubleday, 1983–85).

Each of the fifty-three texts translated is given a brief introduction and some helpful critical notes. Useful with it is

Steve Delamarter, *A Scripture Index to Charlesworth's The Old Testament Pseudepigrapha* (Sheffield: Sheffield Academic Press, 2003).

For information on NT apocryphal and pseudepigraphic literature, see

Wilhelm Schneemelcher, *New Testament Apocrypha*, vol. 1, *Gospels and Related Writings*, rev. ed.; vol. 2, *Writings Relating to the Apostles; Apocalypses and Related Subjects*, rev. ed. (repr., Louisville, KY: Westminster John Knox, 2003–6).

A good coverage of works on Apocrypha and Pseudepigrapha is available via the bibliography in

Joseph A. Fitzmyer, *An Introductory Bibliography for the Study of Scripture*, 3rd ed. (Chicago: Loyola University Press, 1990).

An introduction to Apocrypha and Pseudepigrapha that also addresses other works is found in

Leonhard Rost, *Judaism Outside the Hebrew Canon* (Nashville: Abingdon Press, 1976).

On the Apocrypha, see also

Bruce M. Metzger, *An Introduction to the Apocrypha* (Oxford: Oxford University Press, 1977).

For analysis of how the OT pseudepigraphs relate to the NT, there is

James H. Charlesworth, *The Old Testament Pseudepigrapha and the New Testament: Prolegomena for the Study of Christian Origins* (Harrisburg, PA: Trinity Press International, 1998).

Also helpful are

James H. Charlesworth, P. Dykers, and M. J. H. Charlesworth, *The Pseudepigrapha and Modern Research with a Supplement*, rev. ed. (Chico, CA: Scholars Press, 1981).
Mitchell G. Reddish, ed., *Apocalyptic Literature: A Reader* (Peabody, MA: Hendrickson Publishers, 1996).
John Joseph Collins, *The Apocalyptic Imagination: An Introduction to Jewish Apocalyptic Literature*, 2nd ed. (Grand Rapids: Wm. B. Eerdmans, 1998).

4.9.5. The Old Testament in the New

A demanding task is the analysis of OT themes, doctrines, and so forth as they are reflected in the NT. All too often, OT exegetes neglect the NT data on the grounds that these represent later interpretations, muddying the exegetical waters. Unless you would go so far as to reject NT inspiration and authority, however, in the final analysis you are bound to relate the OT passage to any NT uses or classifications of it. What the NT says about an OT passage is of enormous significance exegetically.

As a general introduction to the principles involved, see the following:

F. F. Bruce, *The New Testament Development of Old Testament Themes* (Grand Rapids: Wm. B. Eerdmans, 1969).
Gregory K. Beale, ed., *The Right Doctrine from the Wrong Texts? Essays on the Use of the Old Testament in the New* (Grand Rapids: Baker Book House, 1994).
C. H. Dodd, *According to the Scriptures: The Sub-structure of New Testament Theology* (New York: Charles Scribner's Sons, 1953).

The following commentary will help you greatly in your task:

G. K. Beale and D. A. Carson, eds. *Commentary on the New Testament Use of the Old Testament* (Grand Rapids: Baker Academic, 2007).

For a comprehensive list of NT citations and allusions to OT passages, consult the "Index of Quotations" (called in some editions "Index of Citations and Allusions") at the back of the latest edition of either the Nestle-Aland or the American Bible Society edition of the Greek NT.

4.10. Theology

4.10.1. Old Testament theologies

Because the major OT theologies attempt a broad coverage of books and passages, it is often possible to use them profitably for exegetical guidance in relating a passage to OT theology as a whole. However, a great diversity of outlook is represented by the various theologies, so they must be used with caution. Some theologies reflect a perspective that downplays the significance or trustworthiness of given portions and passages of the OT in favor of others. Others respect carefully the univocality of the Scriptures. Nevertheless, a recognition of their biases does not mean that the theologies cannot be profitably used. In fact, if your own passage is slighted by the OT theologies, or in your opinion its issues are ignored by them, it becomes precisely your responsibility—and opportunity—to demonstrate whether or not the theologies are derelict in doing so. If the theologies are found wanting, the force of your observations exegetically may be all the more significant and informative.

The theologies listed here are of varying dates. There is not much opportunity for theological concepts to go out of date, so one should not assume that the more recent works are automatically more valuable than the older ones. In general, it would be wise to consult as many of these as possible in preparing a thorough exegesis, because theologies differ from one another relatively more than other types of exegetical aids do.

Bruce K. Waltke with Charles Yu, *An Old Testament Theology: An Exegetical, Canonical, and Thematic Approach* (Grand Rapids: Zondervan Publishing House, 2007).

John Goldingay, *Old Testament Theology: Israel's Faith*, vol. 1, *Israel's Gospel*, vol. 2 (Downers Grove, IL: InterVarsity Press, 2003–6).

Walter Brueggemann, *Theology of the Old Testament: Testimony, Dispute, Advocacy* (Minneapolis: Fortress Press, 1997).

Walther Eichrodt, *Theology of the Old Testament*, 2 vols., Old Testament Library (Philadelphia: Westminster Press, 1961–67).

Gerhard Hasel, *Old Testament Theology*, 4th ed. (Grand Rapids: Wm. B. Eerdmans, 1991).

Paul R. House, *Old Testament Theology* (Downers Grove, IL: InterVarsity Press, 1998).

Edmond Jacob, *Theology of the Old Testament* (New York: Harper & Brothers, 1958).

Walter Kaiser Jr., *Toward an Old Testament Theology* (1978; repr., Grand Rapids: Zondervan Publishing House, 1991).

James Muilenburg, *The Way of Israel: Biblical Faith and Ethics* (New York: Harper & Row, 1961).

Horst Dietrich Preuss, *Old Testament Theology*, 2 vols. (Louisville, KY: Westminster John Knox, 1999).

Gerhard von Rad, *Old Testament Theology*, trans. D. M. G. Stalker, 2 vols., repr. with an introduction by Walter Brueggemann (Louisville, KY: Westminster John Knox Press, 2001).

John H. Sailhamer, *Introduction to Old Testament Theology: A Canonical Approach* (Grand Rapids: Zondervan Publishing House, 1995).

Ralph L. Smith, *Old Testament Theology: Its History, Method, and Message* (Nashville: Broadman & Holman, 1994).

Walther Zimmerli, *Old Testament Theology in Outline* (Atlanta: John Knox Press, 1978).

4.10.2. Christian theologies

Obviously, a Christian theology will give substantial attention to issues beyond the OT and will address some of the OT data less directly than will an OT theology. This broader perspective is valid and necessary for an exegesis to be entirely balanced in its conclusions. A criterion for exegetical value in a Christian theology is that it be biblically based, in constant dialogue with the text. In addition to the famous major theologies of well-known theologians such as Barth and Brunner, several works stand out as keenly biblical in orientation. The following each has various features to commend it to the exegete, and again it must be said that good Christian theologies do not easily go out of date:

Herman Bavinck, *Our Reasonable Faith* (1956; repr., Eugene, OR: Wipf & Stock, 2002).

G. C. Berkouwer, *Studies in Dogmatics*, 14 vols. (Grand Rapids: Wm. B. Eerdmans, 1952–76).

Donald Bloesch, *Christian Foundations*, 4 vols. (Downers Grove, IL: InterVarsity Press, 1992–2000).

Charles W. Carter, ed., *A Contemporary Wesleyan Theology*, 2 vols. (Grand Rapids: Zondervan Publishing House, 1984).

Millard J. Erickson, *Christian Theology*, 2nd ed. (Grand Rapids: Baker Book House, 1998).

Wayne Grudem, *Systematic Theology: An Introduction to Biblical Doctrine* (Grand Rapids: Zondervan Publishing House, 2000; Kindle ebook edition, 2004; also on CD-ROM and within some Bible software modules).

Carl F. H. Henry, *God, Revelation, and Authority*, 6 vols. (Waco, TX: Word Books, 1976–83).

Wolfhart Pannenberg, *Systematic Theology*, 3 vols. (1991–98; repr., New York: T&T Clark International, 2004).

Helmut Thielicke, *The Evangelical Faith*, 3 vols. (1974–82; repr., Macon, GA: Smyth & Helwys Publishing, 1997).

Geerhardus Vos, *Biblical Theology, Old and New Testaments* (Grand Rapids: Wm. B. Eerdmans, 1948).

Otto Weber, *Foundations of Dogmatics*, 2 vols. (Grand Rapids: Wm. B. Eerdmans, 1981–83).

H. Orton Wiley, *Christian Theology*, 3 vols. (Boston: Beacon Hill Press, 1940).

Alister E. McGrath, *Christian Theology: An Introduction*, 4th ed. (Malden, MA: Wiley-Blackwell, 2007).

4.11. Application

4.11.1. Hermeneutics

Hermeneutics is the theory of understanding a passage's meaning. At virtually every stage of an exegesis, you are using hermeneutical (interpretational) principles, whether implicitly or explicitly. At the application stage, however, it is most important of all to be absolutely clear about the interpretational principles you employ since a proper application depends so greatly on reasonable and honest use of good principles. In other words, the rules you go by to interpret the passage will largely determine how accurately you apply the passage.

Traditionally—and simplistically—four different kinds of meanings have been discovered in biblical passages: (1) the literal (historical) meaning; (2) the allegorical (mystical or "spiritual") meaning; (3) the anagogic (typological—especially as relating to the end times and eternity) meaning; and (4) the tropological (moral) meaning. Precisely because the literal meaning was understood so narrowly (as merely the meaning the passage once had, rather than what it may also mean now), interpreters were driven to seek something personal, contemporary, and practical from the latter three types of meaning. After all, we read the Bible for help in our own lives, not just as a historical exercise. The latter types of meaning (allegorical, anagogic, tropological), however, are not usually directly derived from the passage itself, but tend to be more or less invented by the imagination according to rules not always consistently applied. Such kinds of interpretations are often seductively appealing and can allow otherwise "dull" passages to seem to speak personally and practically. However, they usually ignore the intentionality of the text itself, so that what the ancient inspired author meant to be understood from his or her writing is grossly exceeded and indeed eclipsed by almost uncontrolled mystical, typological, and moralizing sorts of over-interpretation.

The delicate task of the interpreter, then, is to be sure that everything the passage means is brought out but that nothing additional is read into the passage. We do not want to miss anything, but we do not want to "find" anything that is not really there either. Hermeneutics properly applied is thus interested in the boundaries of interpretation—the upper and lower limits—that are intended by the Spirit of God for the reader.

The most popular introduction to hermeneutics is the relatively brief
and easy-to-read

Gordon D. Fee and Douglas Stuart, *How to Read the Bible for All Its Worth*, 3rd ed. (Grand
Rapids: Zondervan Publishing House, 2003).

Hundreds of substantial volumes have been written on hermeneutics,
most of them offering at least some helpful methodology. An excellent
introduction to the theoretical issues is

Kevin J. Vanhoozer, *Is There a Meaning in This Text? The Bible, the Reader, and the Morality of
Literary Knowledge* (Grand Rapids: Zondervan, 1998).

The following are certainly among the best substantial works on
hermeneutics, partly because they take seriously the authority and inspiration of the entire Bible:

William Klein, Craig L. Blomberg, and Robert L. Hubbard Jr., *Introduction to Biblical Inter-
pretation*, 2nd ed. (Nashville: Thomas Nelson, 2004).
Anthony C. Thistleton, *New Horizons in Hermeneutics* (Grand Rapids: Zondervan Publishing
House, 1997).
J. Scott Duvall and J. Daniel Hays, *Grasping God's Word: A Hands-On Aproach to Reading, Inter-
preting, and Applying the Bible* (Grand Rapids: Zondervan Publishing House, 2005).
A. Berkeley Mickelsen, *Interpreting the Bible* (repr., Grand Rapids: Wm. B. Eerdmans, 1972).
Grant R. Osborne, *The Hermeneutical Spiral: A Comprehensive Introduction to Biblical Interpre-
tation*, rev. ed. (Downers Grove, IL: IVP Academic, 2006).
Walter C. Kaiser Jr. and Moisés Silva, *An Introduction to Biblical Hermeneutics: The Search for
Meaning* (Grand Rapids: Zondervan Publishing House, 1994).
Roger Lundin, Anthony C. Thiselton, and Clarence Walhout, *The Promise of Hermeneutics*
(Grand Rapids: William B. Eerdmans, 1999).
Roy B. Zuck, ed., *Rightly Divided: Readings in Biblical Hermeneutics* (Grand Rapids: Kregel Pub-
lications, 1996).
D. Brent Sandy and Ronald L. Giese, eds., *Cracking Old Testament Codes* (Nashville: Broad-
man & Holman, 1995).
Robert H. Stein, *A Basic Guide to Interpreting the Bible: Playing by the Rules* (1994; repr., Grand
Rapids: Baker Academic, 1997).
Donald A. Carson, *Exegetical Fallacies*, 2nd ed. (Grand Rapids: Baker Academic, 1996).

A series edited by David M. Howard Jr. titled Handbooks for Old Testament Exegesis has the following works:

Robert B. Chisholm, *Interpreting the Historical Books: An Exegetical Handbook* (Grand Rapids:
Kregel Publications, 2006).
Mark D. Futato, *Interpreting the Psalms: An Exegetical Handbook* (Grand Rapids: Kregel Pub-
lications, 2007).

See also the following reference works on hermeneutics:

David S. Dockery, Robert B. Sloan, and Kenneth A. Matthews, *Foundations for Biblical Interpretation: A Complete Library of Tools and Resources* (Nashville: Broadman & Holman, 1999).
John H. Hayes, ed., *Dictionary of Biblical Interpretation*, 2 vols. (Nashville: Abingdon Press, 1998).

In addition, a number of recent works on the hermeneutical task as it applies to preaching may be cited as particularly useful in their respective categories.

Practical encouragement toward responsibly extracting from a text the features that will bring to a congregation a real sense of involvement with the "original" audience of scriptural events can be found in any of the following:

Wayne E. Ward, *The Word Comes Alive* (Nashville: Broadman Press, 1969).
Haddon W. Robinson, *Biblical Preaching: The Development and Delivery of Expository Messages* (Grand Rapids: Baker Book House, 1980).
George L. Klein, ed., *Reclaiming the Prophetic Mantle: Preaching the Old Testament Faithfully* (Nashville: Broadman Press, 1992).
Sidney Greidanus, *The Modern Preacher and the Ancient Text: Interpreting and Preaching Biblical Literature* (Grand Rapids: Wm. B. Eerdmans, 1988).

Two books on various aspects of OT preaching have been penned by Elizabeth Achtemeier:

Elizabeth Achtemeier, *Preaching from the Old Testament* (Louisville, KY: Westminster John Knox Press, 1989).
Elizabeth Achtemeier, *Preaching Hard Texts of the Old Testament* (Peabody, MA: Hendrickson Publishers, 1998).

Any of the following may also prove helpful to you:

James W. Cox, *A Guide to Biblical Preaching* (Nashville: Abingdon Press, 1976).
James W. Cox, *Preaching* (San Francisco: Harper & Row, 1985).
Haddon W. Robinson, *Biblical Preaching: The Development and Delivery of Expository Messages*, 2nd ed. (Grand Rapids: Baker Academic, 2001).
Sidney Greidanus, *Preaching Christ from the Old Testament: A Contemporary Hermeneutical Method* (Grand Rapids: Wm. B. Eerdmans, 1999).
Bryan Chapell, *Christ-Centered Preaching: Redeeming the Expository Sermon* (Grand Rapids: Baker Academic, 2005).
Jerry Vines and James Shaddix, *Power in the Pulpit: How to Prepare and Deliver Expository Sermons* (Chicago: Moody Press, 1999).
Thomas G. Long, *The Witness of Preaching*, 2nd ed. (Louisville, KY: Westminster John Knox Press, 2005).

4.11.2. Some do's and don'ts in application

1. Do consider the needs and composition of your audience in the way that you construct the application.

2. Do be careful that the application derives directly and logically from the passage (in other words, respect the passage's intentionality).

3. Do try to limit yourself, if possible, to the central or priority application.

4. Do—if your passage functions primarily to illustrate a principle stated elsewhere in Scripture—be sure to demonstrate a genuine relationship between the two.

1. Don't multiply applications needlessly: more is not necessarily better.

2. Don't assume that your audience will automatically make a proper application of the passage just because the rest of your exegesis is good.

3. Don't invent an application if none seems to be forthcoming. Better to say nothing rather than something misleading.

4. Don't confuse illumination with inspiration. The former refers to what you alone, emotionally, existentially, and individually may derive from the passage. The latter refers to what God has intended that the passage say to any of us in general. For illumination, you should diligently appropriate for yourself a most precious, life-sustaining resource of the student and pastor, for which exegesis could never hope to substitute: prayer.

4.12. Secondary Literature

4.12.1. Special reference sources: Using the Web to find books and articles

The Internet has become an essential source for finding out about secondary literature in the field of Old Testament (and most other fields as well). It can be faster and more convenient to search online from your own computer to identify publications relevant to the passage or topic you are working on than by using more traditional means (library catalogs, reference compilations, etc.). But this does not mean that there is anything outdated about libraries and the reference publications their shelves contain. Libraries are the places where most of the publications will actually be physically available to you, and the printed bibliography guides of various sorts found normally in libraries will continue to be essential because they contain lists put together by scholars who have the learning and judgment to include the good and leave out the bad. So unless and until the distant day when everything written in journals and books is also scanned or otherwise rendered into Web-accessible electronic form, we will all be using the Web mainly to find *titles* and sometimes *summaries* or *excerpts* of what has been written on a given passage or topic in books and journals. In many or most cases, we will still have to have the hard copies of books and journals in our hands to be able to find out what they actually say.

The need for hands-on physical access to publications will not go away, especially for full books and commentaries. It costs a lot of money to publish these, and publishers simply cannot put their in-print contents on the Web for free and stay in business. With journals, the situation is somewhat friendlier to an Internet user. First, some journals put their contents online and charge an access fee to users. Others provide journal content at no cost some years after it has been first published in print form. Some journals have also allowed back issues to be scanned into databases that can be accessed either from your own computer if it is linked to a library site (i.e., if a library has paid for a site license that allows it to share such articles with any of its customers) or from a library computer, where it may be printed out or forwarded to your own computer. Some colleges, seminaries, and universities have even begun *requiring* their professors to post their articles online in addition to publishing them in journals, so as to help encourage the dissemination of knowledge. Additionally, many scholars now publish some of their articles *only* online, so that without searching online for information on a passage or topic, you can actually miss these Web-only articles altogether, no matter how well you search the published databases or use your in-library resources.

Here are six categories of online readable resources:

1. *Older books, articles, and commentaries no longer under copyright protection.* Typically, a library or other organization may have scanned these and put them on the Web, and you simply need to find where they are and then read them or download them as you please. Do not be fooled by the mentality that "the new is the true." It is often just the opposite. There are many great publications from the past that deserve to be accessible now, and the fact that many of them are—and so conveniently—is to your advantage.

2. *Parts of current books and commentaries online from certain Web sites.* For example, Amazon.com and several other similar commercial sites often invite you to "look inside this book" and permit you to read excerpts from books and commentaries they have for sale. The percentage of a book that you can read this way depends on what the publisher or author has decided to allow. With good fortune, you may be able to access the part(s) you really need for your research.

3. *Current or recent articles online even though they are also in printed journals.* Some educational institutions now require their employees to double-publish this way, and some scholars do it voluntarily if the journal in question allows it. You get free access to recent, top-quality material.

4. *Articles, and occasionally even books, published* only *online.* Consider the factors: (a) more and more institutions are giving publishing credit to their faculty for articles and books that never appear in print, but solely on the Web; (b) not all scholars are employed by educational institutions; (c) because of backlogs and costs, it can take years for a good article to be printed in a journal; but (d) a scholar can put an article online the minute it is finished and can update it as often as desired thereafter. Some truly fine scholarship is out there *only* on the Web. How do you know it is there and how do you find it? Just by patiently googling for it. Keep trying plausible word combinations (e.g., "Isaiah temple," then "Isaiah prophecy temple," then "Isaiah restoration prophecy," then "Isaiah temple bibliography," then "Old Testament temple bibliography," then "Bible new temple," etc.) and you will be pleased to see how much you can uncover via your diligence. To be sure you have exhausted the possibilities, you must carefully create a list of all possible key words and then google them in sensible small groupings.

5. *Journals and books with restricted access for a fee online.* Some scholarly journals allow you to read their content online if you already have a subscription to the print copy or via a for-cost but nonprofit site (see *ATLA Religion Database,* below). One advantage this provides is the ability to perform topic searches within one or more articles faster and usually more accurately than could be done by reading the printed page. Some journals even give lower rates for just online access, and a few are published only online. The number in this latter category is expected to keep increasing. There are also sites such as *JSTOR, Questia,* and so forth that have assembled a great many books and articles online. You can sometimes get a free trial from these sites to see if you want to become a subscriber; if you subscribe, you pay a monthly or annual fee for access to their holdings, which you can then read online, and usually download (subject to various limits).

6. *Privately generated bibliography lists, sometimes helpfully annotated with evaluations and content descriptions.* Googling for bibliographical listings from personal Web pages, including Web logs (blogs), can lead to surprisingly helpful results. Type the name of almost any biblical book or significant biblical topic word along with the word "bibliography" into a search engine, and you will likely get at least one good list compiled by a professor or grad student or enthusiastic blogger. That site may have links

to others as well. When you find the author and title of an article that looks like it might be helpful to you and copy and paste that into a search engine, you will probably be referred to Web pages that will give you further information, and sometimes either a copy of the article itself or some sort of response to it. With books and commentaries whose identity has been discovered this way, you might even locate some scholar's review of that book or commentary, which will help you know whether or not it is an item you need to get your hands on to use for your research. Print-published bibliographies are out of date as soon as they appear (because of the lag time between writing and publishing), but online bibliographies are often updated regularly by their compilers. Searching online some-times alerts you to newly published articles, books, or commentaries that you probably would not find out about any other way.

Some major bibliographical sites are available online at no cost and are so extensive in their listings that they will usually alert you to almost any article or book actually published in print on the passage or topic you are researching.

Perhaps the most comprehensive of these is

BILDI, http://www.uibk.ac.at/bildi.

BILDI is an acronym for *Bibelwissenschaftliche Literaturdokumentation Inns-bruck*, produced by the Institut für Bibelwissenschaften und Fundamen-taltheologie of the University of Innsbruck, Austria. It is a very large database that allows complex searches covering virtually anything in bib-lical studies and several related fields such as philology and archaeology. *BILDI* keeps track of articles from hundreds of relevant periodicals. Titles are derived from books, articles, and secondhand sources. Usually, this is the database to try first. Here is how you use it:

If you are searching for literature on a verse or passage, just type into the "Basic Index" box the name of the biblical book followed by the word "and" followed by a chapter number (e.g., "Genesis and 1"). This will retrieve all indexed articles and books that have been tagged under the subject "Genesis" or contain the words "Genesis" and "1" in their title. Because articles and books often discuss more than one verse within a bib-lical chapter, this kind of search helps to make sure that you get all possi-ble relevant results. Now, *BILDI* is so large that this will usually yield more references than you want. You will have to sift through the titles to find the articles and books that look as though they may be helpful for your particular research.

An alternative way to find those references that have been tagged in the database with a specific, individual verse is to type in the Basic Index box the abbreviation of the biblical book followed by the chapter number followed by a comma, followed *directly* by the verse number. Every reference must contain two digits except for the Psalms, which must contain three (e.g., Gen 01,16; Ex 03,07; Ps 001,03; etc.). If you are looking for literature on a group of verses, you will have to do this once again for each verse. Careful! You must not put a space between the comma and the following verse number:

Incorrect:	01, 03
Correct:	01,03

The abbreviations for the biblical books must be the ones used by the database. This can be tricky for non-German speakers because *BILDI* does not use the standard SBL abbreviations (see http://sbl-site.org/assets/pdfs/SBLHS.pdf) but rather those common to German tradition. Since these are not listed on the Web site, we list them here:

Genesis	Gen	Exodus	Ex
Leviticus	Lev	Numbers	Num
Deuteronomy	Dtn	Joshua	Jos
Judges	Ri	Ruth	Rut
1 Samuel	1 Sam	2 Samuel	2 Sam
1 Kings	1 Kön	2 Kings	2 Kön
1 Chronicles	1 Chr	2 Chronicles	2 Chr
Ezra	Esr	Nehemiah	Neh
Esther	Est	Job	Hiob
Psalms	Ps	Proverbs	Spr
Ecclesiastes	Pred	Song of Songs	Hld
Isaiah	Jes	Jeremiah	Jer
Lamentations	Klgl	Ezekiel	Ez
Daniel	Dan	Hosea	Hos
Joel	Joel	Amos	Am
Obadiah	Obd	Jonah	Jona
Micah	Mi	Nahum	Nah
Habakkuk	Hab	Zephaniah	Zef
Haggai	Hag	Zechariah	Sach
Malachi	Mal		

You can control the way references appear on the screen and the information they contain by making a selection in the format section to the right of the Basic Index box. You will have several options, including having the references appear in the standard SBL format (a desirable option for anyone—such as a student writing a paper—who needs a bibliography to conform to a proper style; see http://sbl-site.org/assets/pdfs/SBLHS.pdf). The most comprehensive results come from choosing the circle titled "with key words/year" under the "expanded formats" section. This option will give you references along with all key words that were tagged within the database. This will often help you find other closely related references.

Another valuable bibliographic database is

RAMBI, http://jnul.huji.ac.il/rambi.

RAMBI is a modern Hebrew acronym for the equivalent of "Index of Articles on Jewish Studies," produced by the Jewish National and University Library. It is a large database that allows complex searches on Jewish studies and topics related to Israel. The main criterion for inclusion in the bibliography is that the article be based on scientific research. *RAMBI* began in 1966, and there are currently fifty volumes, all online and free to search.

To find references for a biblical verse, select "*RAMBI* Web" at the bottom of the opening page. This will take you to the search page. Then select "Basic Search" at the top left. Under "Search Options" select "Subject starting with . . ." Then type in the "Search For" box the name of the book (e.g., "Genesis") that contains your passage and hit "Go." Several chapters will appear in numerical order (e.g., <Genesis (book of):1>). Select the chapter your passage is in, and you will get all references relevant to that chapter. Sift through the titles to find references on your particular verse or verses or topic. There are several advanced search options for those who are interested, but this is the simplest and quickest way to retrieve references on a particular passage.

Yet another comprehensive datatbase is the

Index Theologicus, http://www.ixtheo.de.

This free database, usually abbreviated as *IxTheo*, is produced by the University of Tübingen in Germany. It is updated daily and now covers more than six hundred periodicals and articles from Festschriften (collections of articles in honor of scholars) and congress publications (collections of articles from scholarly gatherings). Coverage begins in 1980 but is somewhat sketchy until 1984, when it becomes thorough. *IxTheo* covers much of the same ground that the *ATLA Religion Database* does, with one significant difference: It pays attention to some of the European journals and books that the *ATLA Religion Database* does not.

To search for a particular passage, click on "Start English version," then "Scripture References," then "Old Testament," then the name of the biblical book that you want. A text-entry box labeled with that biblical book appears. In that box, type the first verse that you are interested in, such as 1:1. You will see a window showing your results. Then click on each article that looks promising to read more details about it, including the subjects that it covers. You can save all of your results as an RTF file that you can open anytime in such programs as MS Word by clicking on the "Export" button. Once you have saved your results, you can repeat the process for the next verse in your passage or any other verse of interest.

You will also find valuable bibliographical information at

BiBIL, http://www.bibil.net.

BiBIL (*Biblical Bibliography of Lausanne*, produced by the University of Lausanne) covers journals and books related to the OT and NT, as well as early church history. It is free, easy to use, and contains useful links to free online journal articles.

To retrieve articles and/or books related to a particular verse or passage, select the "Simple Search" option on the left side of the *BiBIL* home page. This takes you to a search screen. On the "Biblical Reference" line you will see five boxes in this order: "book," "chapter beginning," "verse," "chapter end," "verse." In the "book" section, type the abbreviation of the biblical book for which you want to find references. The same abbreviations must be used that the database uses, and there is a link to these at the bottom left of the screen. Type into the "chapter beginning" box the chapter number you want to search. Into the "verse" box, type the first verse of the passage you are studying. Leave the "chapter end" box and the final "verse" box empty (e.g., <book: Gen> <chapter beginning: 1> <verse: 1> <chapter end: EMPTY> <verse: EMPTY>). This will retrieve all references relevant to Genesis 1:1 or passages in Genesis 1 that start with verse 1. It will not retrieve references for Genesis 1:2 or 1:3 and so on. You simply follow the same process for every verse in your passage to be sure you retrieve all relevant resources.

The following Web site is especially helpful for textual criticism:

Tov, Emanuel, *Electronic Resources Relevant to the Textual Criticism of Hebrew Scripture*, http://rosetta.reltech.org/TC/vol08/Tov2003.html.

This online source has direct links to dozens of online resources relevant to the exegesis of the Hebrew Bible. It explains how to get free access to the LXX, Targum(s), Peshitta, Samaritan Pentateuch, and Vulgate, as well as other versions, their apparatuses, and credible lexicons. You can copy and paste wordings fairly easily from these versions and put them into a Word document in an interlinear fashion underneath the Hebrew passage being studied, to achieve the same sort of comparison lineup that we illustrate in this book in chapter 2.

Of course, you can do the same thing if you spend enough money for a good set of language modules in *BibleWorks, Accordance*, and others, but the Tov links are free.

You may also have success in finding written resources relevant to your research in

WorldCat, http://www.worldcat.org.

WorldCat is the world's largest library network database. It has over ten thousand libraries registered and contains over a billion cataloged items covering every subject. In addition to written material, it catalogs audio and audiovisual material as well. You can search it online for free. One benefit of *WorldCat* is that it tells you which libraries (if they are registered with *WorldCat*) have the source you are interested in, where they are located, and how many miles they are from where you are doing your search. For instance, as of the date of this writing, for the name Douglas K. Stuart there were 131 hits. Books, articles, and lectures (including lecture series that I have given in various places) were cataloged.

As an example, *WorldCat* shows that my currently out-of-print Harvard Semitic Monograph series book, *Studies in Early Hebrew Meter*, is located in 10 libraries within a 30-mile radius of South Hamilton, Massachusetts—where I teach—and that it is located in 236 libraries that are registered with *WorldCat*. This database will also connect you to a library's Web site so that you can see whether or not the source you want to use is checked out. *WorldCat* is thus a particularly useful tool for students and pastors who do not live close to a seminary or university library and are not sure which local libraries might have the source they are looking for.

A challenge with this database is its size. If you type "Genesis 1:1" into the search box, more than 26,000 items will be retrieved, far too many to sort through efficiently. So try the "Advanced Search" option when researching a biblical passage. Its link is directly under the main search box. When you are at the "Advanced Search" page, find the "Key Word" box at the top, then type in the name of the biblical book, the chapter number, and the first verse of your passage (e.g., Genesis 1:1). In the "Limit results by option" section, click the squares to choose the ways you want your search to be limited. To limit your search even more, use Boolean operators and delimiting words after your Scripture reference in the "Key Word" box. Even after all this limitation, you will probably retrieve more items than you need. You must sift through the lists to find the resources that look as though they will be relevant to your study.

Another online database worth checking is the

Israel Library Network, http://libnet.ac.il/~libnet/malmad-israelnet.htm.

This site contains direct access to the library pages of forty-two colleges and universities in Israel, many of which can be searched at the same time. Most of these sites allow you to use standard searching techniques, although some of them are difficult to use if you do not know at least some modern Hebrew.

If you want to read articles about the Bible online and you are willing to pay an annual fee for the privilege or can get to a library that does, nothing beats the

ATLA Religion Database, http://www.atla.com/products/catalogs/catalogs_rdb.html#general.

The American Theological Library Association has built up this database to the point where, as of this writing, it indexes over 1.6 million journal articles, book reviews, and essays. In their own words, they have: "537,000+ journal article records; 220,000+ essay records from 16,100+ multi-author works; 474,000+ book reviews of 245,500+ books; 1,633 journal titles, 518 of which are currently indexed." You are not limited to a single Web site to use the Religion Database, but you have your pick of three, each of which has been licensed by ATLA to provide access to online users. They have different prices and terms for access, and slightly different interfaces, so you may wish to do a little comparison shopping before making your decision. The ATLA tells you to "contact each of these aggregators directly for information about pricing, subscription terms, trials, features, and technical support":

EBSCO Publishing, www.ebscohost.com.
OCLC FirstSearch, www.oclc.org.
Ovid, www.ovid.com.

The great benefit of this database is the potential it gives you to read, copy, save, and send electronic versions of many articles. Once you have clicked on *ATLA Religion Database with ATLA Serials* on the Web page, you can select "SC Scripture Citation" from a drop-down menu. By typing the verse you want enclosed in quotes into the text box (e.g., "Genesis 1:1") and clicking the "search" button, you will get a page of results. If an electronic copy of the full article is available, you will see a link labeled "Click here for electronic resource." If you want to add the citation information (author, title, publisher, etc.) to your own list, just click on the displayed "Add" link. When you have added all the articles you wish to your list, click on the link labeled "Folder has items." That leads you to a page from which you can e-mail your list of citations to yourself or save them to a disk or both.

Careful: You must search only one verse at a time, and you must enclose your verse in quotation marks: "Genesis 1:1." Leaving out the quotation marks or specifying a range of verses will not give you the results you want.

There is yet another aspect of the ATLA Web site that you can make good use of: searching the *Old Testament Abstracts* (*OTA*) database.

To do this, stay with the same Web page and essentially the same procedure you have already been using to search the *ATLA Database*. Selecting the *Old Testament Abstracts* database, you should then choose *both* "SC Scripture Citation" and "AB Abstract," by putting the same chapter and verse number into both and selecting "OR" from the drop-down menu on the left of the second field.

Warning: The interface permits you to search both *ATLA Database* and *OT Abstracts* at the same time, but if you try to do this, it will eliminate the Scripture citation and abstract fields from your options, so do not do it. Search *ATLA* separately, and then search *OTA* separately.

Another online database is

Questia, Questia.com.

At the present time, *Questia* is the world's largest online library, with holdings of electronic copies of books and articles in a great variety of fields. It requires monthly subscription fees but allows cover-to-cover reading/searching of its holdings. Its religious studies collection is fairly extensive, and compared to buying books and articles you need to use, its costs can seem a bargain.

Consider also

Free Theological Journals on the Web, http://www.atla.com/icc/ejournals.htm.

This site, also provided by the American Theological Library Association, has links to hundreds of journals that allow you to read some or all of their articles online without cost. These are not merely links to the names of articles, but actually to the full text of articles or the journal sites that will allow you eventually to navigate to the article texts. The site suggests ways to search its database by subject, but this has not yet been perfected, so do not rely exclusively on it. Moreover, some of the links are not current. So, some googling of journal names and thoughtful browsing on your own will surely be necessary, but the site is still very informative for all the leads it provides, even if some of the links are flawed.

You will find some useful databases at the following kinds of sites. The two that we select here are merely representative of several others that can be accessed by links from these sites:

The Bible Tool, http://www.crosswire.org/study/.

This is a joint effort of the American Bible Society, CrossWire Bible Society, and the Society of Biblical Literature. It provides searchable databases of Bible translations, older commentaries, lexicons, atlases, glossaries, and other publications of interest to students of the OT.

Bible Gateway, http://www.biblegateway.com/.

This site provides search options for almost fifty modern translations, including about two dozen in English. Often an exegesis project requires precise rendering of a passage accurately in English. When searching for just the right translation, immediate access to virtually all the options that have been chosen by scholar translators is very helpful. Comparing published translations helps to ensure that you have not overlooked a valid translation possibility by reason of the limitations of your own original language skills. Most of these translations are also available in modules of *BibleWorks*, *Accordance*, or others but not free, as they are at such a site as *Bible Gateway*.

The following printed works contain guidance to various online bibliographical resources as well. Consulting them would provide you with a cross-check of what we have said:

Stanislaw Bazylinski, *A Guide to Biblical Research: Introductory Notes* (Rome: Editrice Pontificio Istituto Biblico, 2006). This is a thorough book on biblical research. It covers sources and methodology.

Edith Lubetski, "Online Resources for Biblical Studies: A Sampling," *Currents in Research: Biblical Studies* 8 (2000): 134–45. This article is concise and helpful. It lists several online resources by category and explains how to use them and their relevance for biblical studies.

Patrick Durusau, *High Places in Cyberspace: A Guide to Biblical and Religious Studies, Classics, and Archaeological Resources on the Internet*, 2nd ed. (Atlanta: Scholars Press, 1998). This source is somewhat outdated but still useful.

Printed reference sources

Langevin. For access to most of the significant books and journal articles written on your passage between 1930 and 1983, you can turn to one source that groups them all conveniently so that you do not have to make a year-by-year search for them:

Paul-Émile Langevin, *Bibliographie biblique, Biblical Bibliography, Biblische Bibliographie, Bibliografia biblica, Bibliografía bíblica,* 1 (1930–70); 2 (1930–75); 3 (1975–83) (Quebec: L'Université Laval, 1972, 1978, 1985).

Volume 1 contains references only to Roman Catholic periodicals and books. Volume 2 adds non-Roman Catholic references and brings the Roman Catholic references five years further along (1971–75). Volume 3 brings both up to 1983.

Old Testament Abstracts. A listing and an abstract (a brief summary) of virtually any recent book or article published on an OT topic can be found in *OTA*. Since 1978 it has provided brief summaries of the contents of nearly all significant articles and books written on OT studies year by year. From the abstracts you can get a sense of whether an article or book might be relevant to your study before investing the energy of hunting up the full publication itself. The articles are listed by category, and there are Scripture indexes, author indexes, and key (Hebrew/Aramaic) word indexes added. The *OTA* is so comprehensive that it has almost everything you will likely need after 1978. It is available in electronic version via *EBSCO* (ebscohost.com) or print version. For the print version, consider subscribing. The address is

Old Testament Abstracts, Catholic Biblical Association of America, c/o The Catholic University of America, Washington, DC 20064.

In its electronic form it allows searches for individual Scripture references, key words in any language, authors, and so on. You can even limit your search to works in English if you cannot read other languages.

From 1920 to 1930 all significant OT publications were tabulated yearly and listed both by topic and by Scripture reference in each annual addition of

Elenchus (*Elenchus bibliographicus biblicus*), vols. 1–48 (1920–67) in the journal *Biblica*; then published separately, 1968– (vol. 49–).

For works published after 1930, Langevin and *Old Testament Abstracts* provide virtually the same information, in easier-to-use formats. *Elenchus* has one issue each year, dating back to 1920. There is an electronic version of *Elenchus*, but it goes back only to 1998, and this limitation and its cost mean that relatively fewer libraries have chosen to subscribe to it: www.biblico.it/pubblicazioni/periodicals.html.

SOTS Book List. The *Book List of the British Society for Old Testament Study* is an annual publication listing OT books produced each year since 1946. Its special value is that each book is given a minireview, by which you can gauge something of its potential for your own research. Back copies of the annual *Book List* are on sale at reduced prices: www.sots.ac.uk.

IRBS is of considerable usefulness. The *International Review of Biblical Studies* (also called the *Internationale Zeitschriftenschau für Bibelwissenschaft und Grenzgebiete*) may prove useful to you. Each of its annual volumes contains some 2,000 abstracts and summaries of articles and books on biblical and related literature, including the Dead Sea Scrolls, Pseudepigrapha, noncanonical gospels, and ancient Near Eastern writings. Over 300 of the most important periodicals and book series in or related to biblical studies are abstracted or reviewed. The abstracts are written in any of three langugages (English, German, French) and are arranged topically under headings.

Coverage begins in 1951, and there is one volume per year. To find relevant articles, skim the titles and abstracts in the following sections: "Text—Versions" (Text—Übersetzung) for text and translation issues, the subsection within "Old Testament Exegesis" on your particular biblical book for exegetical issues, and the section on "Philology" (Sprache) for articles that discuss the grammar of your text. *IRBS* is useful, but it is tedious to use because it does not index publications by Bible verse.

Book lists for past years have also been published in various collections, such as those that follow from the Society for Old Testament Study:

H. H. Rowley, ed., *Eleven Years of Bible Bibliography:* . . . *1946–1956* (Indian Hills, CO: Falcon's Wing Press, 1957).
G. W. Anderson, ed., *A Decade of Bible Bibliography:* . . . *1957–1966* (Oxford: Basil Blackwell, Publisher, 1967).

P. R. Ackroyd, ed., *Bible Bibliography, 1967–1973, Old Testament* (Oxford: Basil Blackwell, Publisher, 1974).

IBR Bibliographies. The Institute for Biblical Research (IBR) publishes special bibliographies on various OT topics, and they are valuable for providing judicious listings of works in a given area. Below are some typical examples, via bakeracademic.com.

Ewin C. Hostetter, *Old Testament Introduction,* IBR Bibliographies (Grand Rapids: Baker Book House, 1995).
Elmer A. Martens, *Old Testament Theology,* IBR Bibliographies (Grand Rapids: Baker Book House, 1997).
Peter Enns, *Poetry and Wisdom,* IBR Bibliographies (Grand Rapids: Baker Book House, 1997).
D. Brent Sandy and Daniel M. O'Hare, *Prophecy and Apocalyptic: An Annotated Bibliography,* IBR Bibliographies (Grand Rapids: Baker Academic, 2007).

Hupper's Index. Since most readers of this book will have modern language proficiency mainly in English, the following series is of special note. A very fine, huge listing of OT articles (grouped in hundreds of sections) written in English from 1769 to 1969 has been gathered in eight volumes within the excellent ATLA Bibliography series. The latest volume in the series has added additional articles, still from the time period 1769–1969, and Hupper continues his diligent research, which will result in yet further volumes in the future. In appreciating the latest volume, do not forget that the prior seven are just as superb:

William G. Hupper, ed., *An Index to English Periodical Literature of the Old Testament and Ancient Near East,* vol. 8 (Metuchen, NJ: Scarecrow Press, 1999).

4.12.2. The journals

Dozens of periodicals regularly carry articles related generally to the OT and specifically to OT exegesis. At the risk of slighting some of the best, a *selection* of journals is here recommended for their special attention to exegesis and exegetically important issues. These would likely be carried by most seminary libraries, and by many college and university libraries as well. If you make it a habit to pay attention to these journals, you will be rewarded by exposure to a steady flow of high-level exegetical content. All contain articles in English; most are written exclusively in English. The journals in alphabetical order are

Biblica
Catholic Biblical Quarterly
Expository Times
Interpretation
Journal for the Study of the Old Testament

Journal of Biblical Literature
Revue biblique
Vetus Testamentum
Westminster Theological Journal
Zeitschrift für die alttestamentliche Wissenschaft

4.12.3. Old Testament introductions

Various one-volume introductions to the OT provide helpful access to a discussion of significant critical (exegetically oriented) points related to an OT book. In addition to Eissfeldt's classic *The Old Testament: An Introduction* (4.1.2), several other books are excellent and likely to be of substantial value if consulted. The following list represents some of the best works available in English:

Bernhard W. Anderson and Katheryn Pfisterer Darr, *Understanding the Old Testament*, abridged 4th ed. (Englewood Cliffs, NJ: Prentice-Hall, 1997).
Gleason Archer Jr., *A Survey of Old Testament Introduction*, rev. ed. (Chicago: Moody Press, 1973).
Brevard S. Childs, *Introduction to the Old Testament as Scripture* (Philadelphia: Fortress Press, 1979).
Tremper Longman III and Raymond B. Dillard, *An Introduction to the Old Testament*, 2nd ed. (Grand Rapids: Zondervan Publishing House, 2006).
Georg Fohrer, *Introduction to the Old Testament* (Nashville: Abingdon Press, 1968).
Roland Kenneth Harrison, *Introduction to the Old Testament* (1969; repr., Peabody, MA: Hendrickson Publishers, 2004).
Andrew E. Hill and John H. Walton, *A Survey of the Old Testament* (Grand Rapids: Zondervan Publishing House, 2000).
Paul R. House and Eric Mitchell, *Old Testament Survey*, 2nd ed. (Nashville: B&H Academic, 2007).
William S. LaSor, David A. Hubbard, and Frederic W. Bush, *Old Testament Survey: The Message, Form, and Background of the Old Testament*, 2nd ed. (Grand Rapids: Wm. B. Eerdmans, 1996).
Samuel J. Schultz, *The Old Testament Speaks: A Complete Survey of Old Testament History and Literature*, 5th ed. (San Francisco: HarperSanFrancisco, 2000).
J. Alberto Soggin, *Introduction to the Old Testament*, 3rd ed. (Louisville, KY: Westminster John Knox Press, 1989).
Edward J. Young, *An Introduction to the Old Testament*, rev. ed. (Grand Rapids: Wm. B. Eerdmans, 1964).

4.12.4. Commentaries

Of the dozens of commentary series, certain sets stand out as especially exegetical in format and interest. Commentary series are not consistent;

you must actually evaluate each volume on its own merits. Works that provide a book-by-book listing of commentaries include

Douglas Stuart, *A Guide to Selecting and Using Bible Commentaries* (Dallas: Word Books, 1987).
Tremper Longman III, *Old Testament Commentary Survey* (Grand Rapids: Baker Academic, 2007).
John Glynn, *Commentary and Reference Survey: A Comprehensive Guide to Biblical and Theological Resources* (Grand Rapids: Kregel Academic and Professional, 2007). Glynn includes two chapters specifically on exegetical software.

The following are among the high-quality complete or mostly complete multivolume sets. Dates for the individual volumes are varied. Some are available as modules within Bible software programs.

The Expositor's Bible Commentary (Grand Rapids: Zondervan Publishing House), also on CD-ROM.
Keil and Delitzsch, *Biblical Commentary on the Old Testament* (repr., Peabody, MA: Hendrickson Publishers, 2006), also on CD-ROM.
International Critical Commentary on the Holy Scriptures (London and New York: T&T Clark International), also on CD-ROM and downloadable from logos.com; recent revisions included.
The Interpreter's Bible (Nashville: Abingdon Press), also on CD-ROM.
The New Interpreter's Bible (Nashville: Abingdon Press), also on CD-ROM.
The Anchor Bible (Garden City, NY/New York: Doubleday), also on CD-ROM.
Hermeneia (Minneapolis: Augsburg Fortress), also on CD-ROM.
The New International Commentary on the Old Testament (Grand Rapids: Wm. B. Eerdmans), also on CD-ROM.
The Old Testament Library (Louisville, KY: Westminster John Knox Press).
The Word Biblical Commentary (Nashville: Thomas Nelson), also on CD-ROM and in some Bible software; full revision underway, usually by the original authors.
New American Commentary (Nashville: Broadman & Holman), also on CD-ROM.

Of the several fine one-volume Bible commentaries, four may be mentioned as representative:

The New Bible Commentary: Twenty-first Century Edition (Downers Grove, IL: InterVarsity Press, 2007), also on CD-ROM.
The New Jerome Biblical Commentary (Englewood Cliffs, NJ: Prentice-Hall, 1990), also on CD-ROM.
HarperCollins Bible Commentary, rev. ed. (San Francisco: HarperSanFrancisco, 2000), also on CD-ROM.
Zondervan Bible Commentary (Grand Rapids: Zondervan, 2007), also on CD-ROM.

4.12.5. Bible dictionaries and Bible encyclopedias

A note on nomenclature: The term "Bible encyclopedia" is almost always applied to a multivolume sourcebook with thousands of entries (individual articles on topics). However, the term "Bible dictionary" can be used to indicate anything from a relatively small, single-volume dictionary with a few hundred entries to the most massive of all recent Bible dictionaries or encyclopedias, the *Anchor Bible Dictionary*.

A source for both comprehensive overview articles relating to theology and exegesis, as well as specific articles on individual OT topics, is the *NIDOTTE*:

Willem A. VanGemeren, ed., *New International Dictionary of Old Testament Theology and Exegesis*, 5 vols. (Grand Rapids: Zondervan Publishing House, 1997), also on CD-ROM and available with some Bible software.

See also

Katharine Doob Sakenfeld, Samuel E. Balentine, Kah-Jin Jeffrey Kuan, and Eileen Schuller, eds., 5 vols., *The New Interpreter's Dictionary of the Bible* (Nashville: Abingdon Press, 2006–).

The most comprehensive Bible dictionary is the *ABD*:

David Noel Freedman, ed., *The Anchor Bible Dictionary*, 6 vols. (New York: Doubleday, 1992), also on CD-ROM.

Valuable for many topics and remarkable for its consistency of quality is the fully revised *ISBE*:

G. W. Bromiley, ed., *The International Standard Bible Encyclopedia*, 4 vols. (Grand Rapids: Wm. B. Eerdmans, 1979–88).

Useful, though aging, is the *IDB*:

George A. Buttrick, ed., *The Interpreter's Dictionary of the Bible*, 4 vols. (Nashville: Abingdon Press, 1962).

To this a one-volume supplement was added:

Keith Crim, ed., *The Interpreter's Dictionary of the Bible, Supplementary Volume* (Nashville: Abingdon Press, 1976).

See also

Merrill C. Tenney, ed., *The Zondervan Pictorial Encyclopedia of the Bible*, 5 vols. (Grand Rapids: Zondervan Publishing House, 1975).

A number of good one-volume Bible dictionaries are available. It might be thought that these would have little usefulness in light of the massive scale of giants like the *Anchor Bible Dictionary*. But the size of the giants actually makes the one-volume dictionaries particularly valuable for gaining a judicious overview or digest of the salient information on a topic. The articles in the huge multivolume sets, while prized for their thoroughness, can be so long as to leave the reader wondering what the most important facts really are. The articles in the smaller dictionaries often have the advantage of focus and true summative evaluation of the data by seasoned scholars. It often works well to read an article on a topic first in a one-volume Bible dictionary and then to pursue the topic in more detail via an article in a multivolume set.

Some examples of the one-volume dictionaries are:

The New Bible Dictionary, 3rd ed. (Downers Grove, IL: InterVarsity Press, 1996).
Holman Illustrated Bible Dictionary (Nashville: B&H Publishing Group, 2003).
Nelson's New Illustrated Bible Dictionary, rev. ed. (Nashville: Thomas Nelson, 1995).
The New Unger's Bible Dictionary (Chicago: Moody Press, 2006).
Eerdmans Dictionary of the Bible (Grand Rapids: Wm. B. Eerdmans, 2000).
The New International Bible Dictionary, rev. ed. (Grand Rapids: Zondervan Publishing House, 1999).

4.12.6. Other aids

A series of academic aids has been published by Augsburg Fortress Press. Some of the titles have been mentioned elsewhere in this primer. They explain in a readable, concise format such techniques as textual criticism, form criticism, literary criticism (including source criticism), sociological analysis, structural analysis, archaeology, and poetry criticism. The series is

Guides to Biblical Scholarship: Old Testament Series (Philadelphia till 1988, then Minneapolis: Fortress Press, 1971–).

Most of the individual titles are listed below:

Canon and Community: A Guide to Canonical Criticism, by James A. Sanders (1984).
Cultural Anthropology and the Old Testament, by Thomas W. Overholt (1996).
Folklore and the Hebrew Bible, by Susan Niditch (1993).
Form Criticism of the Old Testament, by Gene Milton Tucker (1971).

The Historical-Critical Method, by Edgar Krentz (1975).
Interpreting Hebrew Poetry, by David L. Petersen and Kent Harold Richards (1992).
Literary Criticism of the Old Testament, by Norman C. Habel (1971).
New Historicism, by Gina Hens-Piazza (2002).
The Old Testament and the Archaeologist, by H. Darrell Lance (1981).
The Old Testament and the Historian, by James Maxwell Miller (1976).
The Old Testament and the Literary Critic, by David A. Robertson (1977).
Psychological Biblical Criticism, by D. Andrew Kille (2001).
Rhetorical Criticism: Context, Method, and the Book of Jonah, by Phyllis Trible (1994).
Sociological Approaches to the Old Testament, by Robert R. Wilson (1984).
Textual Criticism of the Old Testament: The Septuagint after Qumran, by Ralph W. Klein (1974).
Textual Criticism: Recovering the Text of the Hebrew Bible, by P. Kyle McCarter Jr. (1986).
Tradition History and the Old Testament, by Walter E. Rast (1971).
What Is Midrash? by Jacob Neusner (1987).
What Is Narrative Criticism? by Mark Allan Powell (1990).
What Is Postmodern Biblical Criticism? by A. K. M. Adam (1995).
What Is Redaction Criticism? by Norman Perrin (1969).
What Is Social-Scientific Criticism? by John H. Elliott (1993).
What Is Structural Exegesis? by Daniel Patte (1976).

Old Testament illustrations

Collections of illustrations relating to OT studies are often of value to the exegete. If you are analyzing a passage that mentions a site, a coin, a weight, an animal, a piece of furniture, a utensil, a weapon, or any place or object that might just "come alive" if illustrated, check these volumes to see if such an illustration might exist in the case of your topic:

James B. Pritchard, ed., *The Ancient Near East in Pictures Relating to the Old Testament* (Princeton, NJ: Princeton University Press, 1954).
James B. Pritchard, ed., *The Ancient Near East: An Anthology of Texts and Pictures* (Princeton, NJ: Princeton University Press, 1958).
James B. Pritchard, ed., *The Ancient Near East: Supplementary Texts and Pictures Relating to the Old Testament* (Princeton, NJ: Princeton University Press, 1969).
Clifford M. Jones, *Old Testament Illustrations*, The Cambridge Bible Commentary: New English Bible (Cambridge: Cambridge University Press, 1971).
Richard David Barnett, *Illustrations of Old Testament History*, rev. ed. (London: British Museum Publications, 1977).
Trent C. Butler et al., eds., *Holman Illustrated Bible Dictionary* (Nashville: B&H Publishing Group, 2003).
Ronald F. Youngblood, ed., *Nelson's New Illustrated Bible Dictionary*, rev. ed. (Nashville: Thomas Nelson, 1995).
J. D. Douglas and Merrill C. Tenney, eds., *Zondervan's Pictorial Bible Dictionary* (Grand Rapids: Zondervan, 1999).
iLumina, www.livethebible.com.

Life in Bible times

The ability to appreciate daily life, housing, farming, transportation, cooking, and so forth in the agrarian world of Bible times is part of the exegete's skill set while looking at biblical passages that touch on such things. The following, among others, can prove quite valuable in this regard:

Philip J. King and Lawrence E. Stager, *Life in Biblical Israel* (Louisville, KY: Westminster John Knox Press, 2002).

Oded Borowski, *Daily Life in Biblical Times* (Atlanta: Society of Biblical Literature, 2003).

National Geographic Book Service, *Everyday Life in Bible Times*, 2nd ed. (Washington, DC: National Geographic Society, 1977).

Robert Dolezal, *Illustrated Dictionary of Bible Life and Times* (Pleasantville, NY: Reader's Digest, 1997).

J. A. Thompson, *Handbook of Life in Bible Times* (Downers Grove, IL: InterVarsity Press, 1987).

Nelson Reference, *Everyday Living: Bible Life and Times* (Nashville: Thomas Nelson, 2007).

J. I. Packer et al., eds., *Public Life in Bible Times* (Nashville: Thomas Nelson, 1985).

Qumran/Dead Sea Scrolls comparisons

We have already made note of publications on the Dead Sea Scrolls in connection with issues of textual criticism and lexicography. But this does not exhaust the usefulness of the Qumran literature for OT studies. There still remain the cultural, historical, sociological, and theological connections of the scrolls, for which the works below can prove quite helpful. For a good explanation of the materials available as of 1990 (and there were plenty), consider

Joseph A. Fitzmyer, *The Dead Sea Scrolls: Major Publications and Tools for Study*, rev. ed. (Atlanta: Society of Biblical Literature and Scholars Press, 1990).

Fitzmyer introduces the various texts, explains where they and their translations are published, and outlines the contents of some of the major scrolls. He also provides an excellent bibliography and an index to biblical passages in the scrolls.

For an overview of the scrolls and their significance, see the following:

David Noel Freedman and Pam Fox Kuhlken, *What Are the Dead Sea Scrolls and Why Do They Matter?* (Grand Rapids: Wm. B. Eerdmans, 2007).

James VanderKam and Peter Flint, *The Meaning of the Dead Sea Scrolls: Their Significance For Understanding the Bible, Judaism, Jesus, and Christianity* (San Francisco: HarperSanFrancisco, 2002).

C. D. Elledge, *The Bible and the Dead Sea Scrolls* (Atlanta: Society of Biblical Literature, 2005).

For reading through the texts in translation and appreciating their contents, see these works:

Florentino García Martínez and Eibert J. C. Tigchelaar, *The Dead Sea Scrolls Translated: The Qumran Texts in English*, 2nd ed., 2 vols. (Grand Rapids: Wm. B. Eerdmans, 1996).

Theodor H. Gaster, *The Dead Sea Scriptures: In English Translation with Introduction and Notes*, 3rd ed. (Garden City, NJ: Doubleday, Anchor Books, 1976).

Michael O. Wise, Martin G. Abegg Jr., and Edward M. Cook, *The Dead Sea Scrolls: A New Translation*, rev. ed. (San Francisco: HarperSanFrancisco, 2005).

Geza Vermes, trans. and ed., *The Complete Dead Sea Scrolls in English*, rev. ed. (London: Penguin Books, 2004).

Philip R. Davies, George J. Brooke, and Phillip R. Callaway, *The Complete World of the Dead Sea Scrolls* (New York: Thames & Hudson, 2002).

Martin G. Abegg Jr., Peter Flint, and Eugene Ulrich, *The Dead Sea Scrolls Bible: The Oldest Known Bible Translated for the First Time into English* (San Francisco: HarperSanFrancisco, 1999).

Terminology in Old Testament study

For definitions of terminology used in biblical studies, consult the following:

Kevin J. Vanhoozer, ed., *Dictionary for Theological Interpretation of the Bible* (Grand Rapids: Baker Academic, 2005).

F. B. Huey Jr. and Bruce Corley, *A Student's Dictionary for Biblical and Theological Studies* (Grand Rapids: Zondervan Publishing House, 1984).

Donald K. McKim, *Westminster Dictionary of Theological Terms* (Louisville, KY: Westminster John Knox, 1996).

When you need guidance to older bibliographic resources more broadly within the general field of theological study (church history, systematic theology, practical theology, missions, etc.—including biblical studies), consider

David R. Stewart, *The Literature of Theology: A Guide for Students and Pastors*, rev. ed. (Louisville, KY: Westminster John Knox Press, 2003).

4.12.7. Bible software programs and providers

Computer software provides powerful, searchable resources that once were available only in book form. This is a rapidly expanding area, and one that will continue to expand. The following is only a limited sampling of some of the more interesting or valuable or unique software programs and/or providers. Do not rely on this list as if it were exhaustive, because it is hardly that. (Just google "Bible software" and see how great the range of options is.) Instead, check out the full descriptions provided by the publishers at their Web sites, and expect an ever-changing stream of additions, updates, and reconfigurations.

Some Bible software is free, some is pricey. Some is accessed only via interactive online sites; some is available only for purchase either via disks or downloads. Some is geared especially for pods and/or palms and/or cell-receptor devices; some only for desktops or laptops. Some is compatible only with Windows, some with DOS, some with Mac, some with Linux/Unix, some with WinCE, some with Java, and so forth. Any or all may be of benefit to you depending on your needs at any given time.

Some of these Bible software providers even have some of one another's software packages for sale (e.g., see the non-*Accordance* modules within *Accordance*, sampled below). Some are, in fact, mainly resellers. Others charge nothing for unlimited use of their sites. Several have various Web addresses, and since Web addresses are always subject to change, the ones listed below are not necessarily the only ones you may need to use to find their sites. When you reach a Web address listed, you may need to select an option displayed or input words to search for the product.

Accordance Bible Software, www.accordancebible.com.
Ages Library, www.ageslibrary.com.
Alkitab Bible Study, www.kiyut.com/products/alkitab.
ATLA, American Theological Library Association, www.atla.com.
Baker Digital Reference Library, www.amazon.com.
Bible Browser, biblebrowser.com.
Bible Database, bibledatabase.com.
Bible Desktop, crosswire.org/bibledesktop.
Bible Explorer, www.bible-explorer.com.
Bible Reader for Palm, www.gramcord.org.
Bible Research, bible-researcher.com.
Bible Windows, www.silvermnt.com.
Biblesoft.com, www.biblesoft.com.
BibleTime, www.bibletime.info.
BibleWorks, www.bibleworks.com.
Biblical Studies on the Web, www.bsw.org.
Biblos.com, biblos.com.
Center for the Computer Analysis of Texts, ccat.sas.upenn.edu.
Computronic, www.biblecodesplus.com.
DiscountBible.com, www.discountbible.com.
e-Sword, www.e-sword.net.
GMP Soft, www.gmpsoft.com.

GnomeSword, gnomesword.sourceforge.net.
Gramcord/Bible Companion, www.gramcord.org.
IOSCS Site (International Organization for Septuagint and Cognate Studies), ccat.sas.upenn
    .edu/ioscs.
Laridian Bible Software, www.laridian.com.
Logos Bible Software, www.biblesoftware.com.
Logos Bible Software, www.logos.com/mac.
MacSword, macsword.com.
MyBible, www.laridian.com.
Nehemiah Bible Software, www.nehemiahbiblesoftware.com.
Olive Tree Bible Software, www.olivetree.com.
Online Bible, www.onlinebible.net.
Palm Bible Plus, palmbibleplus.sourceforge.net.
Parsons Bible Study Software, www.quickverse.com.
PC Study Bible, www.biblesoft.com.
PocketBible, www.laridian.com.
Quickverse, www.QuickVerse.com.
Scripture 4 All, www.scripture4all.org.
Sword Searcher, www.swordsearcher.com.
The Greek and Hebrew Library 6.0 for Windows, www.zondervan.com.
The Sword Project, www.crosswire.org/sword.
The Word, www.theword.gr/en.
Theophilos Bible Software, www.theophilos.sk.
Tolbss The Online Bible Software Site, www.ccel.org/olb.
Tyndale House, www.tyndalehouse.co.uk.
Word Advanced Study System, http://www-writing.berkeley.edu/chorus/bible/.
WORDsearch, www.wordsearchbible.com.
Zondervan Software, www.zondervan.com.

As an example, here is just a partial listing of some of the sorts of modules that just one of the providers listed above, *Accordance*, can give you. I have omitted mention of most of its dozens of texts and translations, as well as the search programs and so forth, but this list will still give you an idea of the breadth available in a major Bible software product:

Anchor Yale Bible Dictionary
Ancient Christian Commentary on Scripture Series
Apostolic Fathers
BDAG and *HALOT* Bundle
Bible Atlas
Bible Lands PhotoGuide
Bible Reference release 3
Bible Speaks Today Commentary Series
Biblical Archaeology Review Archive
Biblical World in Pictures
Church Fathers and Church History

Context of Scripture (ancient parallels to biblical materials)
Eerdmans Reference (commentaries, etc.)
Essential IVP Reference Collection
Grammatical Supplement
Graphics DVD
Greek-English Lexicon of the New Testament and Other Early Christian Literature
Josephus
Kaufmann Mishna Codex Facsimile
Koehler-Baumgartner's *Hebrew and Aramaic Lexicon*
Mac Emulator for PC
Philo
Pseudepigrapha
Qumran
Society of Biblical Literature (journals, etc.)
Talmud CD-ROM
Targums
Theological Journal Library
Word Biblical Commentary
Zondervan Scholarly Bible Study Suite

A List of Common
Old Testament Exegesis Terms

acrostic: Composed alphabetically, successive verses beginning with successive Hebrew letters (some psalms, sections of Proverbs, Lamentations, etc.).

anacoluthon: Grammatical non sequitur in which the first part of a thought is not completed as expected.

antithetical: Describing poetic parallelism characterized by the pairing of an assertion and its contrast.

Aquila: Translated Hebrew Bible into Greek literalistically around AD 140; included in Hexapla; replaced parts of LXX.

Aramaism: Word or idiom used in Hebrew, supposedly Aramaic in origin, therefore late in date. (Almost all have proved to be Semitisms, not late, and therefore not properly used for dating OT books late.)

assimilation: Replacement of an original text reading by a reading from another document.

asyndeton: Absence of conjunctions or other linking/coordinating words. ("The LORD is my shepherd; I shall not want.") The reader must figure out the relationship of the concepts expressed.

autograph: The original, first copy of a biblical book or portion.

bifid: Organized into two discrete parts. (Many OT books are bifid; their two parts are not early and late respectively, or the products of different authors. They are just convenient ways of organizing the material thematically.)

chiasm (also chiasmus, inverted parallelism, etc.): A pattern of words or concepts in which the first and last are similar, the second and next to last are similar, and so forth, making memorization easy (e.g., Isa. 6:10; Zech. 14; Matt. 7:6a). The middle of a chiasm is not necessarily more important than any other part. Most short chiasms are just stylistic variations within synonymous parallelisms.

codex: An ancient manuscript in book (bound pages) form rather than scroll form.

collate: To compare manuscripts of a given text in order to reconstruct the original.

colon: A single verse unit of poetry. (Usually people mean "one line of a couplet or triplet" by colon, but not always.)

colophon: Title or other summary at the end or beginning of a unit of text. (10 times in Genesis; Lev. 26:46; etc.)

conflation: Combining two variant readings, producing a reading not the same as either of them.

daughter translation: A translation of a translation, usually referring to a translation of the LXX into another language.

deuterograph: Secondary writing/rewriting. (1–2 Chronicles contains deuterographs of 1 Samuel–2 Kings; cf. Pss. 14 and 53; etc.)

dittography: Copy error repeating something accidentally.

doublet: A supposedly parallel narrative, allegedly resulting from retelling in oral tradition (e.g., Gen. 12; 20; 26).

formula: A set of words commonly used in a particular kind of context. ("Thus says the LORD" is a messenger formula.)

hapax legomenon: A word or term that occurs only once in the OT (often making its definition hard to pin down).

haplography: The loss of something during copying (letters, words, sentences, and other units that the copyist accidentally skips).

hendiadys: Expressing a single concept by two or more words or expressions linked by "and" (lord and master; arise and go). (In translating accurately you often have to eliminate or subordinate one of the words, e.g., lord; get going; etc.)

Hexapla: Origen's six-column OT containing (1) the Hebrew, (2) the Hebrew transliterated into Greek; (3) Aquila, (4) Symmachus, (5) the LXX, and (6) Theodotion. (The LXX he produced was highly conflated, with asterisks used to indicate what he had added to the original LXX and obeli used to indicate what he had subtracted from it.)

homoioarchton: Similar beginnings in two words (thus causing the scribe accidentally to skip from the one to the other).

homoioteleuton: Similar endings in two words (thus causing the scribe accidentally to skip from the one to the other).

inclusio: Literary device in which the end and the beginning of a passage are similar, thus sandwiching the rest.

Kethib and *Qere*: Kethib = inferior reading that the Masoretes included in the text by writing only its consonants. Qere = superior reading that the Masoretes imposed over the Kethib consonants by using only its vowels.

lacuna: A physical gap in a manuscript.

meter: The pattern of accents and/or total syllables in a passage of poetry. All musical poetry has meter.

metonymy: A word substitution (e.g., "juice" for electricity; "heaven" for God in Matthew; "crown" for Caesar or emperor in Rev. 12:3).

paleography: Study of ancient writing/penmanship. For example, the style of the letters can tell the age of a document.

parallelism: The logical balances and correspondences between lines of poetry (e.g., synonymous, antithetical, synthetic).

paronomasia: A pun or play on words or word roots (pleasing to the ear, aids memorization).

Peshitta: The most common Syriac version of the OT.

prostaxis: The tendency to start all the clauses in a language in the same way. Hebrew uses prostactic ׀ (*wĕ*, and).

Qinah meter: Supposedly a three-accent + two-accent pattern used in dirges (a misunderstanding of the meter in Lamentations).

rîb form: A literary form (רִיב) by which a nation is imagined to be taken to court, usually to be tried and found guilty.

Septuagint: Greek translation of the Hebrew OT originally made between about 250 and 100 BC, modified often.

Symmachus: Independent, freestyle translation of the OT into Greek around AD 175; influenced Vulgate.

synecdoche: A part used for the whole, or vice versa ("Nice threads!" "Got wheels?" "turning the world upside down").

synonymous: Describing poetic parallelism in which the same essential concept is conveyed by two different wordings that are parallel to each other.

synthetic: Describing poetic parallelism in which the first half of a complete assertion is paralleled and completed by the second half.

Talmud : Huge Jewish rabbinical teaching collection: Mishnah (traditions) and Gemara (commentary on Mishnah), third to fifth centuries AD.

Targum: Aramaic translation of the OT. There are various sections, produced at various times, probably second to fifth centuries AD.

terminus a quo: The earliest possible date for something.

terminus ad quem: The latest possible date for something.

Theodotion: Greek revision of the LXX toward the Hebrew, around AD 175; replaced the old LXX in most Daniel manuscripts.

variant: A different reading (thus requiring the text critic to consider whether it represents the original or not).

Vulgate: Free translation of the OT into Latin by Jerome, completed AD 405 (replaced the older and often better Old Latin).

A List of Frequent Hermeneutical Errors

Allegorizing: Assuming that the components of a passage have meaning only as symbols of Christian truths. ("The 'lover' is Christ; the 'beloved' is the church; the 'daughters of Jerusalem' are the Scriptures.")

Argument from authority: Assuming that the views of "experts" or a pre-ponderance of them must be correct. ("Smith, who has devoted his life to studying Ruth, may be trusted. . . .") ("Since this is held by few schol-ars, it does not seem tenable.")

Argument from silence: Assuming that everything relevant to an issue is mentioned in the Bible every time that issue is mentioned. ("Notice that Paul does not explicitly condemn premarital sex anywhere in his letters.")

Equivocation: Confusing a term or concept with another term or concept, thus misunderstanding its meaning. ("1 Thessalonians 5:22 says to 'abstain from all appearance of evil,' so you can't even ask directions from a prostitute.")

Exemplarizing: Assuming that because someone in the Bible did some-thing, it is an example for us to follow. ("To learn how to tell stories in sermons, let us examine Jesus' storytelling.") ("Let's see how Jesus called disciples and let that be the model for our evangelism.") ("What can we learn about adversity from how the Israelites endured their years as slaves in Egypt?")

False combination: Joining two statements or passages in such a way as to produce a hybrid conclusion. ("In Matthew 25 Jesus calls hell both outer darkness and also fire, so hell fire must be some kind of special divine fire that doesn't give off any light. You can feel it but you can't see it.")

False presupposition: Basing all or part of an argument or conclusion on incorrect assumptions. ("The Hebrew mind thought concretely, the Greek mind abstractly. This is why the OT has more rituals and the NT more symbols.")

Figure of speech confusion: Failure to understand any of the many nonliteral expressions in human speech, especially metaphors. ("Imagine the massive scale of Canaanite dairy farming and beekeeping that led to Canaan's being called a land flowing with milk and honey.")

Genre confusion: Assuming that the interpretational rules for one genre apply to another. ("Jesus' parable of the workers in the vineyard contains seven helpful perspectives on the value of hard work.") ("The Twenty-third Psalm teaches us how to care for those under our authority.") ("According to Deuteronomy 33, if we trust God we'll never lack anything.") ("But Proverbs promises that if we honor God, we'll be well liked by everyone!")

Israel-church confusion: Assuming that things applying to biblical Israel also apply to the church. ("We can learn how to discipline troublesome kids from this law about stoning disobedient children.")

Israel–modern Israel confusion: Assuming that the modern, secular state named Israel in the Near East is the Israel referred to in the Bible. ("How can we support the Saudis when they're the enemies of God's chosen people?")

Israel–modern nation confusion: Assuming that things appling to biblical Israel also apply to modern nations ("According to 2 Chronicles 7:14, if we pray and repent, God will heal America.")

Moralizing: Assuming that principles for living can be derived from all passages. ("We can learn much about parenting by noting how the father of the prodigal son handled his wayward child.") ("The Egyptians drowned at the Red Sea because they had vacillated. You can't vacillate and expect to succeed in this life.")

Personalizing: Assuming that any or all parts of the Bible apply to you or your group in a way that they do not apply to everyone else. ("What Balaam's ass says to me is that I talk too much.") Also known as *individualizing*.

Root fallacy: Assuming that the/an original meaning of a word always attends its usage. ("To be holy means to be set apart." Cf. terrible/terrific/terrifying.)

Spiritualizing: Assuming that events or factors have their real application in some religious truth beyond what they actually say. ("The lovely structure of the Jerusalem temple encourages us to have our own lives well in order.")

Totality transfer: Assuming that all the possible meanings of a word or phrase go with it whenever it is used. ("Head [κεφαλή, *kephalē*], of course, means 'source' here, just as it does in Xenophon's reference to the source of a river.")

Typologizing: Assuming that certain real biblical characters or things are mentioned in order to foreshadow other real—and more important—characters or things. ("Joshua has the same name as Jesus; as a conqueror he points to The Conqueror.") ("Ezra came to his people from afar; entered into Jerusalem on a donkey; prayed before crises; taught what was to many a new law; purified the nation, and so on. His life points directly to the Savior.")

Universalizing: Assuming that something unique or uncommon in the Bible applies to everyone equally. ("We all have our Gethsemanes.") Also known as *generalizing*.

Index of Scripture Passages

Index of Authors

CPSIA information can be obtained
at www.ICGtesting.com
Printed in the USA
BVHW031639080720
583087BV00001B/7

9 780664 233440